Barrier-Free Residential Design

Barrier-Free Residential Design

Albert A. Peloquin, AIA

McGraw-Hill, Inc.
New York San Francisco Washington, D.C. Auckland Bogotá
Caracas Lisbon London Madrid Mexico City Milan
Montreal New Delhi San Juan Singapore
Sydney Tokyo Toronto

Library of Congress Cataloging-in-Publication Data

Peloquin, Albert A.

    Barrier-free residential design / Albert A. Peloquin.
       p.   cm.
    ISBN 0-07-049326-X
    1. Dwellings—United States—Access for the physically
handicapped.   2. Architecture and the physically handicapped—United
States. I. Title.
  NA2545.P5P45   1994
   728'.37042—dc20
                                               94-9150
                                                 CIP

1 2 3 4 5 6 7 8 9 0 KP/KP 9 9 8 7 6 5 4 3

ISBN 0-07-049326-X

The sponsoring editor for this book was Joel E. Stein, the editing supervisor was Caroline Levine, the designer was Susan Maksuta, and the production supervisor was Suzanne W. Babeuf. It was set in Palatino by McGraw-Hill's Professional Book Group composition unit.

Printed and bound by Kingsport Press.

Contents

I dedicate this book to Florence M. Peloquin, my wife

Preface

With the implementation of the Americans with Disabilities Act (ADA), architects, builders, and building owners have suddenly found themselves confronted with the complex and confusing task of ensuring that their new and existing structures comply with these new federally mandated guidelines.

This book is intended as a "how-to" for professionals and for the layperson and architecture student on removal of barriers to the disabled or elderly. The elements of barrier-free design are presented in narrative form as I observe problems of access and their solution while conducting the reader through a tour of an imaginary home.

Each chapter covers a different part of this home, and explanations are given for removal of barriers using the ANSI codes—Federal standard codes that are typically adopted in their entirety by state code councils—and the North Carolina code, which is considered to be one of the best in the country. Throughout the book, I have interpreted the new ADA Guidelines and shown how they may be implemented via simple, easily understood sketches which illustrate problems of access and their solution.

These sketches, which appear together for convenience at the back of the book, are carefully cross-referenced in the text, which itself is illustrated with interior and exterior photographs and examples of products.

I hope that I have made the task of compliance with the ADA easier for architects and builders so that, in turn, the needs of the disabled and the growing number of elderly in this country can be served.

Albert A. Peloquin

Acknowledgments

I would like to express my deep appreciation to those without whose help this book would not have been written.

To Jeffrey, my son, and to James A. Watson, who helped me to formulate the early ideas and who in that sense were co-authors; to my daughters: Mary, who did the early editing, and Jean, who edited the final manuscript. To Pauly Dodd, for her ongoing editing input; Tom Hammer, who was always there when I needed help; and to all who reviewed the early drafts and encouraged me to continue.

Barrier-Free
Residential
Design

INTRODUCTION

What is this book about? It's about residential barrier-free accessibility. It will define and show the barriers that you may find in your own home and describe the changes necessary to attain full accessibility to the extent you may require.

The elderly, the businessperson, the city official, and just about the entire general public, do not recognize many of the barriers that exist in their homes, and many of those who do don't know what is required to make their homes or places of business more accessible.

When we bring an elderly or disabled person into our home, rather than sending him or her to a nursing home or other type of facility, often we do not take these barriers into consideration. Neither do we consider them when we employ the elderly or disabled in our business establishments. Changes may be required to help them to function independently.

Many things can be incorporated into new or renovated construction to make it more livable, more convenient, and safer. Moreover, it can be done without compromising or reducing its inherent beauty of design.

Things can be done to the workplace to make it more convenient, not only for the elderly or disabled, but for everyone. Simple conveniences such as wide doors, wider halls, lever handles instead of knobs on the doors, more space in the kitchen, bathroom, or workplace are just a few of the options available.

This book covers a broad range of ideas that can assist people who need help in a variety of different circumstances. For example, you may need to renovate your present living space, make changes to accommodate an elderly member of your family, build a new house, or even meet the new requirements of the Americans with Disabilities Act (ADA) if you have a facility that is open to the public. There are many things you need to be aware of to know how the Act will affect your facility. Business people now understand how important it is to have their places of business accessible; and there may be issues to address with public officials about accessibility because of increasing numbers of elderly and disabled people who make up a substantial portion of our population.

This book is designed to make it easy to recognize and understand what architectural barriers are and provides information on the recommended ways to remove them. It tells where to obtain additional information and mentions the resources that are available for the asking. It will help to establish those follow-up services that the professional can provide to the homeowner, the real estate agent, the city official, and the businessperson.

After scanning this book you may want to ask yourself a few basic questions to help you determine your particular needs. For this reason, Chapter 12 includes a short questionnaire headed "Checklists." You will find it very useful in defining your particular requirements for accessibility.

In this book you will find sketches and examples illustrating how to remove barriers, and the dimensions necessary for barrier-free accessibility. I have included some product recommendations to help you in the selection process. I have also tried to give you some understanding of what an architectural barrier really is, from the viewpoint of an architect.

Chapters 1 through 8 take you on a hypothetical walk-through of an imaginary home, to identify all the barriers normally found there. They explain how to remove these barriers and give the required space and dimensions necessary for attaining freedom of access. The illustrations included describe how those spaces work and show their respective dimensions.

Chapter 9 describes the design criteria for free movement and increased accessibility for the physically challenged. Chapter 10 explains how the new Americans with Disabilities Act (ADA) will affect almost every aspect of the American population. But it must be understood that this law still does not provide help for the millions of elderly or the physically challenged in their own single-family private residences.

I will go into some detail on how these new laws will affect businesses, the elderly, and the disabled. While the laws pertain to the civil rights of disabled people, it is also very clear that they are designed to help the wheelchair-bound person obtain the barrier-free environment necessary for living an independent life.

Chapter 11 provides an extensive list of the organizations that can supply information on all aspects of housing for the elderly and disabled. It gives information on where to get help from governmental organizations and offers help in selecting products that the elderly and disabled can use.

Chapter 12 includes the checklist I have developed to help you understand and recognize the barriers in and around the home that may have to be removed. The list allows you to organize your search for better accessibility for your residence or business environment. Two survey forms are included, which may be duplicated for your own use. The first is for the site survey for commercial property: this will be useful in determining

A pleasant approach to a home.

whether there are existing architectural barriers, help to identify what they are, and explain how to remove them. This survey is designed in accordance and compliance with Section 504 of the Americans with Disabilities Act of 1990. The second survey form is for use by the homeowner, and will identify barriers that may exist in the home. It can also be used to determine the accessibility of retail establishments and work environments.

It is important to note that those involved in the constructing or renovating of features for accessibility should check their local, state, and government codes such as ANSI A117.1 or others that may apply to their situation. For commercial facilities, meeting federally mandated requirements for accessibility really starts with the evaluation plan of the facility. This is also true for city and town officials who must take measures to make their facilities accessible.

My illustrations will simplify the space requirements for barrier-free accessibility. They show how the space is to be used, as well as how the space permits or limits the free movement needed for free access and independent living.

One of the benefits of good orientation. Looking southeast, the morning sun is wonderful and it's shady in the afternoon.

LAST THINGS FIRST

In the foregoing material I have elaborated on identifying barriers that prevent free accessibility in the home and provided the technical information for eliminating them.

There is one more thing, however, that you may want to consider if you are planning to build. That is, the building lot itself, its location, and the house orientation; that is, how it will be situated on the lot. These considerations can vary according to the climate in your particular area. For example, in moderate climates many people want shade trees on the south side for cooling in the summer; in winter, deciduous trees, that is, those that shed their leaves, are more welcome. In the northern sections of our country, it is recommended that the lots surrounding the buildings have massed evergreen trees on the north side to ward off the winter winds. These last, of course, are for the comfort of everyone, whether physically challenged or not.

In any event, you would be wise to consider your house plan *before* and *after* you select your lot. Discuss this with your builder or architect.

Chapter One
THE PARKING AREA

We begin our walk-through to identify the barriers that may exist in the parking area or driveway. A dirt or gravel driveway poses an obstacle to a person in a wheelchair, a walker, or crutches, and even to those who have trouble walking, such as the elderly. Wheelchair wheels can bog down, and crutches or canes can dig into the dirt or gravel, or perhaps sink into the grass. Rough or uneven material is a great hazard for the visually impaired, possibly causing them to trip, something they have a great fear will happen.

The walkway leads to the front door, but the trip may be very difficult. It may be steep and winding, or filled with grassy holes. Of course, this is not always the case; some walks are set in concrete, easy to traverse, and fill every requirement for the wheelchair-bound person.

Usually, we don't think of the driveway as a barrier, but it can be a problem to the disabled, depending upon the type of materials used in it, the grade, and/or the location.

RESIDENTIAL APARTMENT PARKING

If you have a paved parking area in a residential apartment complex, your parking space should be well marked and have a parking space designed for handicapped parking and a sign that identifies that space as reserved for the handicapped. The distance from your parking space to your front door should be level, with no steps to traverse and no grade too steep. See Fig. 1-1 showing parking-space requirements. (The architectural drawings appear at the end of the book, starting with p. 171.)

BARRIERS IDENTIFIED IN THE PARKING AREA

- Unpaved parking area
- Front walk

How to Remove These Barriers

Unpaved Area. It is best that the paved area be a hard surface of some kind. A concrete or an asphalt driveway usually are the best types of surfaces. If it's a dirt drive, make sure it is made of highly compacted earth. Loose gravel is not a recommended surface. If gravel is used, there should be no stones larger than ½ in., and the driveway should also be compacted and have no ruts at all. It should be as level as possible, or most importantly, at least be level where the vehicle normally is parked.

Front Walk. The walkway should be a continuous, smooth surface, made of the best material available, preferably concrete. An asphalt walk is an

A new house with built-in barriers already present—a steep driveway and no ramp access to the house are the more obvious ones.

An ideal approach to a rear deck, level with no barriers.

A gravel driveway is difficult for the disabled to negotiate.

acceptable alternative. The walkway should be a minimum of 4 ft (48 in.) wide. The maximum grade, or gradient, should be 1 in 20; that is, one with a rise of 1 ft for every 20 ft of distance. The walk should be as level as possible, with no steps of any kind, and should be sloped to one side to prevent any water from collecting. See Fig. 1-2.

Concrete walks should have a minimum number of expansion cracks. Usually, these are spaced about 15 ft apart and are about a half-inch wide. Care should be taken to have the two adjoining concrete surfaces as close as possible to each other in height and never more than ½ in. apart. Again, see Fig. 1-2.

When concrete is placed directly on grade, it is permissible to go to a 1-in-20 rise. If the walk has a drop-off on one or both sides, a ramp is required (see Fig. 1-3). These ramps are calculated differently: We use a gradient or rise of 1 in 12. The grade should not exceed this percentage. See Figs. 1-2, 1-3, 1-4, and 1-5 for details of how ramps are to be designed, installed, and calculated.

Figure 1-6 illustrates various types of ramps and other devices for improving the safety of the trip from the road or driveway to the sidewalk.

A well-designed ramp to the front door. The sidewalk is on the existing grade.

Another example of a well-designed ramp. This is located at the rear of the house.

Imagine having to use this barrier every day.

Chapter Two
THE ENTRANCE

As we approach the front entrance, we come to the front stoop. It may have between 1 and 4 steps, and sometimes has more, but even the lower number is quite a barrier.

We finally make it to the front door and find another barrier: not a high one—only about 2-in. high. As we try to enter the front door, there is a high threshold, and we find that the door itself is too narrow. Some entry doors may only be about 2-ft 8-in. wide or less, certainly not wide enough for a wheelchair. For people using crutches or canes, or those who are visually or hearing impaired, it would be fine, but it has been determined that doors of this size do not permit free access for the wheelchair bound.

There is another common problem regarding most entry doors. If we were arthritic, had a moderate disability, or some form of hand impairment, we would have a lot of trouble with most of the standard types of doorknobs. Often they are awkward to grasp and very difficult to turn. Therefore, it would be difficult to open and/or lock the front door.

We are at the front entrance, trying to figure out how we are going to get in. We back up and almost fall off the stoop. Now we are really afraid to move around on that small stoop. We wonder what we can grab on to just to gain balance.

To solve this potential problem, the area around the entry door (stoop) should have a minimum space of 5 ft × 5 ft (see Fig. 2-1). Since safety is foremost in our minds, we could have a railing installed around the stoop. Railings are always a good idea, and occasionally a must. Railings may also be a code requirement in some states. This requirement usually is determined by how high the stoop or porch is from the ground. And of course the entryway should always be well lit.

BARRIERS IDENTIFIED AT THE FRONT ENTRANCE:

- Steps, stoop, porch
- Threshold
- Door
- Entrance doorknob

How to Remove These Barriers

Steps, Stoop, Porch. The easiest way to remove the steps as a barrier is to provide a ramp. Temporary solutions include the use of portable ramps, which are lightweight, usually made of aluminum, and fairly easy to set in place. They are designed to accommodate a wheelchair and are available for purchase. In the Resource section I have listed some manufacturers of these units. I recommend these portable ramps as a means of providing easy access over a small step.

How would you get to the front door? A new house with little consideration for access.

Another example where little thought was given to access.

All people can travel over this. Right?

If a permanent ramp is chosen, it is necessary to comply with certain design requirements. The ramp may be located at any exterior entrance doorway, and preferably one where the grade-level is as close as possible to the threshold. This will keep the length of the ramp to a minimum. The design of the ramp should be held to a gradient of a 1-in. rise to 12 in. across; this is known as a 1-in-12 rise, or a grade of 8.33 percent. Look again at Figs. 1-3, 1-4, and 1-5. An exterior ramp should be at least 4-ft (48-in.) wide. If a ramp is needed for inside a home, a width of 3 ft (36 in.) is required if space permits. If it doesn't, one must check with the local building inspection official to see if the amount of available space is acceptable.

Exterior ramps that are on grade level can be built with a slope of 1 in 20. These ramps do not require a handrail unless there is a drop-off of 2 in. or more on one or both sides of the ramp. Look again at Fig. 1-3 for a better understanding of the requirements for handrails and ramps.

This slope requirement does not apply to curb ramps or curb cuts leading to accessible walks or parking spaces. See again Fig. 4-6. Handrails, when required, should be set at a height between 30 and 34 in., and have a 12-in. extension on the horizontal ends at the top and bottom landings. The minimum diameter of these handrails should be 1-1/4 to 1-1/2 in.

For children's handrails, use a height of 26 to 28 in. and a diameter of 1-1/4 in. Refer back to Figs. 1-5 and 1-6.

The front stoop or porch should provide a safe area at least 5 ft × 5 ft. See Fig. 2-1. This also will provide a distance of 1 ft 6 in. (18 in.) from the pull or handle of the door, which will allow enough clearance for a person in a wheelchair to reach the handle and be able to pull the door open with relative ease. If this space and distance were not provided, the person in the wheelchair would have to back away from the door-pull, making the door-opening procedure much more difficult.

Portable ramps are useful, but they can be a hazard when used like this.

It is very important, and indeed critical, that in new construction the primary entrance be as close as possible to the grade-level. This will prevent this type of architectural barrier from occurring. If there are existing stoops or porches, and the grade difference is less than 6 in., the preferred approach is to grade the ground to the stoop, preventing any difference in height between the grade-level and the stoop or porch. If a ramp cannot be installed at the front or primary entrance, then one may be installed wherever there is a door at least 36-in. wide and a clear path, or the possibility of installing a 3-ft-wide door, with as short a rise as possible between the ground and the stoop. The new door could then serve as the primary entrance.

The local building code may require handrails around the porch or stoop, depending on the height of the porch or stoop from the natural grade. It might be a good idea to verify this condition before making any changes or installing new handrails or railings.

The Threshold. To prevent the standard threshold from becoming a barrier for the disabled, the construction industry has gone on record as promising to provide barrier-free thresholds for almost every conceivable type of entrance. I recommend that thresholds such as those by Pemko be installed and that you contact the company to ascertain which would be the correct threshold for your entrance. Most of these designs take into account that the maximum height at which exterior doors are to be installed is ½ in. If the entrance is a glass sliding type, the recommended allowance is set at ¾ in. See Fig. 2-2.

Special ramps can be purchased which allow the wheelchair to go over thresholds more than ¾-in. high. For all interior doors with thresholds, the recommended height again is ½ in.

It's amazing how much trouble two inches can be.

Figure 2-3 gives the heights recommended for other types of thresholds such as, for example, a ceramic tile floor in a bathroom or in the entrance area, or a stone or marble threshold that is higher than the required height. If, when you are in the process of your survey and you see a difference of more than ¾ in. in height between the threshold and the floor surface, you must make special provisions to either change the threshold or, better still, remove it entirely. It is still highly recommended that there be no thresholds in the interior of the home.

The Door. The entry door or front entrance, or any door that provides direct access to the home should be of sufficient size to allow the wheelchair-bound person easy access. It has been determined that 2 ft 8 in. (32 in.) of *clear* space is required to clear the hands of a person in a wheelchair. See Fig. 2-4. I personally think this door should be a little wider (42 in.), but this is a personal opinion and not a requirement.

If we look at Fig. 2-5, we notice one additional requirement for entrance doors and their areas if free access is to be maintained. It shows that 3 ft 6 in. (42 in.) is the recommended distance in a corridor, while a 60-in. × 60-in. side width is still the required space.

In a commercial establishment, where self-closing or automatic-opening doors are provided, a 5 ft × 5 ft space is still needed. Other interior doors and their required distances are noted in Fig. 2-6. We must always try to maintain clear access to or a direct route through any area. This is a new ADA requirement for accessibility.

When conditions warrant double-door entries or if airlocks, privacy screens, or covered entrances are the prevailing conditions, then we can look at Figs. 2-7 and 2-8 to help us determine which arrangement will suit our situation best, and use that design. When double doors are required, one of these arrangements will provide the necessary space for easy access. The elderly find that arrangements such as those illustrated here are easy to pass through.

The Entrance Doorknob. For a long time it has been known that the round or common doorknob was not the most practical form of door hardware. It was always thought that the lever handle would be the easiest to operate. That is still true today. Lever handles do cost more than the round type, but if you have arthritis or any other hand mobility impairment, the cost becomes irrelevant. Currently we find that most designers are specifying lever handles for many different purposes, and they are rapidly becoming the standard. I, of course, recommend that you use lever handles wherever you can, and, if possible, on every door. Figures 2-9 and 2-10 show some of the different types of door-pulls, latches, and handles that are available today. A company that is an excellent source for these types of knobs is the Schlage Co. I am not referring to special types of door hardware, such as emergency or panic door devices; these types are called for by code and are requirements for life safety. Ordinary doors are the subject we are discussing here, and easy operation is what we are trying to maintain.

Many doors are very heavy and require special heavy-duty hinges. Keeping these hinges oiled makes these doors much easier to open. In commercial establishments, automatic doors or automatic door closures normally are used. These door openers must be set for normal pulling pressure. Setting the pull pressure at 5-1/2 pounds makes opening them easy.

In areas where heating and/or cooling systems are in operation, it is particularly important that the pressure required to operate automatic

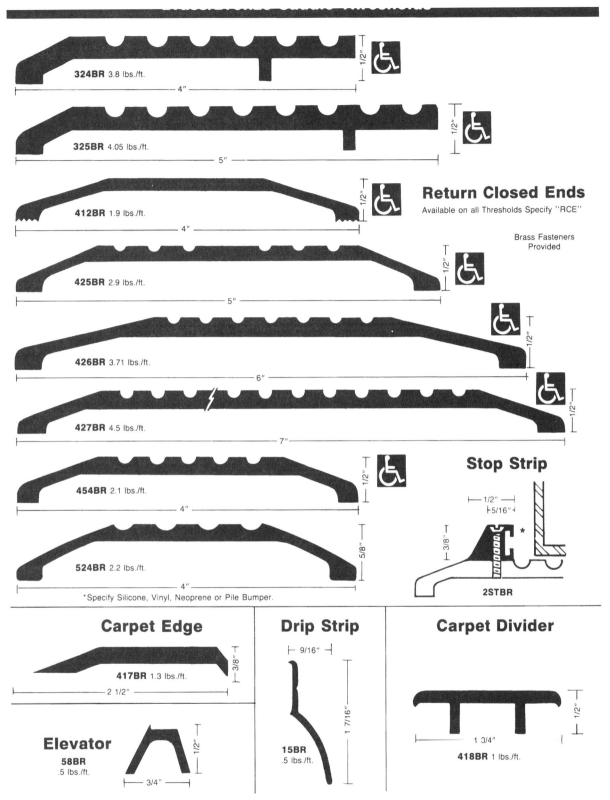

324BR 3.8 lbs./ft. — 4" — 1/2"

325BR 4.05 lbs./ft. — 5" — 1/2"

412BR 1.9 lbs./ft. — 4" — 1/2"

Return Closed Ends

Available on all Thresholds Specify "RCE"

Brass Fasteners Provided

425BR 2.9 lbs./ft. — 5" — 1/2"

426BR 3.71 lbs./ft. — 6" — 1/2"

427BR 4.5 lbs./ft. — 7" — 1/2"

454BR 2.1 lbs./ft. — 4" — 1/2"

Stop Strip

1/2" 5/16" 3/8" *

2STBR

524BR 2.2 lbs./ft. — 4" — 5/8"

*Specify Silicone, Vinyl, Neoprene or Pile Bumper.

Carpet Edge

417BR 1.3 lbs./ft. — 2 1/2" — 3/8"

Elevator

58BR .5 lbs./ft. — 3/4" — 1/2"

Drip Strip

9/16" 1 7/16"

15BR .5 lbs./ft.

Carpet Divider

418BR 1 lbs./ft. — 1 3/4" — 1/2"

Thresholds that allow for easy access. Units manufactured by Natural Guard Products, Inc.

doors not exceed 5-1/2 pounds, because excessive pressure, negative or otherwise, causes them to stay open. The correct way to prevent this is to have the system balanced by the heating/cooling contractor. Automatic doors are the best way to enter any building, but, realistically, not everybody can afford to have them on an individual residence, or, for that matter, not everyone wants one. Figure 2-4 was adapted from the federal guidelines for accessibility, but I feel it gives a clearer picture of what may be needed to provide doors with their most important attribute, accessibility.

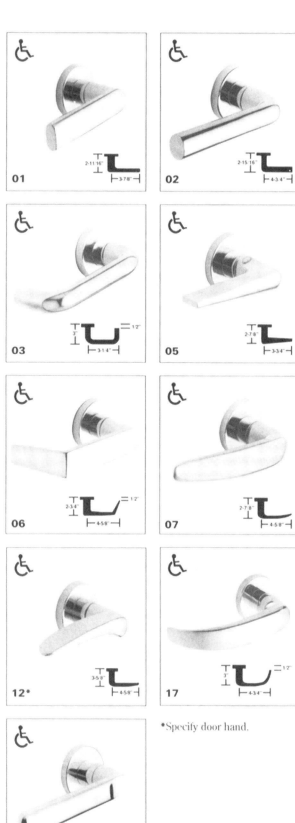

01

02

03

05

06

07

12*

17

*Specify door hand.

18

Lever handles (interior), manufactured by Schlage Lock Co.

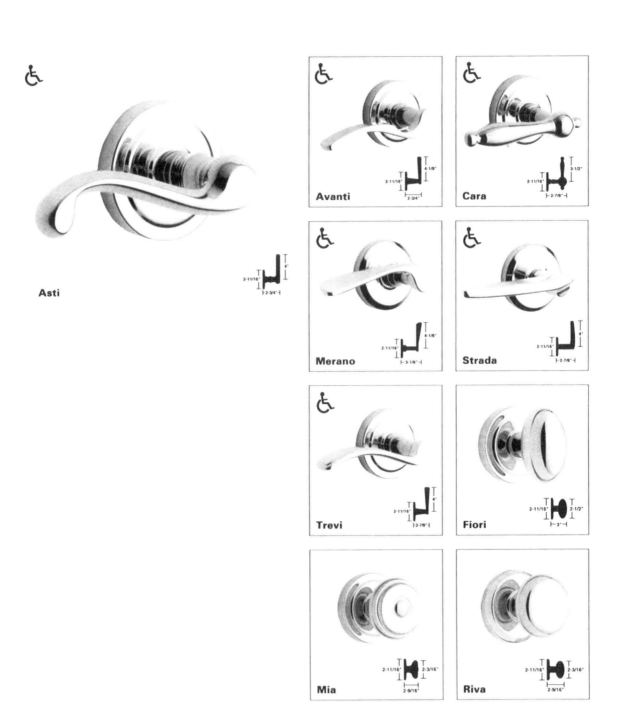

Asti

Avanti

Cara

Merano

Strada

Trevi

Fiori

Mia

Riva

Specify door handing for lever designs.

Lever handles (exterior), manufactured by Schlage Lock Co. (The round handles at the bottom of the chart would pose a problem for many elderly and disabled.)

Chapter Three
THE FOYER

The foyer, sometimes called the front hall, may not pose a problem except to wheelchair-bound persons. The foyer can indeed become a barrier as soon as it becomes clear that there is no space in which to turn around. If there is insufficient space, the wheelchair-bound person can not even close the door. It is frustrating for someone in a wheelchair to hit the wall when trying to turn.

We now continue with our hypothetical walk-through. We get into the house and find out that the chair wheels don't move. This is caused by the deep-pile carpeting in the house; the wheels dig in and can't move. Instead, we may install scatter rungs. If they don't move, fine; but they had better not curl up at the edges. If they do, they become treacherous for the elderly, the blind, or any people who have trouble lifting their legs when they walk. We know that crutches and canes can slip. Actually, it is preferable to have no floor covering at all, since even very smooth floor coverings can cause slippage when the floor is wet.

Removing the wall itself would create more space. While this is a very expensive solution to the removal of a barrier, we need to consider all possible solutions to this problem.

BARRIERS IDENTIFIED IN THE FOYER

- Carpeting or rugs
- Lack of space

How to Remove These Barriers

Carpeting or Rugs. If the carpeting has a deep pile, it would be best to remove it and replace it with carpeting with a low pile and a tight weave. Have it glued to the floor to ensure that it will not move, curl at the edges, or have ridges of any kind. If no carpet can be installed to fit these criteria, go to a smooth floor-covering. See the table in Chapter 7 on the various floor coverings and the slip-resistance of each type. Also, before installing any kind of floor covering, see Fig. 3-1 for some of the problems carpeting can cause.

If you use loose (or scatter) rugs at the front door or foyer, they should be rubber-backed, since rubber-backed rugs offer the greatest slip-resistance. Rugs that curl up at the edges are a hazard to people who use canes, crutches, or walkers, and, incidentally, to everyone. For safety's sake, it's a good idea to go through the entire home, checking wherever there is carpeting, rugs, or surfaces that could become slippery.

Lack of Space. There is not much that can be done to provide additional space for turning around the chair in the foyer. You might consider removing some furniture or a small section of a wall. Wall removal is, of course, quite expensive.

Ideally, when building a new residence, one should provide additional space for turning around in the foyer. (See Fig. 2-6.)

Chapter Four
THE KITCHEN

As we continue our walk-through, we finally make it to the kitchen. It has been said that most of us spend at least half our time in the kitchen to prepare meals, eat, and as an area for visiting. It is a room we use every day in every way.

Most kitchens are not convenient at all! Many of today's kitchens are too small. Usually, there is less than 4 ft between the counters, which does not provide enough space for a wheelchair to turn around.

Wheelchair-bound people can't move about freely, or reach all of the stove controls or the sink faucet. There is insufficient space to put a bag of groceries or store cans or any other everyday items used for cooking. The space is too restrictive and awkward to make their lives enjoyable. It is inconvenient to reach the shelves. In fact it is almost impossible for the wheelchair-bound to put their groceries away.

The many barriers in the kitchen include the stove controls, which are often at the rear of the stove. This condition makes it both difficult and dangerous to reach them from a wheelchair. The water faucet at the sink, again, is at the rear, making it difficult to reach and/or to turn off. If you are arthritic, this action usually is also painful.

The wall oven may be too high, while the stove oven may be too low. It's difficult enough for an able-bodied person to remove a hot object from the oven, so imagine how much harder it would be if you were disabled. The countertops are too high, and every electrical outlet is on that back wall. The kitchen is not user-friendly to those who are physically challenged or elderly.

Quite a bit of research has been done on the kitchen; it has shown that we rely on it much more than it was thought at first. It is a center of family activity, but it is also a place we use to welcome everyone into our homes. Chapter 12 (Fig. 12-3) lists products and ideas on making the kitchen more convenient. There are many things available for the kitchen today to make our lives more enjoyable and easier. There are electrical appliances to open our cans, make our morning coffee, and mix and blend our foods. All of these can make the kitchen one of the happier places in the home.

It is important that we fully utilize this very important area. More and more today, the elderly want to stay in their own homes, so we must make every effort to make the kitchen more accessible.

Let us recap the numerous barriers we have identified to see exactly what we can do to make things more accessible. It is satisfying to know that help is on the way.

BARRIERS IDENTIFIED IN THE KITCHEN

- Inadequate space
- Lack of shelving

Wouldn't a dropped counter be nice in this kitchen?

- Lack of shelving at proper height
- Appliances hard to reach and operate
- Inaccessible sinks
- Difficult-to-reach storage areas
- Countertops at improper heights
- Wall receptacles, switches, thermostats
- Floor coverings

How to Remove These Barriers

Inadequate Space. This is a difficult barrier to eliminate because the cost of enlarging a space is so high. It comes close to being a major renovation.

I have included some space requirements that I highly recommend be followed. See Figs. 4-1, 4-2, and 4-3 and follow along with me. Figure 4-1 describes how the toe space can add to the space you have, so that it is easier to move the wheelchair around. Obviously, it is important that one is able to move around in the kitchen. The 30" × 48" clear space that is recommended will allow free movement to the appliances, the fixtures, and the storage shelves. As Fig. 4-2 shows, the 60-in. × 60-in. space can overlap the 30-in. × 30-in. space. Figure 4-3, which is adapted from the federal guidelines, explains reach limits. You must survey your own kitchen to see what space you have and decide whether there is any way you can utilize extra space. All this should be done before any attempt is made to seek outside help in planning for renovations.

Lack of Shelving. The lack of shelving is not a barrier solely for the disabled. Really, it is an acknowledged condition of many homes. Most homeowners simply complain that they do not have enough shelving to satisfy their particular needs. The question of what constitutes sufficient shelving can be answered only by you.

Lack of Shelving at the Proper Height. Shelving that can be reached with relative ease is fully usable, but shelving that is too high to reach merely becomes dead storage, a place to put those pots and pans you use once a year, or other items you rarely use. This places a premium on the remaining accessible shelving. Figure 4-4 gives the recommended dimensions for accessible shelving. The bottom shelf of the upper wall cabinet should be no higher than 48 in. from the floor. The wall cabinets above refrigerators may be considered dead storage space.

If you feel that more shelving is required, check every corner you have, to see where additional shelving could be installed. A pantry makes an excellent addition for extra storage and shelving, but always make sure that you are not just adding another barrier, in just a different area, one that will cause you problems later on.

Appliances Difficult to Reach and to Operate. It has become a major concern to appliance manufacturers that units be more accessible to the disabled, because they can see that there is a strong market for this type of unit. The controls of most "handicapped" appliances are now in the front and are very easy to see and operate. Most of the newer models stress this advantage in their advertising. It is to our benefit that we, in turn, make known what we want in these new appliances. Look at Figs. 4-5, 4-6, 4-7, and 4-8 to gain an understanding of the space required to operate appliances safely.

Let us look at Fig. 4-5 again. It states that ovens, as well as microwave units, should have the door latch or handle located on the same side of the oven as worktop space. It should be a maximum distance of 4 ft 8 in. (54 in.) above the finished floor. The figure also shows that the door latch or handle could be at the top of the oven if its distance from the floor is no more than 54 in. On a standard oven, controls at the front are the preferred type, but stoves of this type should always be located next to an accessible worktop. This allows the disabled person to place a hot item directly from the oven onto the worktop. As we see in Fig. 4-6, the worktop space next to the oven should always be insulated to prevent it from burning.

When refrigerators are placed near a wing-wall or a kitchen end-wall, care must be taken to allow the door to swing a complete 180 degrees without meeting any obstruction.

Dishwashers should be placed next to an accessible sink. If possible, provide units that have the controls in front, bottom-hinged doors, and doors that lock by lever or pushbutton. See Fig. 4-7.

Kitchen garbage disposal/grinder units should always be placed under the deeper sink, with the activating switch at a height of 48 in. if on a sidewall, and 26 in. if at the front of a cabinet. See Fig. 4-8.

Inaccessible Sinks. We may say that the sink should be accessible, but do we know what the requirements for that are? But, we might ask, why all the fuss over what is an accessible sink? If you are in a wheelchair, or become wheelchair-bound in the future, you will never again ask that question. One cannot describe the frustration of trying to reach the faucet for a glass of water; or the frustration of trying to wash that dish at a sink you can't reach.

Studies have shown the reach of a chair-bound person. Figure 4-3 is a copy of the federal regulations that show the reach limitations. I agree that it is very confusing. Let us simplify it. The maximum reach of a person in a chair is approximately 48 in. This will vary according to the size of the person, but 48 in. is typical for a person whose reach is about 25 in. along the countertop or level plane. This distance would increase if one's legs could get closer to the wall or barrier. Again to reiterate, you can reach up and forward 48 in., and sideways up to 54 in., allowing you to reach closer and still be able to reach horizontally 25 inches. By allowing the legs to go under the counter, items at the rear can be reached more easily. Twenty-five in. is still the maximum reach, but access is improved to provide more of a reachable area.

Sinks for the physically challenged are open at the bottom since this open space allows the legs to pass under the countertop, so they can get closer to the sink, the faucet, and any other objects they would normally use at the sink.

When you refer to Fig. 4-9 you will note the dimensions needed for better access. Be certain that the hot water pipes are insulated or covered with a removable metallic baffle if hot water temperatures are over 120°F. To prevent leg burns from these hot pipes, it is always safer to have the temperature set at about 112°F. See Fig. 4-10.

Difficult to Reach Storage Areas. When the physically challenged or the elderly start to think about storage in their homes, they begin to realize that they may have more than they thought. The critical dimensions of storage space include the distance from the shelves to the floor, and the ease of reaching for items at the rear portion of the shelves. If you can't reach it, you can't use it.

Look all around your home; inside, outside, and in every corner. I cannot emphasize the importance of being able to reach and use all this space. A home can never have enough storage space to satisfy everyone.

Countertops at the Improper Height. Many people now recognize that counter heights are an important element in accessibility. We need to provide more workspace on counters so that the disabled can prepare their own food and do the hundred and one things that need to be done in the kitchen. Figure 4-5 shows that an adjustable work countertop is recommended, that it be at least 30 in. wide, and be located next to an oven. Figure 4-6 again will show that a clear workspace of 30 in. is recommended on at least one side of the sink. I recommend that at least one adjustable area of countertop be provided. I would like to see another space identical to it somewhere in the kitchen, preferably opposite the kitchen sink, next to the refrigerator, or the place where food is prepared. See Figs. 4-11 and 4-12.

If you do not have a table that is close to a height of 30 in., it is critical that this be provided to allow the wheelchair to get under the table; a table height of 30 in. allows the chair to fit nicely under it. If you have other disabilities that require special provisions in the kitchen and I have

Another beautiful kitchen, but inaccessible.

not addressed them here, I suggest that you contact your local rehabilitation office or the occupational therapist at your local hospital. Either of these would be of great assistance in determining your specific needs.

Wall Receptacles, Switches, and Thermostats. Electrical wall receptacles in the kitchen or anywhere else in the house must be accessible. You do not need to be in a wheelchair to know the frustration of not being able to reach a receptacle. If you will look at Fig. 4-13, you can check on the recommended height for all receptacles, switches, and other electrical controls.

Receptacles over the back-splash of the counter are another problem. It is almost impossible to reach these receptacles when you are in a chair. We need to extend them to within easy reach. Extension cords that provide three or four additional plugs are useful and usually safe if they are not overloaded. Never put more than one extension cord into each outlet; that is the cause of many of the fires in the home today.

Locate some receptacles as close as possible to the edge of a wing wall or on the back wall. This allows the disabled to use those plugs when preparing foods or cooking.

If a major renovation is being planned, I strongly recommend that a professional electrical contractor be employed to install the electrical additions. Stress the fact that you are disabled, and for independent living require access to all the kitchen receptacles. You should request that the electrician follow the recommendations in your local and state building codes for the electrical needs of the disabled. This will ensure that the receptacle heights are correct and are located in the best possible places for easy access.

Floor Coverings. Did you ever think that the kind of floor covering you have in your home could be a barrier? To consider what type of flooring is best suited to your needs, you must first understand how slippery floors affect the disabled, and precisely what constitutes a slippery floor.

Most vinyls (that would include floor tiles) have some form of adhesive backing that is inherent to that type of floor covering. We call this type of flooring *slip resistant.* Sheet vinyl is very common today, and is the flooring most often installed in the kitchen, halls, laundries, and bathrooms.

When selecting flooring for your home, look for the type that offers the most slip resistance. When vinyl gets wet, it can be very slippery, but in the manufacture of some vinyl, a slip resistant material is added to it. This may be quartz, graphite crystals, or another material that provides slip resistance.

The table in Chapter 7 lists a number of well-known floor coverings and provides a chart showing their slip resistance. You may wish to review this list to see which ones will serve you best.

Chapter Five
THE LAUNDRY

The laundry room might be a washing machine and a dryer located in a small alcove or large utility room, or it might be no more than a portable washing machine hooked up to a faucet. Laundry rooms usually are located off a hallway or even in the garage. Wherever they are, often they are the cause of frustration, and are a definite barrier to the disabled. Water spills are dangerous to those on walkers or crutches; exposed hot water pipes can burn or scald people. There also are many electrical hazards associated with the laundry; switches and receptacles are too high and/or unreachable, and they may not be grounded properly.

Inefficient methods of heating hot water, coupled with a work space that is very tight for the wheelchair can lead to dangerous practices, and inadequate ventilation could be a health problem. The local codes in your area will provide you with information on the correct amount of air exchange or forced ventilation that is recommended for safety.

BARRIERS IDENTIFIED IN THE LAUNDRY AREA

- Inadequate space
- Water spills
- Receptacles, switches
- Insufficient storage
- Ventilation deficiencies

How to Remove These Barriers

Inadequate Space. Always allow as much space as possible in the laundry. If it is possible to allocate a room to function just as a laundry, it would be easier for the elderly or almost any disabled person. The location of the laundry room depends on your own work style and circumstances.

Provide as much space as possible to store such items as detergent and bleach; and a table of some sort to separate and fold laundry is very helpful. If you do not have a sink that can be used for presoaking, hand washing, or as a mop sink, have one installed if possible. Call for the services of a licensed plumber to install a new sink.

Indoor clothes racks and clotheslines are useful for drying small items. Details on exterior clotheslines are in Chapter 8.

A collapsible ironing board can be installed on a wall close to your laundry or the place where you do most of your ironing. When set at the proper height, these collapsible boards are very useful. If they are installed against a wall, they should be easy to pull out. Before having a built-in ironing board installed, though, verify the amount of space you would have around the ironing board when it is open. Also check to see whether this installation creates any additional barriers, such as there not being enough room to move about, cords laying on the floor that would cause a tripping problem, and so on.

For your safety, a telephone should be nearby, too, possibly in some area of the laundry. It must be set at the proper height and be easy to reach. Perhaps the most important part of making the laundry accessible is ensuring that it have as much space as possible.

Water Spills. The floor is bound to get wet at some point, and when it gets wet, it gets very slippery. When this happens, it becomes not just a barrier, but a very dangerous situation for the disabled, the elderly, or people hampered by crutches, canes, or a walker.

To control this, you could have floor drains installed to get rid of the water, but this may not always be practical. One possibility is to have non-slip flooring installed. A less costly solution is making sure that water spills are wiped up quickly. This barrier is a condition that is very hard to eliminate, but, as long as you understand how dangerous it is, you can control it.

Electrical Receptacles, Switches, Thermostats. If you look back at Fig. 4.13 again, you will notice that most problems are the result of controls at inaccessible heights. If all receptacles and switches were set at 40 in., it would be very easy. If this problem can not be solved in some other way, the only recourse is to have some renovations done to move them to the correct height.

Typical laundry appliances, with controls in the rear, making operation difficult for the disabled.

A practical laundry setup, with accessible controls; manufactured by Whirlpool.

Insufficient Storage Space. To remove the barrier of insufficient storage space, one must look into every nook and cranny to see if there is any place to put those extra things away. I wish there were a magic way to get extra storage. The only way I know is to add on or renovate, and that, unfortunately, is expensive. Architects, home builders, and occupational and physical therapists can offer some ideas on what may be done to provide the extra storage.

Ventilation Deficiencies. Adequate ventilation is imperative in the laundry. Not only does air movement help the drying process, it also provides a cooling effect from the steam or heat usually found in the laundry room. Therefore ventilation is useful in alleviating any stress on the disabled or the elderly caused by the steam. Adequate ventilation, then, becomes an important element in making things easier for the elderly or the disabled. To check whether there is a code or regulation that tells how much ventilation is required, it is important to contact your local building inspection official. If you are involved in providing housing or other buildings for the elderly, there are specific ventilation requirements that must be met.

Chapter Six
THE BATHROOM

Next in our walk-through is the bathroom, another very important area. Research is ongoing as to what we should expect our bathrooms to provide, how they should look, and what we may expect in the bathrooms of the future. There are many publications available that attempt to tell us what our bathrooms should look like and how they should function.

Why is the bathroom such a barrier to the disabled? Why does it cause so many problems? It's hard to believe that a room that is a relative newcomer to the place we call a home can cause so many problems. Maybe it is because in the past, in an effort to minimize the cost of residences and commercial spaces, many designers, architects, and home builders reduced the space allocated to bathrooms. The result was toilets that were small, compact, and utilitarian. Designers have striven to make them very convenient to get to, but the bathrooms themselves became hard to get into. Since most doors were designed to be 24 to 28-in wide, designers have built in space problems for the wheelchair-bound person. See Fig. 6-1. Figures 6-2, 6-3, 6-4, and 6-5 show Federal guidelines, directly applicable to bathroom design, for wheelchair space allowances, reach ranges, and accessible routes.

If you can get through the door, you consider yourself lucky, since most doors are less than 2-ft 4-in. wide (28 in.). You may not be able to use the vanity or get up to the sink or faucet. The counter is too high to use comfortably. You cannot see into the mirror, and you have trouble reaching the towel. You feel restricted and closed in. The main function of the bathroom is the use of the commode, but it sits over in the corner, so you can barely reach it, and there is nothing to grab onto for support. A grab-bar would make it easier for you to transfer from the wheelchair to the commode and then back. You know there has to be a better way.

The bathtub again offers some formidable barriers. If you can get up to it, you find there is no grab bar of any kind to use, no seat in the tub, and no way you can use the water controls even if you can manage to get into the tub. There is a danger of being scalded, and the controls, if there are any, are too high for you to reach. While you are in the tub, the water controls are too high or low for you to use, and it is difficult to reach up that high or low enough to turn those controls on.

Some of you may be lucky enough to have a shower unit instead of a tub. There are barriers here for the disabled as well. The doorway may be too narrow, the shower may not have an inside seat to sit on while showering, or enough space for the wheelchair to fit inside the shower there. The shower has become a necessity and you depend on it. You ask why all the things you rely on are so difficult to use? This is especially true for those who are disabled.

BARRIERS IDENTIFIED IN THE BATHROOM

- Narrow entrance door
- Inaccessible lavatory (sink)

A typical bathroom door; too narrow when it is only 2-ft wide.

A unique bathroom, but unsuitable for the disabled, who would find the sink and bathtub difficult to use.

The radiator is too close to the commode. This can be very hazardous to the elderly and disabled.

- Mirrors, shelves, and towel bars
- Inaccessible commodes
- Missing grab bars
- Bathtub access; grab bars in the tub
- Slippery surfaces
- No seat provided
- Controls too high
- Shower access too narrow
- Lack of temperature controls

How to Remove These Barriers

Narrow Entrance Door. There is no denying it, if the doorway to your bathroom has less than 32 in. of clear width (see Fig. 6.2), and you are in a wheelchair, the door needs to be wider if you are to have free access. You may say that you got by in the past and can continue to do so now, or that it's too expensive to change, but, if your goal is independent living, then the door will have to be changed.

If you do decide to change the doors to get access, I suggest that you contact your local building inspection official and ask for the names of local contractors who can do this work for you.

If you have a small bathroom (most of those in the residences in the United States are small, usually around 80 to 100 sq ft), I suggest that you study Figs. 6-6 and 6-7 to get some feeling of the space relationship you can follow to attain the required accessibility.

When and if you do exchange your door for one of the correct size, at the same time you should change the doorknob to one of the lever type. This type of doorknob is best for people with any kind of disability to use. As a matter of fact, lever-action knobs are the easiest to use of all the types of doorknobs.

Inaccessible Lavatory (Sink). The area of clear floor space that will allow a wheelchair-bound person to physically get closer to the vanity and to reach the faucets is 30 in. × 40 in. You can get your legs closer if you have an open vanity. (Open vanities are those with no base cabinet). If you will look at Fig. 6-8, you will see the configuration requirements.

Notice that it's better to have the open space beneath the lavatory, which permits a wide approach to the vanity. See Figs. 6-9 and 6-10. Pedestal sinks, which offer the greatest freedom of access, are also known as free-standing lavatories, and they are not as expensive as you might think.

Figure 6.8 also shows the recommended treatments for the hot and cold water supply lines. Remember, it is best to have the hot water temperature set at less than 112°. You may wish to have hotter water, but if you do, the water pipes must be covered with some form of insulation to protect the disabled from having their legs burned. The rim of the lavatory must be no higher than 30 in. from the floor.

Mirrors, Shelves, and Towel Bars. Mirrors are a necessity in the bathroom, and when placed above the lavatory, should be no higher than 34 in. from the finished floor. Fig. 6-11 shows how they are set. Shelves should also be set at the same height. This height affords those in wheelchairs easier access.

Accessories that are located in many other areas around the home should also be placed within easy reach. This makes for more convenient

A beautiful bathroom, but with no access for the disabled to the commode, lavatory, or even the medicine cabinet.

Invitation™ lavatory, which overhangs the counter, provides improved access; manufactured by Kohler.

living. When commercial applications are needed, Fig. 6.11 provides the correct heights for such things as towel bars, cup dispensers, paper towels, or any other coin-, lever-, or push-button-operated dispensers. Installing them at 36 in. from the floor makes these accessories easy to reach for all the disabled. See Fig. 6.11 for additional information.

If you are planning to either build a new residence, or make major renovations on your existing home, I recommend that you explore the advantages of going into an "adaptable house." Plan for such things as having the blocking for grab-bars installed in the walls before the wall construction is complete. Also plan for wider halls and doors that have 32 in. of clear width. The house should be built close to the ground, and have either very low thresholds or none at all. Many of the barriers I have already discussed are removed from or designed out of an adaptable house. Figure 6-12 gives the details on the blocking for grab-bars.

Inaccessible Commodes. Much has been written on how to make the commode, water closet, toilet, or whatever we may call it, accessible. I will attempt to keep things relatively simple.

For the disabled, the most important problem is transferring from the wheelchair to the commode. Ideally, there should be 60 in. × 60 in. (5 ft × 5 ft) of space in front of the commode. Many of my sketches call for this space as a specific requirement, since it has become the standard because it allows a wheelchair to make a complete turn. It also provides the maximum ease in making the transfer.

Figures 6.6 and 6.7 give the recommended space requirements for toilets with showers. These drawings depict small toilet rooms, and can be used to determine the space requirements for your own bathroom. Figures 6-13, 6-14, and 6-15 show different space arrangements, and how the door may swing in or out, or slide, in each. Figure 6-16 depicts a bathroom that offers accessibility in a very small space.

It is important to remember that the type of approach used in the transfer from the wheelchair to the commode will help you to determine the amount of the space you need for making the transfer. These sketches will help you to understand the amount of space necessary for safe and easy transfers when using the commode. Unless some space is definitely allocated, the bathroom will always be an area that causes frustration and anger.

Missing Grab Bars. Why must we have grab bars? The answer is that grab bars are necessary for the safety of the disabled. They instill a sense of security when maintaining balance is a problem. They normally are installed around the commode, where they provide the most security and help in transferring to and from it. Figure 6-17 shows where grab bars are mounted, at a height of between 33 and 36 in. from the floor. Figures 6-18 and 6-19 show the recommended locations.

Grab bars can and should be installed in all places where people might require assistance in maintaining their balance. In another portion of this book, I will describe the required locations of the grab bar in the tub and shower area.

If you are planning to build or renovate your existing home or commercial facility, look into the possibility of using the *Adaptable House* manual as an additional guide. The main idea is to have the blocking installed during initial construction for the installation of grab bars in the future, should they become necessary. This manual is included in my list of resources in Chapter 11.

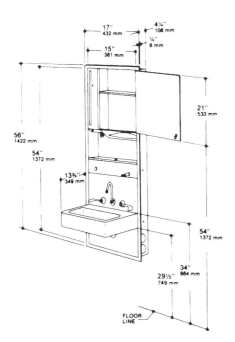

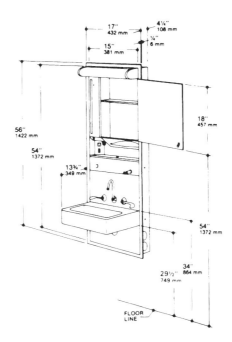

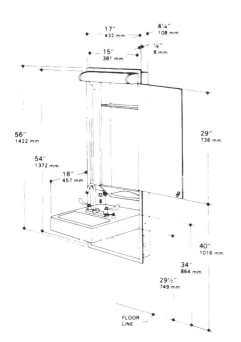

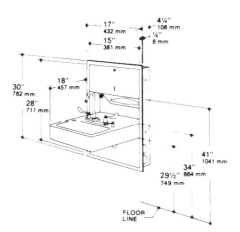

Console units for the disabled; manufactured by Bobrick Washroom Equipment.

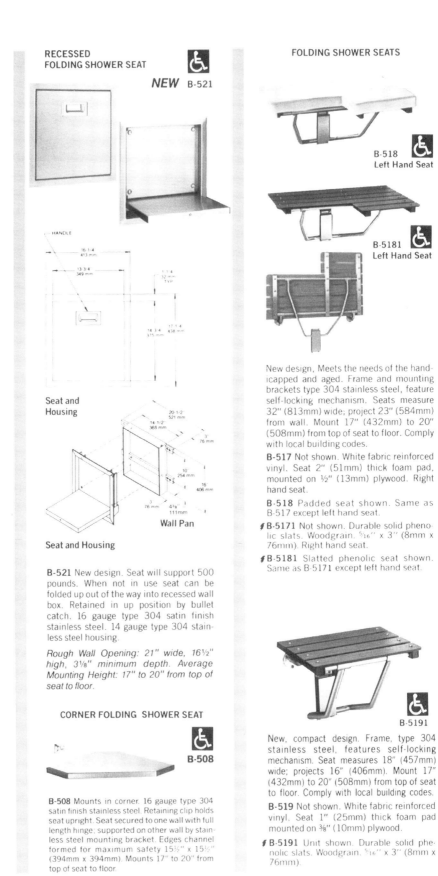

RECESSED FOLDING SHOWER SEAT

NEW B-521

Seat and Housing

Seat and Housing

Wall Pan

B-521 New design. Seat will support 500 pounds. When not in use seat can be folded up out of the way into recessed wall box. Retained in up position by bullet catch. 16 gauge type 304 satin finish stainless steel. 14 gauge type 304 stainless steel housing.

Rough Wall Opening: 21" wide, 16½" high, 3⅛" minimum depth. Average Mounting Height: 17" to 20" from top of seat to floor.

CORNER FOLDING SHOWER SEAT

B-508

B-508 Mounts in corner. 16 gauge type 304 satin finish stainless steel. Retaining clip holds seat upright. Seat secured to one wall with full length hinge; supported on other wall by stainless steel mounting bracket. Edges channel formed for maximum safety 15½" x 15½" (394mm x 394mm). Mounts 17" to 20" from top of seat to floor.

FOLDING SHOWER SEATS

B-518
Left Hand Seat

B-5181
Left Hand Seat

New design. Meets the needs of the handicapped and aged. Frame and mounting brackets type 304 stainless steel, feature self-locking mechanism. Seats measure 32" (813mm) wide; project 23" (584mm) from wall. Mount 17" (432mm) to 20" (508mm) from top of seat to floor. Comply with local building codes.

B-517 Not shown. White fabric reinforced vinyl. Seat 2" (51mm) thick foam pad, mounted on ½" (13mm) plywood. Right hand seat.

B-518 Padded seat shown. Same as B-517 except left hand seat.

ƒ B-5171 Not shown. Durable solid phenolic slats. Woodgrain. ⁵⁄₁₆" x 3" (8mm x 76mm). Right hand seat.

ƒ B-5181 Slatted phenolic seat shown. Same as B-5171 except left hand seat.

B-5191

New, compact design. Frame, type 304 stainless steel, features self-locking mechanism. Seat measures 18" (457mm) wide; projects 16" (406mm). Mount 17" (432mm) to 20" (508mm) from top of seat to floor. Comply with local building codes.

B-519 Not shown. White fabric reinforced vinyl. Seat 1" (25mm) thick foam pad mounted on ⅜" (10mm) plywood.

ƒ B-5191 Unit shown. Durable solid phenolic slats. Woodgrain. ⁵⁄₁₆" x 3" (8mm x 76mm).

Accessories for the bath and shower; manufactured by Bobrick Washroom Equipment.

The height of this toilet, manufactured by Kohler, makes it more accessible to the elderly and disabled.

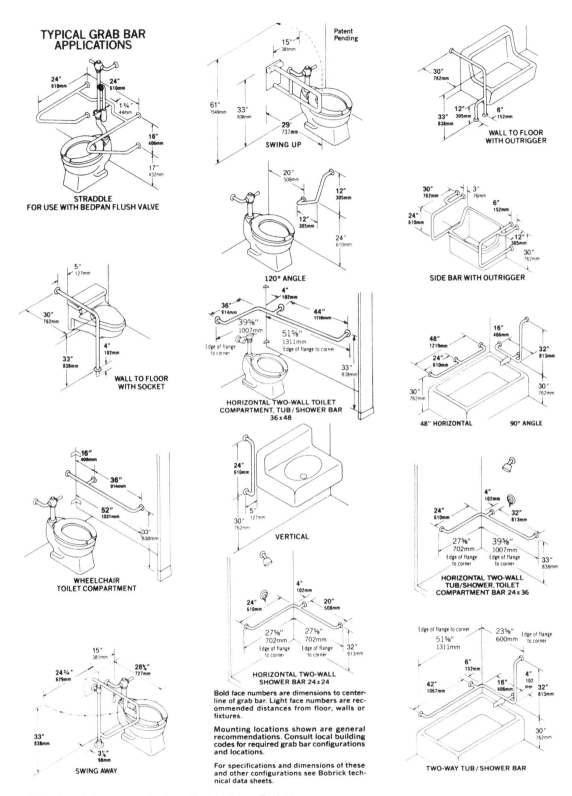

TYPICAL GRAB BAR APPLICATIONS

STRADDLE
FOR USE WITH BEDPAN FLUSH VALVE

SWING UP

WALL TO FLOOR WITH OUTRIGGER

120° ANGLE

SIDE BAR WITH OUTRIGGER

WALL TO FLOOR WITH SOCKET

HORIZONTAL TWO-WALL TOILET COMPARTMENT, TUB/SHOWER BAR 36 x 48

48" HORIZONTAL   **90° ANGLE**

WHEELCHAIR TOILET COMPARTMENT

VERTICAL

HORIZONTAL TWO-WALL TUB/SHOWER, TOILET COMPARTMENT BAR 24 x 36

HORIZONTAL TWO-WALL SHOWER BAR 24 x 24

Bold face numbers are dimensions to centerline of grab bar. Light face numbers are recommended distances from floor, walls or fixtures.

Mounting locations shown are general recommendations. Consult local building codes for required grab bar configurations and locations.

For specifications and dimensions of these and other configurations see Bobrick technical data sheets.

SWING AWAY

TWO-WAY TUB/SHOWER BAR

Typical grab bars; manufactured by McKinney Parker.

In commercial buildings, the law is quite specific. All public toilets must provide either an accessible commode with partitions, or, in small toilet rooms, have the required grab bars installed in accordance with the new ADA laws such as the Rehabilitation Acts, Sections 503 and 504, and the new Americans with Disabilities Act of 1990; both of these spell out these requirements very clearly. Commercial applications can follow Fig. 6-20 for the installation of urinals, and Fig. 6-21 for the requirements of the ANSI code.

While the *Adaptable Housing* manual may not give you all the answers you need, it will help you to understand what barrier-free housing is, and will lead you to other resources that contain additional information.

Bathtub Access and Grab Bars in the Tub. Figure 6-22 shows the amount of clear opening necessary for access to an enclosed bathtub.

The location of the grab bars for the bathtub should conform to a particular set of requirements. When you look at Figs. 6-23 and 6-24, you will see that they specify that two bars be installed parallel to the finished floor, and that they be on the wall parallel to the length of the tub. If a seat is provided in the tub, the grab bars should be 24-in. long. If a built-up seat is provided, the grab bars should be 48-in. long. Bars are needed at the control side of the tub and at the end opposite the controls. Figure 6-25 shows grab bars in a different configuration. Check with your local code official to see which configuration is recommended.

There have been some disagreements on the number of grab bars that should be required or installed in the tub area. The important thing is to use the number that makes you feel most secure and comfortable.

Slippery Surfaces. Most of the newer manufactured bathtubs have a non-slip surface built into the tubs themselves. If you have an older tub that does not have this safety feature, you can install rubber or plastic appliqués on the surface of the tub. Whatever is installed should be of a non-slip character and have been tested in the past and proven to be safe.

There is a new product on the market today that I recommended very highly. It is called "Soft-Tub," and is made of a material that has a built-in type of cushion. Look for it in the resource list in Chapter 11.

No Tub Seat Provided. When a tub seat is to be installed in a bathtub, the type of approach used by the person in the wheelchair will determine the type of seat best-suited to the transfer. My sketches show this requirement more clearly. See Figs. 6-26 through 6-29. Because of the many types of seats that can be installed, I recommend that you contact your local plumbing contractor or supply house and ask for assistance. I also strongly recommend that you work closely with your local occupational therapist or contact your local rehabilitation office. Much of the help you will need can also be obtained from your local building inspection department.

Controls Too High. Review Figs. 6.21 and 6.23 to see the correct heights for the shower controls in bathtubs. Control units like the ones shown are available at plumbing hardware stores, and construction equipment outlets such as Lowe's, Moore's, Hechingers, and Homequarters (HQ's). If you are unable to find one, in Chapter 11 I have listed some product manufacturers that you may contact directly.

Shower Access. The shower stall is fast becoming the most frequently installed fixture in the home. Since it is easy to install, can be put almost anywhere, and is relatively inexpensive, most people request one. Yet, many stall showers are placed incorrectly, or are of no use to the disabled or the wheelchair-bound person.

Most stock shower units have narrow doors that are approximately 2-ft wide. One must make certain that the shower unit is specifically designed for the disabled. The newer designs take into account the space required to allow free access for the wheelchair. Kohler and American Standard are but two of the nationally recognized firms that have handicapped-accessible shower units. You might check to see which ones your local plumber can provide. While the curb is a barrier on most of the ceramic tile shower units, it can be removed. One must make sure that if it is removed, the water is not allowed to run out onto the floor, which, of course would cause other problems.

If the shower unit is new, the surfaces inside it have been designed to be nonslip. If yours is old, you will have to follow the procedure described for the tub. Applying nonslip patches to the shower floor will provide that additional measure of safety.

All of the units intended for the disabled that are being manufactured now allow for the installation of the safety controls necessary. These units are readily available through your local plumbing contractor. Again, I

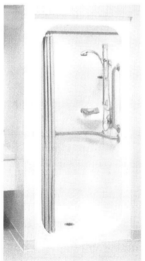

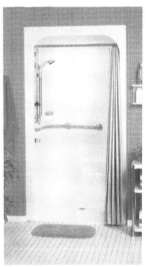

Shower units for the elderly and disabled.

A sit-down shower unit; manufactured by Lasco.

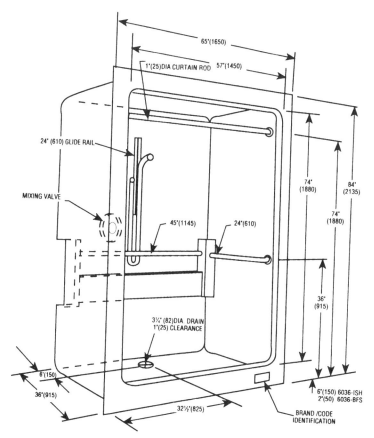

Dimensions of a sit-down shower unit manufactured by Lasco.

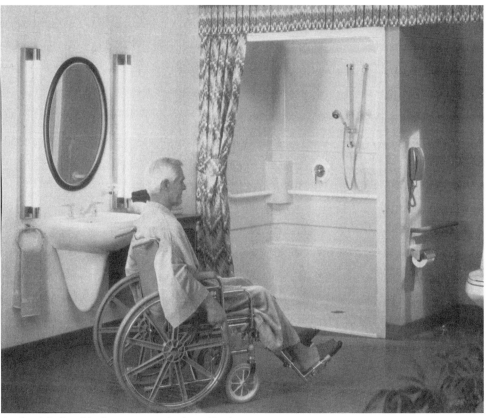

A wheelchair-roll-in shower manufactured by Lasco.

can't stress enough that help is available from your local occupational therapist or rehabilitation office. They are trained to assist you with all of these problems.

See Figs. 6-30 through 6-34 for useful information on shower units and installation.

Lack of Temperature Controls. You should contact the same plumbing supply sources mentioned for bathtubs and showers to obtain the various types of temperature controls that are available. They usually are not very expensive and are easy to install. There are many types on the market today. Perhaps the hardest thing is choosing the one that best suits your purpose.

Chapter Seven
OTHER SPACES: DINING ROOM, LIVING ROOM, HALLS, BEDROOMS, AND CARPETING AND FLOORING

DINING ROOM AND LIVING ROOM

The dining room is an area where most disabled people do not expect to encounter any barriers. Still, it does pose some unique problems. In addition to furniture that may be misplaced or in the way, the carpet may lie too deep, or the floor too slippery. The light switches are usually too high for the wheelchair-bound to reach.

You can adjust the furniture to meet your needs and take care of the slippery floor, just as you did at the front entrance, and take stock in the furniture.

It may help to reduce the amount of furniture you have, a very good way of providing freer access through the house. You may need to replace the type of carpet you currently have with low-pile carpeting, and provide lower light switches, which should be 40 in. from the floor. You could use smaller tables for general use; the kind that fold up are useful. The main point is to provide as much free area as possible for the wheelchair to maneuver around the dining room or the living room.

HALLS

Halls offer a problem that is different from that presented by most other areas in the home. As we go down the hall towards the bedroom, we notice that the hall is a bit tight. It may be 3-ft wide as is recommended, but what we have here is a problem created by the items placed along the sides of the hall, such as a table with a lamp, bookcases, perhaps a mirror on the wall, or shelves holding knickknacks. Radiators, of course, take up lots of space.

The flooring again may be too smooth; if so, you might slip and fall. If it is too loose, you can trip. If it's too thick, you are unable to maneuver the wheelchair or walker.

There are more barriers in the hall than was first imagined. Objects that protrude into the hall and in other places create hazards for the visually impaired. Although guide dogs are trained to avoid such hazards, people with visual impairments also use a cane to identify these objects. Any object that is higher than 27 in. from the floor cannot be detected by canes at all, so the blind may bump into them. The best way to prevent this hazard is to remove any objects the handicapped may bump into.

BEDROOMS

The bedroom represents many additional barriers. Not much thought is given to how a physically disabled or an elderly person actually uses the bedroom. Most bedroom doors are too narrow to allow a wheelchair to enter. There may be extremely tight areas around the bed. How close is the telephone to the bed? Is it easy to reach? Is the carpet, or rug nonslip? Are the light switches easy to reach? Can other lights be controlled from the bedroom? Can they be turned on and off? You need to consider the problem of security, and its impact on your life. Can you hear the front doorbell and can tell who's there?

The closet and the closet shelves may not meet your storage requirements. All of the design requirements for closets can be found in Fig. 7-1.

Again, refer to Figs. 6.2, 6.3, and 6.4 for the space requirements for maneuvering; refer back to Fig. 4.12 again for the requirements for switches and other controls.

Carpeting and Flooring. I have discussed carpeting in general terms in the many instances where carpeting, rugs, and flooring are used in the home. Now I would like to explain the design criteria for carpeting.

While more needs to be done to develop both quantitative and qualitative criteria for carpeting, certain functional characteristics are well established. When both carpeting and padding are used, it is desirable to have minimal movement between the pad and the carpet. In areas of very heavy traffic, thick, soft (plush) padding or cushioning, especially when it is used with a deep-pile carpet, makes it very difficult for people in wheelchairs to move about. This does not preclude the use of carpeting in the home, or in commercial establishments. Carpeting that is safe for the disabled can be achieved by using low-pile carpeting and the correct combination of pad and carpet, and, of course, proper installation.

People who are unsteady on their feet, or those who have difficulty maintaining their balance, are more prone to slipping and tripping, so these are the hazards most feared by the elderly and the disabled. A stable surface is required for walking, especially on stairs, where anything loose spells disaster. It is debatable as to which is the best nonslip surface to use, and it does depend on the individual preference. Table 7-1 is a list of nonslip floor coverings and finishes for outside use and for use inside the house. This table will provide you with some of the characteristics of different types of flooring, and will help you to decide which may be the best for you.

Table 7-1 Indoor and outdoor floor coverings and finishes.

Material	Slip resistance	Notes on use
Carpet	VG	Where carpet adjoins a different floor finish at doorways, a dividing strip or threshold should be provided.
Clay tiles	G—F	Poor when polished. Exceptionally poor when polished and wet.
Clay tiles—textured finish	VG	Suitable for external stairs or steps. Panelled finish easier to clean than ribbed. Tiles are also available with a carborundum finish.
Concrete	G	Slippery when wet unless a textured finish is applied or non-slip aggregate used.
Concrete paving slabs	G	`Ripple Finish' is non-slip even when wet. Slabs available with carborundum or other non-slip finish.
Cork carpet	VG	Susceptible to damp. Threshold or dividing strip necessary where cork carpet adjoins a different floor finish.
Cork tiles	VG	Susceptible to damp.
Flexible PVC	VG—G	Slippery when wet, unless textured. Susceptible to damp. Sheets liable to come up at edges, making a tripping edge if not fixed to base. Threshold or dividing strip necessary as for carpet.
Felt-backed flexible PVC	VG—G	Susceptible to damp; slippery when wet unless textured.
Flexible PVC incorporating non-slip granules	VG	Non-slip even when wet. Hessian-backed types are susceptible to damp.
Granolithic	G	Poor when wet. On external steps a carborundum finish should be specified.
Linoleum	G	Susceptible to damp. Sheets liable to come up at edges, making a tripping edge if not fixed to base. Threshold or dividing strip necessary as for carpet.
Mastic asphalt	G—F	
Rubber—sheet or tiles	VG (VP when wet)	Unsuitable for areas connected with cooking, washing, or laundering or in spaces near entrance doors.
Terrazzo	G (VP when polished)	Exceptionally slippery when polished. Polish should be avoided on surfaces adjacent to terrazzo as it can be transferred by treading. On stairs non-slip nosing is necessary.
Thermoplastic tiles	G	Slip-resistance fair when wet. Although not completely grease-resistant, suitable for domestic kitchens except under cooker.
Timber—softwood boards or blocks	G	Poor if wax-polished.
Timber—hardwood boards or blocks	F	Very poor if wax-polished. On stairtreads a non-slip nosing is necessary.
Vinyl asbestos tiles	G—VG	Slip-resistance fair when wet. Have rather better abrasion-resistance than thermoplastic tiles, good grease- and oil-resistance and suitable for domestic kitchens.

Chapter Eight
OUTDOOR LIVING

At times we need to go outdoors, perhaps just to hang our clothes on the line or do some gardening, or perhaps to cook a meal on the grill.

Whatever the reason, we go outdoors to enjoy ourselves in what we feel is our private world. The path from the back door to wherever we intend to go in our yard has many barriers that interfere with even the simple tasks mentioned above. We may not find the surface hard enough for the wheelchair, or we may discover that the ground is too soft for our crutches or canes. Although benches are useful, they may be difficult to use because they are at incorrect heights. A table may be difficult for a chair to get close to. There is little protection from the sun or rain. Where is that telephone if we need it? We may not get inside fast enough to answer it if it rings. What kind of lights have we provided for our safety and security?

What have we done to make our life easy in the outdoor area of our home? Can we get at our gardening tools? Is there some protection against insects?

We know that the outdoors can be fun, and we deserve to use it, but we must provide safety and security for the disabled, the elderly, or anyone else, and we must know what to provide. We must not let these barriers restrict us keeping us housebound, taking away our right to use our own property.

BARRIERS IDENTIFIED OUTDOORS

- Steps to the ground, high thresholds
- Soft ground
- No rest areas
- No protection from the rain or sun
- Telephone inaccessible
- Improper lighting
- Lack of security

How to Remove These Barriers

Steps to the Ground, High Thresholds. Look at your threshold again and remember that anything over ½-in. high is too high. Any threshold that is higher should be removed and replaced with one at the correct height. You might also install a small ramp, depending on the number of steps you have to cover. You can accomplish this only after you have studied your conditions and determined what is needed.

Set clotheslines low enough to allow a person in a wheelchair to reach them, and provide a smooth, hard surface below the line as well, so that the wheelchair can travel along the clothesline.

A 3-ft-wide doorway; an invitation for free access.

Soft Ground. In discussing outdoor areas, many things must be considered. In the case of soft ground, some sort of hard pavement must be provided, such as a concrete patio. If this is not possible, consider installing compacted gravel, with no stones larger than ¾-in.

The Resting Place. Providing a resting place in your yard involves thinking of how you intend to use the area. There should be enough space around benches to provide ample space for the wheelchair to clear. Tables must have enough clearance below to allow the chair to reach under the table. Know how far you can travel before you become too tired to move, and place some sort of seating at regular intervals to compensate for the limited distance.

No Protection From the Rain or Sun. If you want to set up some form of protection against the element, remember that the local climate needs to be considered. If the wind can cause problems, you might need professional help for constructing a shelter.

Telephone Inaccessible. With the arrival of the portable telephone, no one need be anxious about being without the security of a phone close at hand. It will provide for any emergency situations that may arise, and allow free access to police, the doctor, and relatives.

Improper Lighting. Lighting is another thing that is necessary for security. Perhaps only the person affected can decide whether it needs correcting. You must look over the complete area around the house to see if there are any places where someone can hide. Also consider how you move about outside your home. Lighting can provide that extra bit of safety, especially to provide the light you need to see any steps or drop-offs that might cause problems. Lighting around the front entrance is very important for the safety of all involved, and cannot be stressed often enough.

Lack of Security. Provide peepholes in the doors to see who is outside; better yet, install a home security system that is designed to provide the maximum amount of security for the home. See Fig. 8-1. Security systems, however, are very expensive; check them out to see the actual cost of having one installed in your home.

We can never do enough to provide for the security of the elderly. The fear most elderly have, though, is their isolation and the fear that nobody will know when they may need help. You can go only as far as your finances will permit; you must decide how you view your security needs and how much you are willing or able to pay for security.

Chapter Nine
DESIGN CRITERIA

Included in this chapter is the latest copy of the new *Americans with Disabilities Act Accessibility Guidelines for Buildings and Facilities*. These guidelines were issued on July 17, 1991. They are the result of a careful study requested by the Justice Department on how to enforce the ADA laws.

There are many points to consider when you start the design process, because when a building environment calls for major changes, a professional should be contacted. It could be an architect, an engineer, or a building contractor. Before entering into any sort of design agreement, be certain that the contractor is fully acquainted with the regulations and capable of complying with them, because there are many requirements associated with complying with the codes.

The laws pertaining to accessibility require more study pertaining to the floor space and the travel routes. Most commercial applications need to conform to the state and local building codes in your area, laws that cover egress, exit requirements, fire safety, life safety, energy conservation, and access for the disabled.

There are many fine design professionals such as landscape and interior designers, and we must be careful to select those with the proper qualifications. Be sure that the professional you choose is well-versed in the federal standards as well as the local building codes. Only then can they provide the best design solutions.

Housing for the elderly and accessible housing for the disabled have fast become sought-after markets for design professionals. This market, produced by the graying of America, has great potential in providing for housing for a great number of people; there are estimates that there were over 20 million in 1970, but by the year 2000 there will be in excess of 31 million people over the age of sixty. Many of the elderly and quite a few of the disabled do not want to stay in institutional facilities, and prefer to live independently at home, so you can understand why the potential for work in this sector is growing at a tremendous rate.

Housing design has shifted away from high-rise apartment dwellings and institutionalized forms of housing. We do a better job today of design and construction for the physically challenged. The architectural students in our schools are striving to provide them with better designs, and that awareness is being strengthened. The new articles on design, the concept of adaptable housing, and the new civil rights laws are all making an impact on what and how to design accessible housing. There is an all new environment for the disabled and the elderly.

Approaching a residence like this is a pleasant experience..

ADA ACCESSIBILITY GUIDELINES
FOR BUILDINGS AND FACILITIES
TABLE OF CONTENTS

i

ii

1. PURPOSE.

This document sets guidelines for accessibility to places of public accommodation and commercial facilities by individuals with disabilities. These guidelines are to be applied during the design, construction, and alteration of such buildings and facilities to the extent required by regulations issued by Federal agencies, including the Department of Justice, under the Americans with Disabilities Act of 1990.

The technical specifications 4.2 through 4.35, of these guidelines are the same as those of the American National Standard Institute's document A117.1-1980, except as noted in this text by italics. However, sections 4.1.1 through 4.1.7 and sections 5 through 10 are different from ANSI A117.1 in their entirety and are printed in standard type.

The illustrations and text of ANSI A117.1 are reproduced with permission from the American National Standards Institute. Copies of the standard may be purchased from the American National Standards Institute at 1430 Broadway, New York, New York 10018.

2. GENERAL.

2.1 Provisions for Adults. *The specifications in these guidelines are based upon adult dimensions and anthropometrics.*

2.2* Equivalent Facilitation. *Departures from particular technical and scoping requirements of this guideline by the use of other designs and technologies are permitted where the alternative designs and technologies used will provide substantially equivalent or greater access to and usability of the facility.*

3. MISCELLANEOUS INSTRUCTIONS AND DEFINITIONS.

3.1 Graphic Conventions. Graphic conventions are shown in Table 1. Dimensions that are not marked minimum or maximum are absolute, unless otherwise indicated in the text or captions.

Table 1
Graphic Conventions

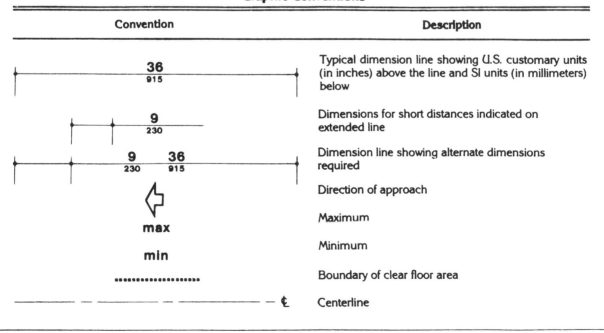

Convention	Description
36 / 915	Typical dimension line showing U.S. customary units (in inches) above the line and SI units (in millimeters) below
9 / 230	Dimensions for short distances indicated on extended line
9 36 / 230 915	Dimension line showing alternate dimensions required
	Direction of approach
max	Maximum
min	Minimum
●●●●●●●●●●●●	Boundary of clear floor area
— — — ₵	Centerline

1

3.2 Dimensional Tolerances. All dimensions are subject to conventional building industry tolerances for field conditions.

3.3 Notes. The text of *these guidelines* does not contain notes or footnotes. Additional information, explanations, and advisory materials are located in the Appendix. Paragraphs marked with an asterisk have related, non-mandatory material in the Appendix. In the Appendix, the corresponding paragraph numbers are preceded by an A.

3.4 General Terminology.

comply with. Meet one or more specifications of *these guidelines*.

if. if ... then. Denotes a specification that applies only when the conditions described are present.

may. Denotes an option or alternative.

shall. Denotes a mandatory specification or requirement.

should. Denotes an advisory specification or recommendation.

3.5 Definitions.

Access Aisle. An accessible pedestrian space between elements, such as parking spaces, seating, and desks, that provides clearances appropriate for use of the elements.

Accessible. Describes a site, building, facility, or portion thereof that complies with *these guidelines*.

Accessible Element. An *element* specified by *these guidelines* (for example, telephone, controls, and the like).

Accessible Route. A continuous unobstructed path connecting all accessible elements and spaces of a building or facility. Interior accessible routes may include corridors, floors, ramps, elevators, lifts, and clear floor space at fixtures. Exterior accessible routes may include parking access aisles, curb ramps, *crosswalks at vehicular ways*, walks, ramps, and lifts.

Accessible Space. *Space that complies with these guidelines.*

Adaptability. The ability of certain building spaces and elements, such as kitchen counters, sinks, and grab bars, to be added or altered so as to accommodate the needs of *individuals with or without disabilities* or to accommodate the needs of persons with different types or degrees of disability.

Addition. *An expansion, extension, or increase in the gross floor area of a building or facility.*

Administrative Authority. A governmental agency that adopts or enforces regulations and *guidelines* for the design, construction, or *alteration* of buildings and facilities.

Alteration. *An alteration is a change to a building or facility made by, on behalf of, or for the use of a public accommodation or commercial facility, that affects or could affect the usability of the building or facility or part thereof. Alterations include, but are not limited to, remodeling, renovation, rehabilitation, reconstruction, historic restoration, changes or rearrangement of the structural parts or elements, and changes or rearrangement in the plan configuration of walls and full-height partitions. Normal maintenance, reroofing, painting or wallpapering, or changes to mechanical and electrical systems are not alterations unless they affect the usability of the building or facility.*

Area of Rescue Assistance. *An area, which has direct access to an exit, where people who are unable to use stairs may remain temporarily in safety to await further instructions or assistance during emergency evacuation.*

Assembly Area. A room or space accommodating a *group of* individuals for recreational, educational, political, social, or amusement purposes, or for the consumption of food and drink.

Automatic Door. A door equipped with a power-operated mechanism and controls that open and close the door automatically upon receipt of a momentary actuating signal. The switch that begins the automatic cycle may be a photoelectric device, floor mat, or manual switch (see power-assisted door).

2

Building. Any structure used and intended for supporting or sheltering any use or occupancy.

Circulation Path. An exterior or interior way of passage from one place to another for pedestrians, including, but not limited to, walks, hallways, courtyards, stairways, and stair landings.

Clear. Unobstructed.

Clear Floor Space. *The minimum unobstructed floor or ground space required to accommodate a single, stationary wheelchair and occupant.*

Closed Circuit Telephone. *A telephone with dedicated line(s) such as a house phone, courtesy phone or phone that must be used to gain entrance to a facility.*

Common Use. Refers to those interior and exterior rooms, spaces, or elements that are made available for the use of a restricted group of people (for example, *occupants of a homeless shelter*, the occupants of an office building, or the guests of such occupants).

Cross Slope. The slope that is perpendicular to the direction of travel (see running slope).

Curb Ramp. A short ramp cutting through a curb or built up to it.

Detectable Warning. *A standardized surface feature built in or applied to walking surfaces or other elements to warn visually impaired people of hazards on a circulation path.*

Dwelling Unit. A single unit which provides a kitchen or food preparation area, in addition to rooms and spaces for living, bathing, sleeping, and the like. *Dwelling units include a single family home or a townhouse used as a transient group home; an apartment building used as a shelter; guestrooms in a hotel that provide sleeping accommodations and food preparation areas; and other similar facilities used on a transient basis. For purposes of these guidelines, use of the term "Dwelling Unit" does not imply the unit is used as a residence.*

Egress, Means of. *A continuous and unobstructed way of exit travel from any point in a building or facility to a public way. A means of egress comprises vertical and horizontal travel* and may include intervening room spaces, doorways, hallways, corridors, passageways, balconies, ramps, stairs, enclosures, lobbies, horizontal exits, courts and yards. An accessible means of egress is one that complies with these guidelines and does not include stairs, steps, or escalators. Areas of rescue assistance or evacuation elevators may be included as part of accessible means of egress.

Element. *An architectural or mechanical component of a building, facility, space, or site, e.g., telephone, curb ramp, door, drinking fountain, seating, or water closet.*

Entrance. Any access point to a building or portion of a building or facility used for the purpose of entering. An entrance includes the approach walk, the vertical access leading to the entrance platform, the entrance platform itself, vestibules if provided, the entry door(s) or gate(s), and the hardware of the entry door(s) or gate(s).

Facility. *All or any portion of buildings, structures, site improvements, complexes, equipment, roads, walks, passageways, parking lots, or other real or personal property located on a site.*

Ground Floor. *Any occupiable floor less than one story above or below grade with direct access to grade. A building or facility always has at least one ground floor and may have more than one ground floor as where a split level entrance has been provided or where a building is built into a hillside.*

Mezzanine or Mezzanine Floor. *That portion of a story which is an intermediate floor level placed within the story and having occupiable space above and below its floor.*

Marked Crossing. A crosswalk or other identified path intended for pedestrian use in crossing a vehicular way.

Multifamily Dwelling. Any building containing more than two dwelling units.

Occupiable. *A room or enclosed space designed for human occupancy in which individuals congregate for amusement, educational or similar purposes, or in which occupants are engaged at labor, and which is equipped with means of egress, light, and ventilation.*

3

Operable Part. A part of a piece of equipment or appliance used to insert or withdraw objects, or to activate, deactivate, or adjust the equipment or appliance (for example, coin slot, pushbutton, handle).

Path of Travel. (Reserved).

Power-assisted Door. A door used *for human passage* with a mechanism that helps to open the door, or relieves the opening resistance of a door, upon the activation of a switch or a continued force applied to the door itself.

Public Use. Describes interior or exterior rooms or spaces that are made available to the general public. Public use may be provided at a building or facility that is privately or publicly owned.

Ramp. A walking surface which has a running slope greater than 1:20.

Running Slope. The slope that is parallel to the direction of travel (see cross slope).

Service Entrance. An entrance intended primarily for delivery of goods or services.

Signage. *Displayed* verbal, symbolic, *tactile,* and pictorial information.

Site. A parcel of land bounded by a property line or a designated portion of a public right-of-way.

Site Improvement. Landscaping, paving for pedestrian and vehicular ways, outdoor lighting, recreational facilities, and the like, added to a site.

Sleeping Accommodations. Rooms in which people sleep; for example, dormitory and hotel or motel guest rooms or suites.

Space. *A definable area, e.g., room, toilet room, hall, assembly area, entrance, storage room, alcove, courtyard, or lobby.*

Story. *That portion of a building included between the upper surface of a floor and upper surface of the floor or roof next above. If such* portion of a building does not include occupiable space, it is not considered a story for purposes of these guidelines. There may be more than one floor level within a story as in the case of a mezzanine or mezzanines.

Structural Frame. The structural frame shall be considered to be the columns and the girders, beams, trusses and spandrels having direct connections to the columns and all other members which are essential to the stability of the building as a whole.

Tactile. Describes an object that can be perceived using the sense of touch.

Text Telephone. *Machinery or equipment that employs interactive graphic (i.e., typed) communications through the transmission of coded signals across the standard telephone network. Text telephones can include, for example, devices known as TDD's (telecommunication display devices or telecommunication devices for deaf persons) or computers.*

Transient Lodging. *A building, facility, or portion thereof, excluding inpatient medical care facilities, that contains one or more dwelling units or sleeping accommodations. Transient lodging may include, but is not limited to, resorts, group homes, hotels, motels, and dormitories.*

Vehicular Way. A route intended for vehicular traffic, such as a street, driveway, or parking lot.

Walk. An exterior pathway with a prepared surface intended for pedestrian use, including general pedestrian areas such as plazas and courts.

NOTE: Sections 4.1.1 through 4.1.7 are different from ANSI A117.1 in their entirety and are printed in standard type (ANSI A117.1 does not include scoping provisions).

4

4. ACCESSIBLE ELEMENTS AND SPACES: SCOPE AND TECHNICAL REQUIREMENTS.

4.1 Minimum Requirements

4.1.1* Application.

(1) General. All areas of newly designed or newly constructed buildings and facilities required to be accessible by 4.1.2 and 4.1.3 and altered portions of existing buildings and facilities required to be accessible by 4.1.6 shall comply with these guidelines, 4.1 through 4.35, unless otherwise provided in this section or as modified in a special application section.

(2) Application Based on Building Use. Special application sections 5 through 10 provide additional requirements for restaurants and cafeterias, medical care facilities, business and mercantile, libraries, accessible transient lodging, and transportation facilities. When a building or facility contains more than one use covered by a special application section, each portion shall comply with the requirements for that use.

(3)* Areas Used Only by Employees as Work Areas. Areas that are used only as work areas shall be designed and constructed so that individuals with disabilities can approach, enter, and exit the areas. These guidelines do not require that any areas used only as work areas be constructed to permit maneuvering within the work area or be constructed or equipped (i.e., with racks or shelves) to be accessible.

(4) Temporary Structures. These guidelines cover temporary buildings or facilities as well as permanent facilities. Temporary buildings and facilities are not of permanent construction but are extensively used or are essential for public use for a period of time. Examples of temporary buildings or facilities covered by these guidelines include, but are not limited to: reviewing stands, temporary classrooms, bleacher areas, exhibit areas, temporary banking facilities, temporary health screening services, or temporary safe pedestrian passageways around a construction site. Structures,

sites and equipment directly associated with the actual processes of construction, such as scaffolding, bridging, materials hoists, or construction trailers are not included.

(5) General Exceptions.

(a) In new construction, a person or entity is not required to meet fully the requirements of these guidelines where that person or entity can demonstrate that it is structurally impracticable to do so. Full compliance will be considered structurally impracticable only in those rare circumstances when the unique characteristics of terrain prevent the incorporation of accessibility features. If full compliance with the requirements of these guidelines is structurally impracticable, a person or entity shall comply with the requirements to the extent it is not structurally impracticable. Any portion of the building or facility which can be made accessible shall comply to the extent that it is not structurally impracticable.

(b) Accessibility is not required to (i) observation galleries used primarily for security purposes; or (ii) in non-occupiable spaces accessed only by ladders, catwalks, crawl spaces, very narrow passageways, or freight (non-passenger) elevators, and frequented only by service personnel for repair purposes; such spaces include, but are not limited to, elevator pits, elevator penthouses, piping or equipment catwalks.

4.1.2 Accessible Sites and Exterior Facilities: New Construction. An accessible site shall meet the following minimum requirements:

(1) At least one accessible route complying with 4.3 shall be provided within the boundary of the site from public transportation stops, accessible parking spaces, passenger loading zones if provided, and public streets or sidewalks, to an accessible building entrance.

(2) At least one accessible route complying with 4.3 shall connect accessible buildings, accessible facilities, accessible elements, and accessible spaces that are on the same site.

(3) All objects that protrude from surfaces or posts into circulation paths shall comply with 4.4.

5

(4) Ground surfaces along accessible routes and in accessible spaces shall comply with 4.5.

(5) (a) If parking spaces are provided for self-parking by employees or visitors, or both, then accessible spaces complying with 4.6 shall be provided in each such parking area in conformance with the table below. Spaces required by the table need not be provided in the particular lot. They may be provided in a different location if equivalent or greater accessibility, in terms of distance from an accessible entrance, cost and convenience is ensured.

Total Parking in Lot	Required Minimum Number of Accessible Spaces
1 to 25	1
26 to 50	2
51 to 75	3
76 to 100	4
101 to 150	5
151 to 200	6
201 to 300	7
301 to 400	8
401 to 500	9
501 to 1000	2 percent of total
1001 and over	20 plus 1 for each 100 over 1000

Except as provided in (b), access aisles adjacent to accessible spaces shall be 60 in (1525 mm) wide minimum.

(b) One in every eight accessible spaces, but not less than one, shall be served by an access aisle 96 in (2440 mm) wide minimum and shall be designated "van accessible" as required by 4.6.4. The vertical clearance at such spaces shall comply with 4.6.5. All such spaces may be grouped on one level of a parking structure.

EXCEPTION: Provision of all required parking spaces in conformance with "Universal Parking Design" (see appendix A4.6.3) is permitted.

(c) If passenger loading zones are provided, then at least one passenger loading zone shall comply with 4.6.6.

(d) At facilities providing medical care and other services for persons with mobility impairments, parking spaces complying with 4.6 shall

be provided in accordance with 4.1.2(5)(a) except as follows:

(i) Outpatient units and facilities: 10 percent of the total number of parking spaces provided serving each such outpatient unit or facility;

(ii) Units and facilities that specialize in treatment or services for persons with mobility impairments: 20 percent of the total number of parking spaces provided serving each such unit or facility.

(e)*Valet parking: Valet parking facilities shall provide a passenger loading zone complying with 4.6.6 located on an accessible route to the entrance of the facility. Paragraphs 5(a), 5(b), and 5(d) of this section do not apply to valet parking facilities.

(6) If toilet facilities are provided on a site, then each such public or common use toilet facility shall comply with 4.22. If bathing facilities are provided on a site, then each such public or common use bathing facility shall comply with 4.23.

For single user portable toilet or bathing units clustered at a single location, at least 5% but no less than one toilet unit or bathing unit complying with 4.22 or 4.23 shall be installed at each cluster whenever typical inaccessible units are provided. Accessible units shall be identified by the International Symbol of Accessibility.

EXCEPTION: Portable toilet units at construction sites used exclusively by construction personnel are not required to comply with 4.1.2(6).

(7) Building Signage. Signs which designate permanent rooms and spaces shall comply with 4.30.1, 4.30.4, 4.30.5 and 4.30.6. Other signs which provide direction to, or information about, functional spaces of the building shall comply with 4.30.1, 4.30.2, 4.30.3, and 4.30.5. Elements and spaces of accessible facilities which shall be identified by the International Symbol of Accessibility and which shall comply with 4.30.7 are:

(a) Parking spaces designated as reserved for individuals with disabilities;

6

(b) Accessible passenger loading zones;

(c) Accessible entrances when not all are accessible (inaccessible entrances shall have directional signage to indicate the route to the nearest accessible entrance);

(d) Accessible toilet and bathing facilities when not all are accessible.

4.1.3 Accessible Buildings: New Construction. Accessible buildings and facilities shall meet the following minimum requirements:

(1) At least one accessible route complying with 4.3 shall connect accessible building or facility entrances with all accessible spaces and elements within the building or facility.

(2) All objects that overhang or protrude into circulation paths shall comply with 4.4.

(3) Ground and floor surfaces along accessible routes and in accessible rooms and spaces shall comply with 4.5.

(4) Interior and exterior stairs connecting levels that are not connected by an elevator, ramp, or other accessible means of vertical access shall comply with 4.9.

(5)* One passenger elevator complying with 4.10 shall serve each level, including mezzanines, in all multi-story buildings and facilities unless exempted below. If more than one elevator is provided, each full passenger elevator shall comply with 4.10.

EXCEPTION 1: Elevators are not required in facilities that are less than three stories or that have less than 3000 square feet per story unless the building is a shopping center, a shopping mall, or the professional office of a health care provider, or another type of facility as determined by the Attorney General. The elevator exemption set forth in this paragraph does not obviate or limit in any way the obligation to comply with the other accessibility requirements established in section 4.1.3. For example, floors above or below the accessible ground floor must meet the requirements of this section except for elevator service. If toilet or bathing facilities are provided on a level not served by an elevator, then toilet or bathing facilities must be provided on the accessible ground floor. In new construction if a building or facility is eligible for this exemption but a full passenger elevator is nonetheless planned, that elevator shall meet the requirements of 4.10 and shall serve each level in the building. A full passenger elevator that provides service from a garage to only one level of a building or facility is not required to serve other levels.

EXCEPTION 2: Elevator pits, elevator penthouses, mechanical rooms, piping or equipment catwalks are exempted from this requirement.

EXCEPTION 3: Accessible ramps complying with 4.8 may be used in lieu of an elevator.

EXCEPTION 4: Platform lifts (wheelchair lifts) complying with 4.11 of this guideline and applicable state or local codes may be used in lieu of an elevator only under the following conditions:

(a) To provide an accessible route to a performing area in an assembly occupancy.

(b) To comply with the wheelchair viewing position line-of-sight and dispersion requirements of 4.33.3.

(c) To provide access to incidental occupiable spaces and rooms which are not open to the general public and which house no more than five persons, including but not limited to equipment control rooms and projection booths.

(d) To provide access where existing site constraints or other constraints make use of a ramp or an elevator infeasible.

(6) Windows: (Reserved).

(7) Doors:

(a) At each accessible entrance to a building or facility, at least one door shall comply with 4.13.

(b) Within a building or facility, at least one door at each accessible space shall comply with 4.13.

(c) Each door that is an element of an accessible route shall comply with 4.13.

7

(d) Each door required by 4.3.10, Egress, shall comply with 4.13.

(8) In new construction, at a minimum, the requirements in (a) and (b) below shall be satisfied independently:

(a)(i) At least 50% of all public entrances (excluding those in (b) below) must be accessible. At least one must be a ground floor entrance. Public entrances are any entrances that are not loading or service entrances.

(ii) Accessible entrances must be provided in a number at least equivalent to the number of exits required by the applicable building/fire codes. (This paragraph does not require an increase in the total number of entrances planned for a facility.)

(iii) An accessible entrance must be provided to each tenancy in a facility (for example, individual stores in a strip shopping center).

One entrance may be considered as meeting more than one of the requirements in (a). Where feasible, accessible entrances shall be the entrances used by the majority of people visiting or working in the building.

(b)(i) In addition, if direct access is provided for pedestrians from an enclosed parking garage to the building, at least one direct entrance from the garage to the building must be accessible.

(ii) If access is provided for pedestrians from a pedestrian tunnel or elevated walkway, one entrance to the building from each tunnel or walkway must be accessible.

One entrance may be considered as meeting more than one of the requirements in (b).

Because entrances also serve as emergency exits whose proximity to all parts of buildings and facilities is essential, it is preferable that all entrances be accessible.

(c) If the only entrance to a building, or tenancy in a facility, is a service entrance, that entrance shall be accessible.

(d) Entrances which are not accessible shall have directional signage complying with 4.30.1,

4.30.2, 4.30.3, and 4.30.5, which indicates the location of the nearest accessible entrance.

(9)* In buildings or facilities, or portions of buildings or facilities, required to be accessible, accessible means of egress shall be provided in the same number as required for exits by local building/life safety regulations. Where a required exit from an occupiable level above or below a level of accessible exit discharge is not accessible, an area of rescue assistance shall be provided on each such level (in a number equal to that of inaccessible required exits). Areas of rescue assistance shall comply with 4.3.11. A horizontal exit, meeting the requirements of local building/life safety regulations, shall satisfy the requirement for an area of rescue assistance.

EXCEPTION: Areas of rescue assistance are not required in buildings or facilities having a supervised automatic sprinkler system.

(10)* Drinking Fountains:

(a) Where only one drinking fountain is provided on a floor there shall be a drinking fountain which is accessible to individuals who use wheelchairs in accordance with 4.15 and one accessible to those who have difficulty bending or stooping. (This can be accommodated by the use of a "hi-lo" fountain; by providing one fountain accessible to those who use wheelchairs and one fountain at a standard height convenient for those who have difficulty bending; by providing a fountain accessible under 4.15 and a water cooler; or by such other means as would achieve the required accessibility for each group on each floor.)

(b) Where more than one drinking fountain or water cooler is provided on a floor, 50% of those provided shall comply with 4.15 and shall be on an accessible route.

(11) Toilet Facilities: If toilet rooms are provided, then each public and common use toilet room shall comply with 4.22. Other toilet rooms provided for the use of occupants of specific spaces (i.e., a private toilet room for the occupant of a private office) shall be adaptable. If bathing rooms are provided, then each public and common use bathroom shall comply with 4.23. Accessible toilet rooms and bathing facilities shall be on an accessible route.

8

(12) Storage, Shelving and Display Units:

(a) If fixed or built-in storage facilities such as cabinets, shelves, closets, and drawers are provided in accessible spaces, at least one of each type provided shall contain storage space complying with 4.25. Additional storage may be provided outside of the dimensions required by 4.25.

(b) Shelves or display units allowing self-service by customers in mercantile occupancies shall be located on an accessible route complying with 4.3. Requirements for accessible reach range do not apply.

(13) Controls and operating mechanisms in accessible spaces, along accessible routes, or as parts of accessible elements (for example, light switches and dispenser controls) shall comply with 4.27.

(14) If emergency warning systems are provided, then they shall include both audible alarms and visual alarms complying with 4.28. Sleeping accommodations required to comply with 9.3 shall have an alarm system complying with 4.28. Emergency warning systems in medical care facilities may be modified to suit standard health care alarm design practice.

(15) Detectable warnings shall be provided at locations as specified in 4.29.

(16) Building Signage:

(a) Signs which designate permanent rooms and spaces shall comply with 4.30.1, 4.30.4, 4.30.5 and 4.30.6.

(b) Other signs which provide direction to or information about functional spaces of the building shall comply with 4.30.1, 4.30.2, 4.30.3, and 4.30.5.

EXCEPTION: Building directories, menus, and all other signs which are temporary are not required to comply.

(17) Public Telephones:

(a) If public pay telephones, public closed circuit telephones, or other public telephones are provided, then they shall comply with 4.31.2 through 4.31.8 to the extent required by the following table:

Number of each type of telephone provided on each floor	Number of telephones required to comply with 4.31.2 through 4.31.8[1]
1 or more single unit	1 per floor
1 bank[2]	1 per floor
2 or more banks[2]	1 per bank. Accessible unit may be installed as a single unit in proximity (either visible or with signage) to the bank. At least one public telephone per floor shall meet the requirements for a forward reach telephone[3].

[1] Additional public telephones may be installed at any height. Unless otherwise specified, accessible telephones may be either forward or side reach telephones.

[2] A bank consists of two or more adjacent public telephones, often installed as a unit.

[3] EXCEPTION: For exterior installations only, if dial tone first service is available, then a side reach telephone may be installed instead of the required forward reach telephone (i.e., one telephone in proximity to each bank shall comply with 4.31).

(b)* All telephones required to be accessible and complying with 4.31.2 through 4.31.8 shall be equipped with a volume control. In addition, 25 percent, but never less than one, of all other public telephones provided shall be equipped with a volume control and shall be dispersed among all types of public telephones, including closed circuit telephones, throughout the building or facility. Signage complying with applicable provisions of 4.30.7 shall be provided.

(c) The following shall be provided in accordance with 4.31.9:

(i) if a total number of four or more public pay telephones (including both interior and exterior phones) is provided at a site, and at least one is in an interior location, then at least one interior public text telephone shall be provided.

(ii) if an interior public pay telephone is provided in a stadium or arena, in a convention center, in a hotel with a convention center, or

9

in a covered mall, at least one interior public text telephone shall be provided in the facility.

(iii) If a public pay telephone is located in or adjacent to a hospital emergency room, hospital recovery room, or hospital waiting room, one public text telephone shall be provided at each such location.

(d) Where a bank of telephones in the interior of a building consists of three or more public pay telephones, at least one public pay telephone in each such bank shall be equipped with a shelf and outlet in compliance with 4.31.9(2).

(18) If fixed or built-in seating or tables (including, but not limited to, study carrels and student laboratory stations), are provided in accessible public or common use areas, at least five percent (5%), but not less than one, of the fixed or built-in seating areas or tables shall comply with 4.32. An accessible route shall lead to and through such fixed or built-in seating areas, or tables.

(19)* Assembly areas:

(a) In places of assembly with fixed seating accessible wheelchair locations shall comply with 4.33.2, 4.33.3, and 4.33.4 and shall be provided consistent with the following table:

Capacity of Seating in Assembly Areas	Number of Required Wheelchair Locations
4 to 25	1
26 to 50	2
51 to 300	4
301 to 500	6
over 500	6, plus 1 additional space for each total seating capacity increase of 100

In addition, one percent, but not less than one, of all fixed seats shall be aisle seats with no armrests on the aisle side, or removable or folding armrests on the aisle side. Each such seat shall be identified by a sign or marker. Signage notifying patrons of the availability of such seats shall be posted at the ticket office. Aisle seats are not required to comply with 4.33.4.

(b) This paragraph applies to assembly areas where audible communications are integral to the use of the space (e.g., concert and lecture halls, playhouses and movie theaters, meeting rooms, etc.). Such assembly areas, if (1) they accommodate at least 50 persons, or if they have audio-amplification systems, and (2) they have fixed seating, shall have a permanently installed assistive listening system complying with 4.33. For other assembly areas, a permanently installed assistive listening system, or an adequate number of electrical outlets or other supplementary wiring necessary to support a portable assistive listening system shall be provided. The minimum number of receivers to be provided shall be equal to 4 percent of the total number of seats, but in no case less than two. Signage complying with applicable provisions of 4.30 shall be installed to notify patrons of the availability of a listening system.

(20) Where automated teller machines (ATMs) are provided, each ATM shall comply with the requirements of 4.34 except where two or more are provided at a location, then only one must comply.

EXCEPTION: Drive-up-only automated teller machines are not required to comply with 4.27.2, 4.27.3 and 4.34.3.

(21) Where dressing and fitting rooms are provided for use by the general public, patients, customers or employees, 5 percent, but never less than one, of dressing rooms for each type of use in each cluster of dressing rooms shall be accessible and shall comply with 4.35.

Examples of types of dressing rooms are those serving different genders or distinct and different functions as in different treatment or examination facilities.

4.1.4 (Reserved).

4.1.5 Accessible Buildings: Additions.
Each addition to an existing building or facility shall be regarded as an alteration. Each space or element added to the existing building or facility shall comply with the applicable provisions of 4.1.1 to 4.1.3, Minimum Requirements (for New Construction) and the applicable technical specifications of 4.2 through 4.35 and sections 5 through 10. Each addition that

10

affects or could affect the usability of an area containing a primary function shall comply with 4.1.6(2).

4.1.6 Accessible Buildings: Alterations.

(1) General. Alterations to existing buildings and facilities shall comply with the following:

(a) No alteration shall be undertaken which decreases or has the effect of decreasing accessibility or usability of a building or facility below the requirements for new construction at the time of alteration.

(b) If existing elements, spaces, or common areas are altered, then each such altered element, space, feature, or area shall comply with the applicable provisions of 4.1.1 to 4.1.3 Minimum Requirements (for New Construction). If the applicable provision for new construction requires that an element, space, or common area be on an accessible route, the altered element, space, or common area is not required to be on an accessible route except as provided in 4.1.6(2) (Alterations to an Area Containing a Primary Function.)

(c) If alterations of single elements, when considered together, amount to an alteration of a room or space in a building or facility, the entire space shall be made accessible.

(d) No alteration of an existing element, space, or area of a building or facility shall impose a requirement for greater accessibility than that which would be required for new construction. For example, if the elevators and stairs in a building are being altered and the elevators are, in turn, being made accessible, then no accessibility modifications are required to the stairs connecting levels connected by the elevator. If stair modifications to correct unsafe conditions are required by other codes, the modifications shall be done in compliance with these guidelines unless technically infeasible.

(e) At least one interior public text telephone complying with 4.31.9 shall be provided if:

(i) alterations to existing buildings or facilities with less than four exterior or interior public pay telephones would increase the total number to four or more telephones with at least one in an interior location; or

(ii) alterations to one or more exterior or interior public pay telephones occur in an existing building or facility with four or more public telephones with at least one in an interior location.

(f) If an escalator or stair is planned or installed where none existed previously and major structural modifications are necessary for such installation, then a means of accessible vertical access shall be provided that complies with the applicable provisions of 4.7, 4.8, 4.10, or 4.11.

(g) In alterations, the requirements of 4.1.3(9), 4.3.10 and 4.3.11 do not apply.

(h)*Entrances: If a planned alteration entails alterations to an entrance, and the building has an accessible entrance, the entrance being altered is not required to comply with 4.1.3(8), except to the extent required by 4.1.6(2). If a particular entrance is not made accessible, appropriate accessible signage indicating the location of the nearest accessible entrance(s) shall be installed at or near the inaccessible entrance, such that a person with disabilities will not be required to retrace the approach route from the inaccessible entrance.

(i) If the alteration work is limited solely to the electrical, mechanical, or plumbing system, or to hazardous material abatement, or automatic sprinkler retrofitting, and does not involve the alteration of any elements or spaces required to be accessible under these guidelines, then 4.1.6(2) does not apply.

(j) EXCEPTION: In alteration work, if compliance with 4.1.6 is technically infeasible, the alteration shall provide accessibility to the maximum extent feasible. Any elements or features of the building or facility that are being altered and can be made accessible shall be made accessible within the scope of the alteration.

Technically Infeasible. Means, with respect to an alteration of a building or a facility, that it has little likelihood of being accomplished because existing structural conditions would require removing or altering a load-bearing member which is an essential part of the structural frame; or because other existing physical or site constraints prohibit modification or

11

addition of elements, spaces, or features which are in full and strict compliance with the minimum requirements for new construction and which are necessary to provide accessibility.

(k) EXCEPTION:

(i) These guidelines do not require the installation of an elevator in an altered facility that is less than three stories or has less than 3,000 square feet per story unless the building is a shopping center, a shopping mall, the professional office of a health care provider, or another type of facility as determined by the Attorney General.

(ii) The exemption provided in paragraph (i) does not obviate or limit in any way the obligation to comply with the other accessibility requirements established in these guidelines. For example, alterations to floors above or below the ground floor must be accessible regardless of whether the altered facility has an elevator. If a facility subject to the elevator exemption set forth in paragraph (i) nonetheless has a full passenger elevator, that elevator shall meet, to the maximum extent feasible, the accessibility requirements of these guidelines.

(2) Alterations to an Area Containing a Primary Function: In addition to the requirements of 4.1.6(1), an alteration that affects or could affect the usability of or access to an area containing a primary function shall be made so as to ensure that, to the maximum extent feasible, the path of travel to the altered area and the restrooms, telephones, and drinking fountains serving the altered area, are readily accessible to and usable by individuals with disabilities, unless such alterations are disproportionate to the overall alterations in terms of cost and.scope (as determined under criteria established by the Attorney General).

(3) Special Technical Provisions for Alterations to Existing Buildings and Facilities:

(a) Ramps: Curb ramps and interior or exterior ramps to be constructed on sites or in existing buildings or facilities where space limitations prohibit the use of a 1:12 slope or less may have slopes and rises as follows:

(i) A slope between 1:10 and 1:12 is allowed for a maximum rise of 6 inches.

(ii) A slope between 1:8 and 1:10 is allowed for a maximum rise of 3 inches. A slope steeper than 1:8 is not allowed.

(b) Stairs: Full extension of handrails at stairs shall not be required in alterations where such extensions would be hazardous or impossible due to plan configuration.

(c) Elevators:

(i) If safety door edges are provided in existing automatic elevators, automatic door reopening devices may be omitted (see 4.10.6).

(ii) Where existing shaft configuration or technical infeasibility prohibits strict compliance with 4.10.9, the minimum car plan dimensions may be reduced by the minimum amount necessary, but in no case shall the inside car area be smaller than 48 in by 48 in.

(iii) Equivalent facilitation may be provided with an elevator car of different dimensions when usability can be demonstrated and when all other elements required to be accessible comply with the applicable provisions of 4.10. For example, an elevator of 47 in by 69 in (1195 mm by 1755 mm) with a door opening on the narrow dimension, could accommodate the standard wheelchair clearances shown in Figure 4.

(d) Doors:

(i) Where it is technically infeasible to comply with clear opening width requirements of 4.13.5, a projection of 5/8 in maximum will be permitted for the latch side stop.

(ii) If existing thresholds are 3/4 in high or less, and have (or are modified to have) a beveled edge on each side, they may remain.

(e) Toilet Rooms:

(i) Where it is technically infeasible to comply with 4.22 or 4.23, the installation of at least one unisex toilet/bathroom per floor, located in the same area as existing toilet facilities, will be permitted in lieu of modifying existing toilet facilities to be accessible. Each unisex toilet room shall contain one water closet complying with 4.16 and one lavatory complying with 4.19, and the door shall have a privacy latch.

12

(ii) Where it is technically infeasible to install a required standard stall (Fig. 30(a)), or where other codes prohibit reduction of the fixture count (i.e., removal of a water closet in order to create a double-wide stall), either alternate stall (Fig.30(b)) may be provided in lieu of the standard stall.

(iii) When existing toilet or bathing facilities are being altered and are not made accessible, signage complying with 4.30.1, 4.30.2, 4.30.3, 4.30.5, and 4.30.7 shall be provided indicating the location of the nearest accessible toilet or bathing facility within the facility.

(f) Assembly Areas:

(i) Where it is technically infeasible to disperse accessible seating throughout an altered assembly area, accessible seating areas may be clustered. Each accessible seating area shall have provisions for companion seating and shall be located on an accessible route that also serves as a means of emergency egress.

(ii) Where it is technically infeasible to alter all performing areas to be on an accessible route, at least one of each type of performing area shall be made accessible.

(g) Platform Lifts (Wheelchair Lifts): In alterations, platform lifts (wheelchair lifts) complying with 4.11 and applicable state or local codes may be used as part of an accessible route. The use of lifts is not limited to the four conditions in exception 4 of 4.1.3(5).

(h) Dressing Rooms: In alterations where technical infeasibility can be demonstrated, one dressing room for each sex on each level shall be made accessible. Where only unisex dressing rooms are provided, accessible unisex dressing rooms may be used to fulfill this requirement.

4.1.7 Accessible Buildings: Historic Preservation.

(1) Applicability:

(a) General Rule. Alterations to a qualified historic building or facility shall comply with 4.1.6 Accessible Buildings: Alterations, the applicable technical specifications of 4.2

through 4.35 and the applicable special application sections 5 through 10 unless it is determined in accordance with the procedures in 4.1.7(2) that compliance with the requirements for accessible routes (exterior and interior), ramps, entrances, or toilets would threaten or destroy the historic significance of the building or facility in which case the alternative requirements in 4.1.7(3) may be used for the feature.

EXCEPTION: (Reserved).

(b) Definition. A qualified historic building or facility is a building or facility that is:

(i) Listed in or eligible for listing in the National Register of Historic Places; or

(ii) Designated as historic under an appropriate State or local law.

(2) Procedures:

(a) Alterations to Qualified Historic Buildings and Facilities Subject to Section 106 of the National Historic Preservation Act:

(i) Section 106 Process. Section 106 of the National Historic Preservation Act (16 U.S.C. 470 f) requires that a Federal agency with jurisdiction over a Federal, federally assisted, or federally licensed undertaking consider the effects of the agency's undertaking on buildings and facilities listed in or eligible for listing in the National Register of Historic Places and give the Advisory Council on Historic Preservation a reasonable opportunity to comment on the undertaking prior to approval of the undertaking.

(ii) ADA Application. Where alterations are undertaken to a qualified historic building or facility that is subject to section 106 of the National Historic Preservation Act, the Federal agency with jurisdiction over the undertaking shall follow the section 106 process. If the State Historic Preservation Officer or Advisory Council on Historic Preservation agrees that compliance with the requirements for accessible routes (exterior and interior), ramps, entrances, or toilets would threaten or destroy the historic significance of the building or facility, the alternative requirements in 4.1.7(3) may be used for the feature.

(b) Alterations to Qualified Historic Buildings and Facilities Not Subject to Section 106 of the National Historic Preservation Act. Where alterations are undertaken to a qualified historic building or facility that is not subject to section 106 of the National Historic Preservation Act, if the entity undertaking the alterations believes that compliance with the requirements for accessible routes (exterior and interior), ramps, entrances, or toilets would threaten or destroy the historic significance of the building or facility and that the alternative requirements in 4.1.7(3) should be used for the feature, the entity should consult with the State Historic Preservation Officer. If the State Historic Preservation Officer agrees that compliance with the accessibility requirements for accessible routes (exterior and interior), ramps, entrances or toilets would threaten or destroy the historical significance of the building or facility, the alternative requirements in 4.1.7(3) may be used.

(c) Consultation With Interested Persons. Interested persons should be invited to participate in the consultation process, including State or local accessibility officials, individuals with disabilities, and organizations representing individuals with disabilities.

(d) Certified Local Government Historic Preservation Programs. Where the State Historic Preservation Officer has delegated the consultation responsibility for purposes of this section to a local government historic preservation program that has been certified in accordance with section 101(c) of the National Historic Preservation Act of 1966 (16 U.S.C. 470a (c)) and implementing regulations (36 CFR 61.5), the responsibility may be carried out by the appropriate local government body or official.

(3) Historic Preservation: Minimum Requirements:

(a) At least one accessible route complying with 4.3 from a site access point to an accessible entrance shall be provided.

EXCEPTION: A ramp with a slope no greater than 1:6 for a run not to exceed 2 ft (610 mm) may be used as part of an accessible route to an entrance.

(b) At least one accessible entrance complying with 4.14 which is used by the public shall be provided.

EXCEPTION: If it is determined that no entrance used by the public can comply with 4.14, then access at any entrance not used by the general public but open (unlocked) with directional signage at the primary entrance may be used. The accessible entrance shall also have a notification system. Where security is a problem, remote monitoring may be used.

(c) If toilets are provided, then at least one toilet facility complying with 4.22 and 4.1.6 shall be provided along an accessible route that complies with 4.3. Such toilet facility may be unisex in design.

(d) Accessible routes from an accessible entrance to all publicly used spaces on at least the level of the accessible entrance shall be provided. Access shall be provided to all levels of a building or facility in compliance with 4.1 whenever practical.

(e) Displays and written information, documents, etc., should be located where they can be seen by a seated person. Exhibits and signage displayed horizontally (e.g., open books), should be no higher than 44 in (1120 mm) above the floor surface.

NOTE: The technical provisions of sections 4.2 through 4.35 are the same as those of the American National Standard Institute's document A117.1-1980, except as noted in the text.

4.2 Space Allowance and Reach Ranges.

4.2.1* Wheelchair Passage Width. The minimum clear width for single wheelchair passage shall be 32 in (815 mm) at a point and 36 in (915 mm) continuously (see Fig. 1 and 24(e)).

4.2.2 Width for Wheelchair Passing. The minimum width for two wheelchairs to pass is 60 in (1525 mm) (see Fig. 2).

4.2.3* Wheelchair Turning Space. The space required for a wheelchair to make a 180-degree turn is a clear space of 60 in (1525 mm)

14

diameter (see Fig. 3(a)) or a T-shaped space (see Fig. 3(b)).

4.2.4* Clear Floor or Ground Space for Wheelchairs.

4.2.4.1 Size and Approach. The minimum clear floor or ground space required to accommodate a single, stationary wheelchair and occupant is 30 in by 48 in (760 mm by 1220 mm) (see Fig. 4(a)). The minimum clear floor or ground space for wheelchairs may be positioned for forward or parallel approach to an object (see Fig. 4(b) and (c)). Clear floor or ground space for wheelchairs may be part of the knee space required under some objects.

4.2.4.2 Relationship of Maneuvering Clearance to Wheelchair Spaces. One full unobstructed side of the clear floor or ground space for a wheelchair shall adjoin or overlap an accessible route or adjoin another wheelchair clear floor space. If a clear floor space is located in an alcove or otherwise confined on all or part of three sides, additional maneuvering clearances shall be provided as shown in Fig. 4(d) and (e).

4.2.4.3 Surfaces for Wheelchair Spaces. Clear floor or ground spaces for wheelchairs shall comply with 4.5.

4.2.5* Forward Reach. If the clear floor space only allows forward approach to an object, the maximum high forward reach allowed shall be 48 in (1220 mm) (see Fig. 5(a)). *The minimum low forward reach is 15 in (380 mm).* If the high forward reach is over an obstruction, reach and clearances shall be as shown in Fig. 5(b).

4.2.6* Side Reach. If the clear floor space allows parallel approach by a person in a wheelchair, the maximum high side reach allowed shall be 54 in (1370 mm) and the low side reach shall be no less than 9 in (230 mm) above the floor (Fig. 6(a) and (b)). If the side reach is over an obstruction, the reach and clearances shall be as shown in Fig 6(c).

4.3 Accessible Route.

4.3.1* General. All walks, halls, corridors, aisles, *skywalks, tunnels,* and other spaces

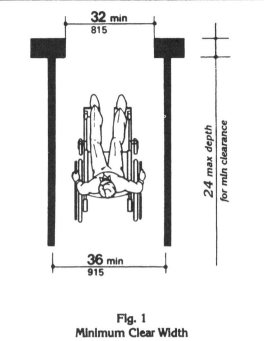

Fig. 1
Minimum Clear Width
for Single Wheelchair

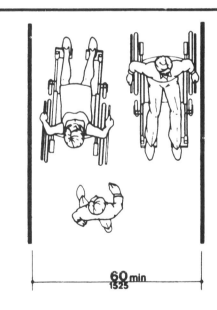

Fig. 2
Minimum Clear Width
for Two Wheelchairs

15

that are part of an accessible route shall comply with 4.3.

4.3.2 Location.

(1) At least one accessible route *within the boundary of the site* shall be provided from public transportation stops, accessible parking, and accessible passenger loading zones, and public streets or sidewalks to the accessible building entrance they serve. *The accessible route shall, to the maximum extent feasible, coincide with the route for the general public.*

(2) At least one accessible route shall connect accessible buildings, facilities, elements, and spaces that are on the same site.

(3) At least one accessible route shall connect accessible building or facility entrances with all accessible spaces and elements and with all accessible dwelling units within the building or facility.

(4) An accessible route shall connect at least one accessible entrance of each accessible dwelling unit with those exterior and interior spaces and facilities that serve the accessible dwelling unit.

4.3.3 Width.
The minimum clear width of an accessible route shall be 36 in (915 mm) except at doors (see 4.13.5 and 4.13.6). If a person in a wheelchair must make a turn around an obstruction, the minimum clear width of the accessible route shall be as shown in Fig. 7(a) and (b).

4.3.4 Passing Space.
If an accessible route has less than 60 in (1525 mm) clear width, then passing spaces at least 60 in by 60 in (1525 mm by 1525 mm) shall be located at reasonable intervals not to exceed 200 ft (61 m). A T-intersection of two corridors or walks is an acceptable passing place.

4.3.5 Head Room.
Accessible routes shall comply with 4.4.2.

4.3.6 Surface Textures.
The surface of an accessible route shall comply with 4.5.

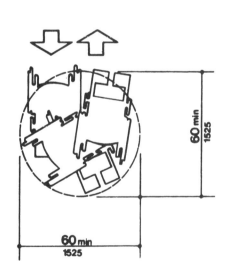

(a)
60-in (1525-mm)-Diameter Space

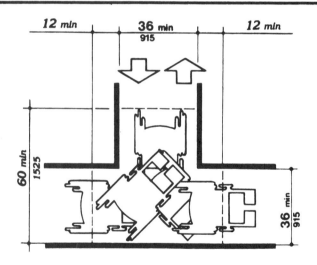

(b)
T-Shaped Space for 180° Turns

Fig. 3
Wheelchair Turning Space

16

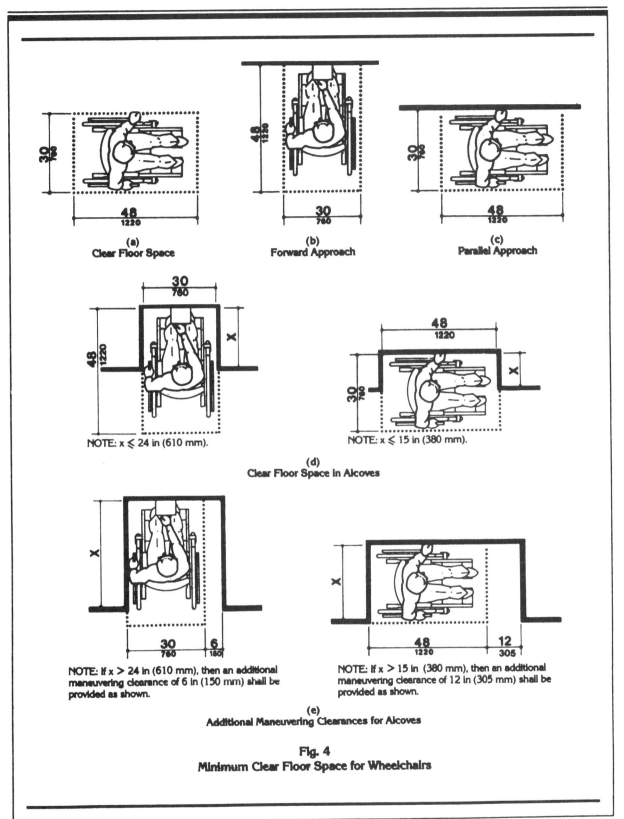

NOTE: x ≤ 24 in (610 mm).

(d)
Clear Floor Space in Alcoves

NOTE: If x > 24 in (610 mm), then an additional maneuvering clearance of 6 in (150 mm) shall be provided as shown.

NOTE: If x > 15 in (380 mm), then an additional maneuvering clearance of 12 in (305 mm) shall be provided as shown.

(e)
Additional Maneuvering Clearances for Alcoves

Fig. 4
Minimum Clear Floor Space for Wheelchairs

17

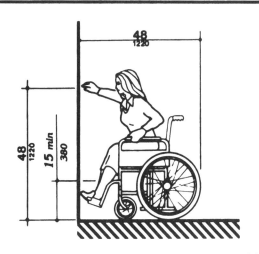

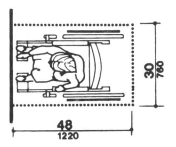

(a)
High Forward Reach Limit

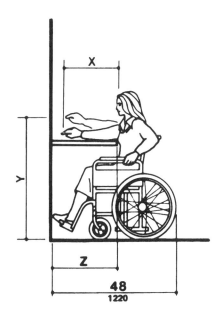

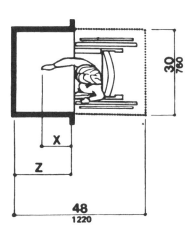

NOTE: x shall be ≤ 25 in (635 mm); z shall be ≥ x. When x < 20 in (510 mm), then y shall be 48 in (1220 mm) maximum. When x is 20 to 25 in (510 to 635 mm), then y shall be 44 in (1120 mm) maximum.

(b)
Maximum Forward Reach over an Obstruction

Fig. 5
Forward Reach

18

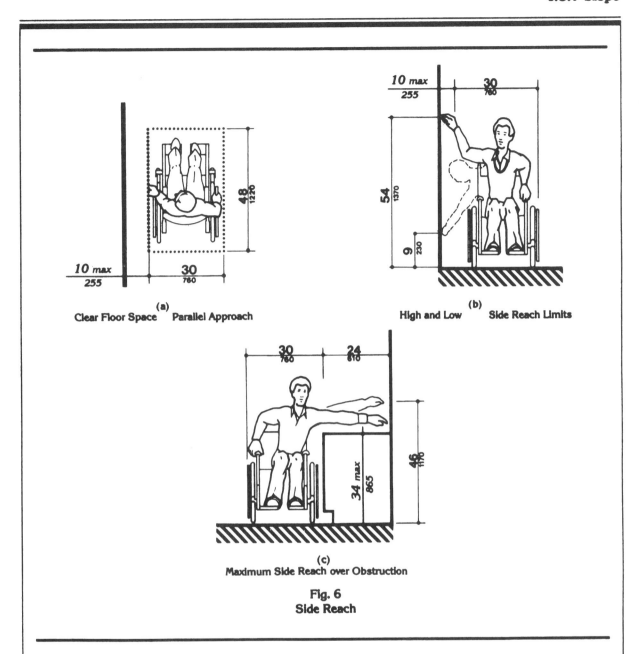

(a)
Clear Floor Space   Parallel Approach

(b)
High and Low   Side Reach Limits

(c)
Maximum Side Reach over Obstruction

Fig. 6
Side Reach

4.3.7 Slope. An accessible route with a running slope greater than 1:20 is a ramp and shall comply with 4.8. Nowhere shall the cross slope of an accessible route exceed 1:50.

4.3.8 Changes in Levels. Changes in levels along an accessible route shall comply with 4.5.2. If an accessible route has changes in level greater than 1/2 in (13 mm), then a curb ramp, ramp, elevator, or platform lift *(as permitted in 4.1.3 and 4.1.6)* shall be provided that complies with 4.7, 4.8, 4.10, or 4.11, respectively. An accessible route does not include stairs, steps, or escalators. See definition of "egress, means of" in 3.5.

4.3.9 Doors. Doors along an accessible route shall comply with 4.13.

19

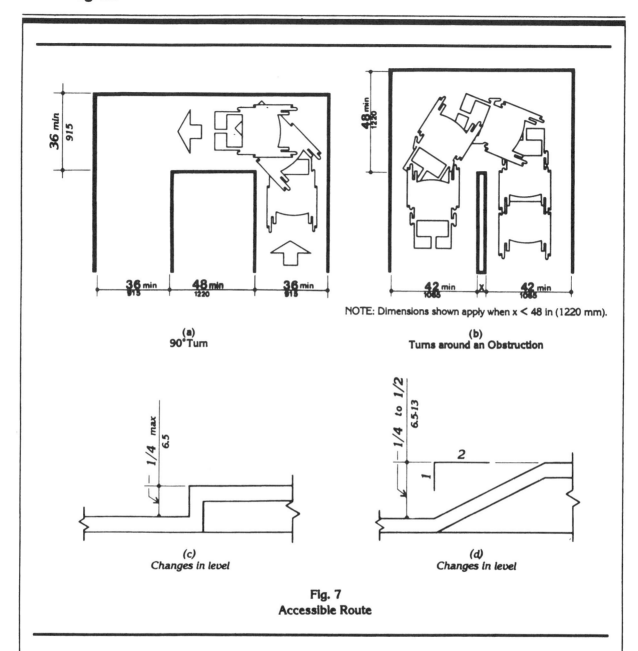

(a)
90°Turn

(b)
Turns around an Obstruction

NOTE: Dimensions shown apply when x < 48 in (1220 mm).

(c)
Changes in level

(d)
Changes in level

Fig. 7
Accessible Route

4.3.10* Egress. Accessible routes serving any accessible space or element shall also serve as a means of egress for emergencies or connect to an accessible area of *rescue assistance.*

4.3.11 Areas of Rescue Assistance.

4.3.11.1 Location and Construction. *An area of rescue assistance shall be one of the following:*

(1) A portion of a stairway landing within a smokeproof enclosure (complying with local requirements).

(2) A portion of an exterior exit balcony located immediately adjacent to an exit stairway when the balcony complies with local requirements for exterior exit balconies. Openings to the interior of the building located within 20 feet (6 m) of the

20

area of rescue assistance shall be protected with fire assemblies having a three-fourths hour fire protection rating.

(3) A portion of a one-hour fire-resistive corridor (complying with local requirements for fire-resistive construction and for openings) located immediately adjacent to an exit enclosure.

(4) A vestibule located immediately adjacent to an exit enclosure and constructed to the same fire-resistive standards as required for corridors and openings.

(5) A portion of a stairway landing within an exit enclosure which is vented to the exterior and is separated from the interior of the building with not less than one-hour fire-resistive doors.

(6) When approved by the appropriate local authority, an area or a room which is separated from other portions of the building by a smoke barrier. Smoke barriers shall have a fire-resistive rating of not less than one hour and shall completely enclose the area or room. Doors in the smoke barrier shall be tight-fitting smoke- and draft-control assemblies having a fire-protection rating of not less than 20 minutes and shall be self-closing or automatic closing. The area or room shall be provided with an exit directly to an exit enclosure. Where the room or area exits into an exit enclosure which is required to be of more than one-hour fire-resistive construction, the room or area shall have the same fire-resistive construction, including the same opening protection, as required for the adjacent exit enclosure.

(7) An elevator lobby when elevator shafts and adjacent lobbies are pressurized as required for smokeproof enclosures by local regulations and when complying with requirements herein for size, communication, and signage. Such pressurization system shall be activated by smoke detectors on each floor located in a manner approved by the appropriate local authority. Pressurization equipment and its duct work within the building shall be separated from other portions of the building by a minimum two-hour fire-resistive construction.

4.3.11.2 Size. Each area of rescue assistance shall provide at least two accessible areas each being not less than 30 inches by 48 inches (760 mm by 1220 mm). The area of rescue

assistance shall not encroach on any required exit width. The total number of such 30-inch by 48-inch (760 mm by 1220 mm) areas per story shall be not less than one for every 200 persons of calculated occupant load served by the area of rescue assistance.

EXCEPTION: The appropriate local authority may reduce the minimum number of 30-inch by 48-inch (760 mm by 1220 mm) areas to one for each area of rescue assistance on floors where the occupant load is less than 200.

4.3.11.3* Stairway Width. Each stairway adjacent to an area of rescue assistance shall have a minimum clear width of 48 inches between handrails.

4.3.11.4* Two-way Communication. A method of two-way communication, with both visible and audible signals, shall be provided between each area of rescue assistance and the primary entry. The fire department or appropriate local authority may approve a location other than the primary entry.

4.3.11.5 Identification. Each area of rescue assistance shall be identified by a sign which states "AREA OF RESCUE ASSISTANCE" and displays the international symbol of accessibility. The sign shall be illuminated when exit sign illumination is required. Signage shall also be installed at all inaccessible exits and where otherwise necessary to clearly indicate the direction to areas of rescue assistance. In each area of rescue assistance, instructions on the use of the area under emergency conditions shall be posted adjoining the two-way communication system.

4.4 Protruding Objects.

4.4.1* General. Objects projecting from walls (for example, telephones) with their leading edges between 27 in and 80 in (685 mm and 2030 mm) above the finished floor shall protrude no more than 4 in (100 mm) into walks, halls, corridors, passageways, or aisles (see Fig. 8(a)). Objects mounted with their leading edges at or below 27 in (685 mm) above the finished floor may protrude any amount (see Fig. 8(a) and (b)). Free-standing objects mounted on posts or pylons may overhang 12 in (305 mm) maximum from 27 in to 80 in (685 mm to 2030 mm) above the ground or

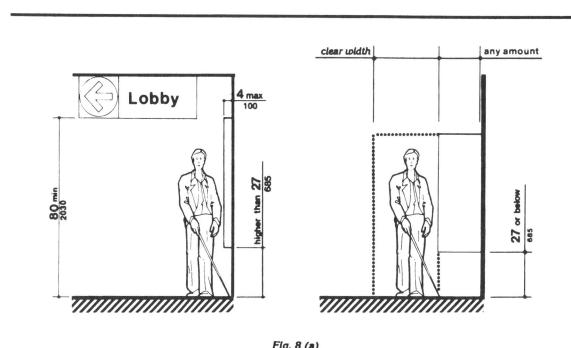

Fig. 8 (a)
Walking Parallel to a Wall

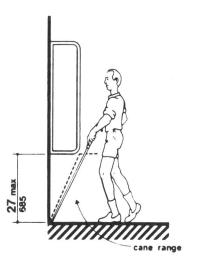

Fig. 8 (b)
Walking Perpendicular to a Wall

Fig. 8
Protruding Objects

finished floor (see Fig. 8(c) and (d)). Protruding objects shall not reduce the clear width of an accessible route or maneuvering space (see Fig. 8(e)).

4.4.2 Head Room. Walks, halls, corridors, passageways, aisles, or other circulation spaces shall have 80 in (2030 mm) minimum clear head room (see Fig. 8(a)). *If vertical clearance of an area adjoining an accessible route is reduced to less than 80 in (nominal dimension), a barrier to warn blind or visually-impaired persons shall be provided (see Fig. 8(c-1)).*

4.5 Ground and Floor Surfaces.

4.5.1* General. Ground and floor surfaces along accessible routes and in accessible rooms and spaces including floors, walks, ramps, stairs, and curb ramps, shall be stable, firm, slip-resistant, and shall comply with 4.5.

4.5.2 Changes in Level. Changes in level up to 1/4 in (6 mm) may be vertical and without edge treatment *(see Fig. 7(c)).* Changes in level between 1/4 in and 1/2 in (6 mm and 13 mm)

22

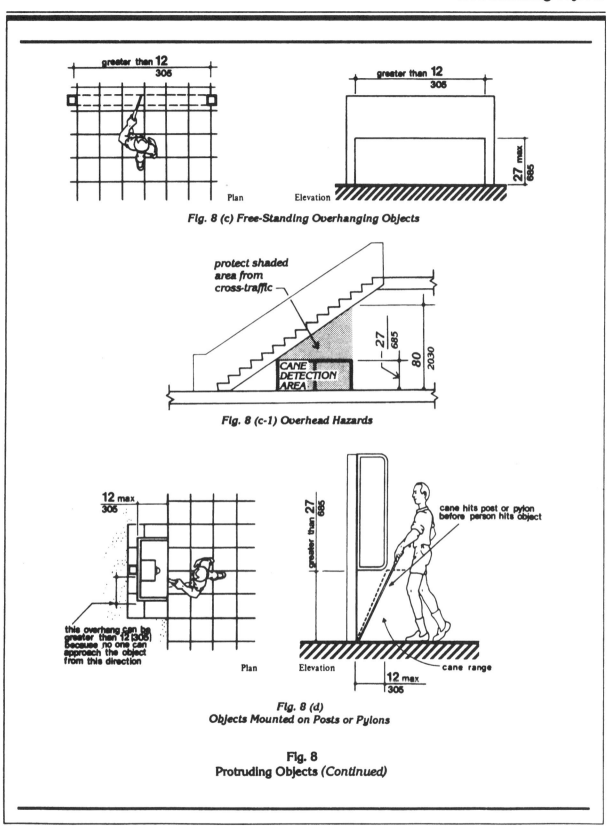

Fig. 8 (c) Free-Standing Overhanging Objects

Fig. 8 (c-1) Overhead Hazards

Fig. 8 (d)
Objects Mounted on Posts or Pylons

Fig. 8
Protruding Objects (Continued)

23

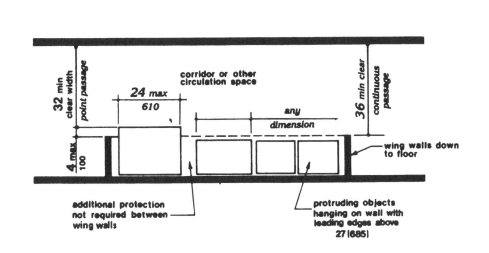

Fig. 8 (e)
Example of Protection around Wall-Mounted Objects and Measurements of Clear Widths

Fig. 8
Protruding Objects *(Continued)*

shall be beveled with a slope no greater than
1:2 *(see Fig. 7(d))*. Changes in level greater than
1/2 in (13 mm) shall be accomplished by
means of a ramp that complies with 4.7 or 4.8.

4.5.3* Carpet. If carpet or carpet tile is used
on a ground or floor surface, then it shall be
securely attached; have a firm cushion, pad, or
backing, or no cushion or pad; and have a level
loop, textured loop, level cut pile, or level cut/
uncut pile texture. The maximum pile *thickness* shall be 1/2 in (13 mm) (see Fig. 8(f)).
Exposed edges of carpet shall be fastened to
floor surfaces and have trim along the entire
length of the exposed edge. Carpet edge trim
shall comply with 4.5.2.

4.5.4 Gratings. If gratings are located in
walking surfaces, then they shall have spaces
no greater than 1/2 in (13 mm) wide in one
direction *(see Fig. 8(g))*. If gratings have elongated openings, then they shall be placed so
that the long dimension is perpendicular to the
dominant direction of travel *(see Fig. 8(h))*.

**4.6 Parking and Passenger Loading
Zones.**

4.6.1 Minimum Number. *Parking spaces
required to be accessible by 4.1 shall comply
with 4.6.2 through 4.6.5. Passenger loading
zones required to be accessible by 4.1 shall
comply with 4.6.5 and 4.6.6.*

24

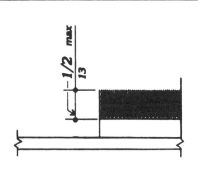

Fig. 8 (f)
Carpet Pile Thickness

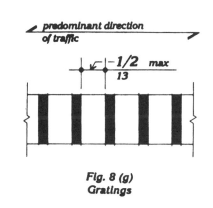

predominant direction
of traffic

Fig. 8 (g)
Gratings

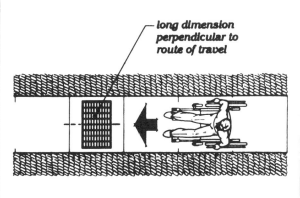

long dimension
perpendicular to
route of travel

Fig. 8 (h)
Grating Orientation

4.6.2 Location. *Accessible parking spaces serving* a particular building shall be located on the shortest accessible route of travel *from adjacent parking* to an accessible entrance. *In parking facilities* that do not serve a particular building, *accessible parking* shall be located on the shortest accessible route *of travel* to an accessible pedestrian entrance of the parking facility. *In buildings with multiple accessible entrances with adjacent parking, accessible parking spaces shall be dispersed and located closest to the accessible entrances.*

4.6.3* Parking Spaces. *Accessible* parking spaces shall be at least 96 in (2440 mm) wide. Parking access aisles shall be part of an accessible route to the building or facility entrance and shall comply with 4.3. Two accessible parking spaces may share a common access aisle (see Fig. 9). Parked vehicle overhangs shall not reduce the clear width of an accessible route. *Parking spaces and access aisles shall be level with surface slopes not exceeding 1:50 (2%) in all directions.*

4.6.4* Signage. Accessible parking spaces shall be designated as reserved by a sign showing the symbol of accessibility (see 4.30.7). *Spaces complying with 4.1.2(5)(b) shall have an additional sign "Van-Accessible" mounted below the symbol of accessibility.* Such signs shall be located so they cannot be obscured by a vehicle parked in the space.

4.6.5* Vertical Clearance. *Provide minimum vertical clearance of 114 in (2895 mm) at accessible passenger loading zones and along at least one vehicle access route to such areas from site entrance(s) and exit(s). At parking spaces complying with 4.1.2(5)(b), provide minimum vertical clearance of 98 in (2490 mm) at the parking space and along at least one vehicle access route to such spaces from site entrance(s) and exit(s).*

4.6.6 Passenger Loading Zones. Passenger loading zones shall provide an access aisle at least 60 in (1525 mm) wide and 20 ft (240 in) (6100 mm) long adjacent and parallel to the vehicle pull-up space (see Fig. 10). If there are curbs between the access aisle and the vehicle pull-up space, then a curb ramp complying with 4.7 shall be provided. *Vehicle standing spaces and access aisles shall be level with*

25

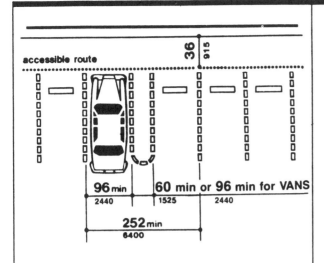

accessible route

96 min
2440

60 min or 96 min for VANS
1525

2440

252 min
6400

36
915

Fig. 9
Dimensions of Parking Spaces

surface slopes not exceeding 1:50 (2%) in all directions.

4.7 Curb Ramps.

4.7.1 Location. Curb ramps complying with 4.7 shall be provided wherever an accessible route crosses a curb.

4.7.2 Slope. Slopes of curb ramps shall comply with 4.8.2. The slope shall be measured as shown in Fig. 11. *Transitions from ramps to walks, gutters, or streets shall be flush and free of abrupt changes. Maximum slopes of adjoining gutters, road surface immediately adjacent to the curb ramp, or accessible route shall not exceed 1:20.*

4.7.3 Width. The minimum width of a curb ramp shall be 36 in (915 mm), exclusive of flared sides.

4.7.4 Surface. Surfaces of curb ramps shall comply with 4.5.

4.7.5 Sides of Curb Ramps. If a curb ramp is located where pedestrians must walk across the ramp, *or where it is not protected by handrails or guardrails,* it shall have flared sides; the maximum slope of the flare shall be 1:10 (see Fig. 12(a)). Curb ramps with returned curbs

may be used where pedestrians would not normally walk across the ramp (see Fig. 12(b)).

4.7.6 Built-up Curb Ramps. Built-up curb ramps shall be located so that they do not project into vehicular traffic lanes (see Fig. 13).

4.7.7 Detectable Warnings. A curb ramp shall have a *detectable* warning complying with 4.29.2. *The detectable warning shall extend the full width and depth of the curb ramp.*

4.7.8 Obstructions. Curb ramps shall be located or protected to prevent their obstruction by parked vehicles.

4.7.9 Location at Marked Crossings. Curb ramps at marked crossings shall be wholly contained within the markings, excluding any flared sides (see Fig. 15).

4.7.10 Diagonal Curb Ramps. If diagonal (or corner type) curb ramps have returned curbs or other well-defined edges, such edges shall be parallel to the direction of pedestrian flow. The bottom of diagonal curb ramps shall have 48 in (1220 mm) minimum clear space as shown in Fig. 15(c) and (d). If diagonal curb ramps are provided at marked crossings, the 48 in (1220 mm) clear space shall be within the markings (see Fig. 15(c) and (d)). If diagonal curb ramps have flared sides, they shall also have at least a 24 in (610 mm) long segment of straight curb located on each side of the curb ramp and within the marked crossing (see Fig. 15(c)).

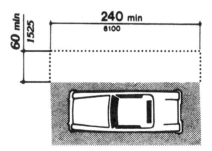

60 min
1525

240 min
6100

Fig. 10
Access Aisle at Passenger Loading Zones

26

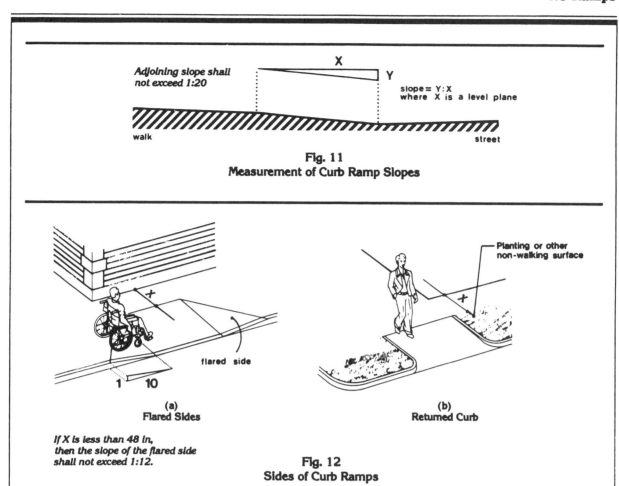

Fig. 11
Measurement of Curb Ramp Slopes

*If X is less than 48 in,
then the slope of the flared side
shall not exceed 1:12.*

**(a)
Flared Sides**

**(b)
Returned Curb**

Fig. 12
Sides of Curb Ramps

4.7.11 Islands. Any raised islands in crossings shall be cut through level with the street or have curb ramps at both sides and a level area at least 48 in (1220 mm) long between the curb ramps in the part of the island intersected by the crossings (see Fig. 15(a) and (b)).

4.8 Ramps.

4.8.1* General. Any part of an accessible route with a slope greater than 1:20 shall be considered a ramp and shall comply with 4.8.

4.8.2* Slope and Rise. The least possible slope shall be used for any ramp. The maximum slope of a ramp in new construction shall be 1:12. The maximum rise for any run shall be 30 in (760 mm) (see Fig. 16). Curb ramps

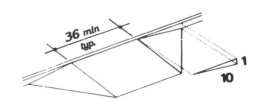

Fig. 13
Built-Up Curb Ramp

and ramps to be constructed on existing sites or in existing buildings or facilities may have slopes and rises as *allowed in 4.1.6(3)(a)* if space limitations prohibit the use of a 1:12 slope or less.

27

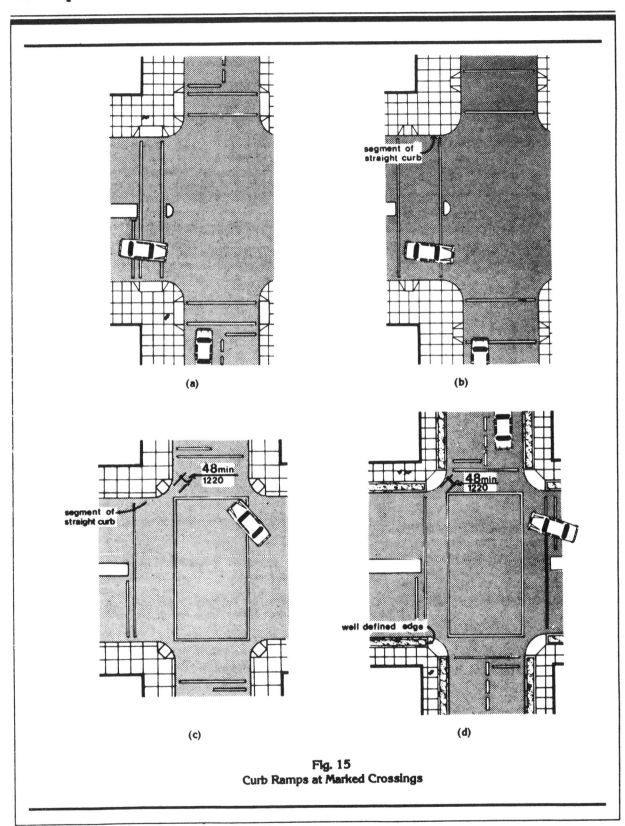

Fig. 15
Curb Ramps at Marked Crossings

28

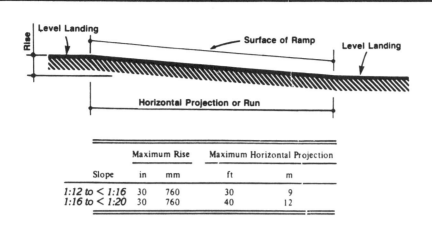

	Maximum Rise		Maximum Horizontal Projection	
Slope	in	mm	ft	m
1:12 to < 1:16	30	760	30	9
1:16 to < 1:20	30	760	40	12

Fig. 16
Components of a Single Ramp Run and Sample Ramp Dimensions

4.8.3 Clear Width. The minimum clear width of a ramp shall be 36 in (915 mm).

4.8.4* Landings. Ramps shall have level landings at bottom and top of *each ramp and each ramp* run. Landings shall have the following features:

(1) The landing shall be at least as wide as the ramp run leading to it.

(2) The landing length shall be a minimum of 60 in (1525 mm) clear.

(3) If ramps change direction at landings, the minimum landing size shall be 60 in by 60 in (1525 mm by 1525 mm).

(4) If a doorway is located at a landing, then the area in front of the doorway shall comply with 4.13.6.

4.8.5* Handrails. If a ramp run has a rise greater than 6 in (150 mm) or a horizontal projection greater than 72 in (1830 mm), then it shall have handrails on both sides. Handrails are not required on curb ramps *or adjacent to seating in assembly areas.* Handrails shall comply with 4.26 and shall have the following features:

(1) Handrails shall be provided along both sides of ramp segments. The inside handrail on switchback or dogleg ramps shall always be continuous.

(2) If handrails are not continuous, they shall extend at least 12 in (305 mm) beyond the top and bottom of the ramp segment and shall be parallel with the floor or ground surface (see Fig. 17).

(3) The clear space between the handrail and the wall shall be 1 - 1/2 in (38 mm).

(4) Gripping surfaces shall be continuous.

(5) *Top of handrail gripping surfaces shall be mounted between 34 in and 38 in (865 mm and 965 mm) above ramp surfaces.*

(6) *Ends of handrails shall be either rounded or returned smoothly to floor, wall, or post.*

(7) *Handrails shall not rotate within their fittings.*

4.8.6 Cross Slope and Surfaces. The cross slope of ramp surfaces shall be no greater than 1:50. Ramp surfaces shall comply with 4.5.

4.8.7 Edge Protection. Ramps and landings with drop-offs shall have curbs, walls, railings, or projecting surfaces that prevent people from slipping off the ramp. Curbs shall be a minimum of 2 in (50 mm) high (see Fig. 17).

4.8.8 Outdoor Conditions. Outdoor ramps and their approaches shall be designed so that water will not accumulate on walking surfaces.

4.9 Stairs.

4.9.1* Minimum Number. *Stairs required to be accessible by 4.1 shall comply with 4.9.*

4.9.2 Treads and Risers. On any given flight of stairs, all steps shall have uniform riser heights and uniform tread widths. Stair treads shall be no less than 11 in (280 mm) wide, measured from riser to riser (see Fig. 18(a)). *Open risers are not permitted.*

4.9.3 Nosings. The undersides of nosings shall not be abrupt. The radius of curvature at the leading edge of the tread shall be no greater than 1/2 in (13 mm). Risers shall be sloped or the underside of the nosing shall have an angle not less than 60 degrees from the horizontal. Nosings shall project no more than 1-1/2 in (38 mm) (see Fig. 18).

4.9.4 Handrails. Stairways shall have handrails at both sides of all stairs. Handrails shall comply with 4.26 and shall have the following features:

(1) Handrails shall be continuous along both sides of stairs. The inside handrail on switchback or dogleg stairs shall always be continuous (see Fig. 19(a) and (b)).

(2) If handrails are not continuous, they shall extend at least 12 in (305 mm) beyond the top riser and at least 12 in (305 mm) plus the width of one tread beyond the bottom riser. At the top, the extension shall be parallel with the floor or ground surface. At the bottom, the handrail shall continue to slope for a distance of the width of one tread from the bottom riser; the remainder of the extension shall be horizontal (see Fig. 19(c) and (d)). Handrail extensions shall comply with 4.4.

(3) The clear space between handrails and wall shall be 1-1/2 in (38 mm).

(4) Gripping surfaces shall be uninterrupted by newel posts, other construction elements, or obstructions.

(5) *Top of handrail gripping surface shall be mounted between 34 in and 38 in (865 mm and 965 mm) above stair nosings.*

(6) *Ends of handrails shall be either rounded or returned smoothly to floor, wall or post.*

(7) *Handrails shall not rotate within their fittings.*

4.9.5 Detectable Warnings at Stairs. *(Reserved).*

4.9.6 Outdoor Conditions. Outdoor stairs and their approaches shall be designed so that water will not accumulate on walking surfaces.

4.10 Elevators.

4.10.1 General. *Accessible* elevators shall be on an accessible route and shall comply with 4.10 and with the *ASME A17.1-1990, Safety Code for Elevators and Escalators. Freight elevators shall not be considered as meeting the requirements of this section unless the only elevators provided are used as combination passenger and freight elevators for the public and employees.*

4.10.2 Automatic Operation. Elevator operation shall be automatic. Each car shall be equipped with a self-leveling feature that will automatically bring the car to floor landings within a tolerance of 1/2 in (13 mm) under rated loading to zero loading conditions. This self-leveling feature shall be automatic and independent of the operating device and shall correct the overtravel or undertravel.

4.10.3 Hall Call Buttons. Call buttons in elevator lobbies and halls shall be centered at 42 in (1065 mm) above the floor. Such call buttons shall have visual signals to indicate when each call is registered and when each call is answered. Call buttons shall be a minimum of 3/4 in (19 mm) in the smallest dimension. The button designating the up direction shall be on top. (See Fig. 20.) *Buttons shall be raised or flush. Objects mounted beneath hall call buttons shall not project into the elevator lobby more than 4 in (100 mm).*

30

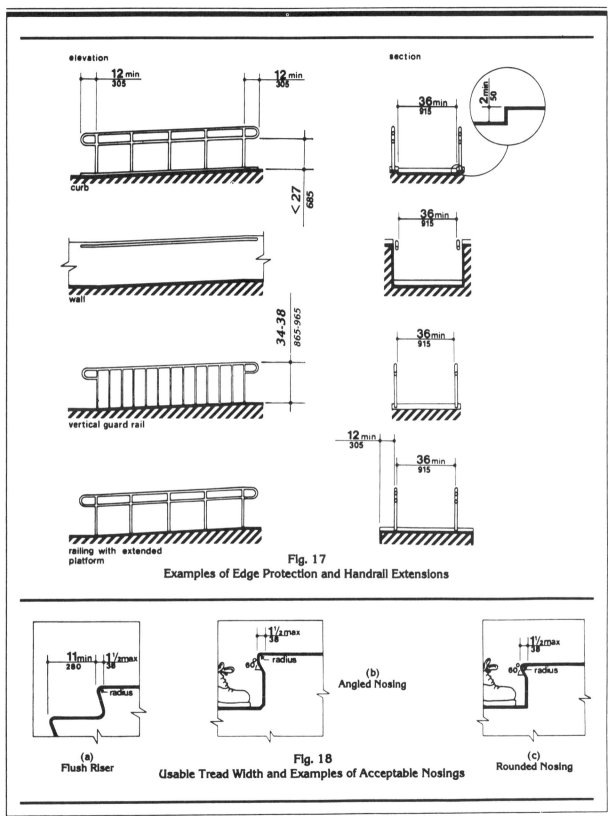

Fig. 17
Examples of Edge Protection and Handrail Extensions

Fig. 18
Usable Tread Width and Examples of Acceptable Nosings

(a) Flush Riser

(b) Angled Nosing

(c) Rounded Nosing

31

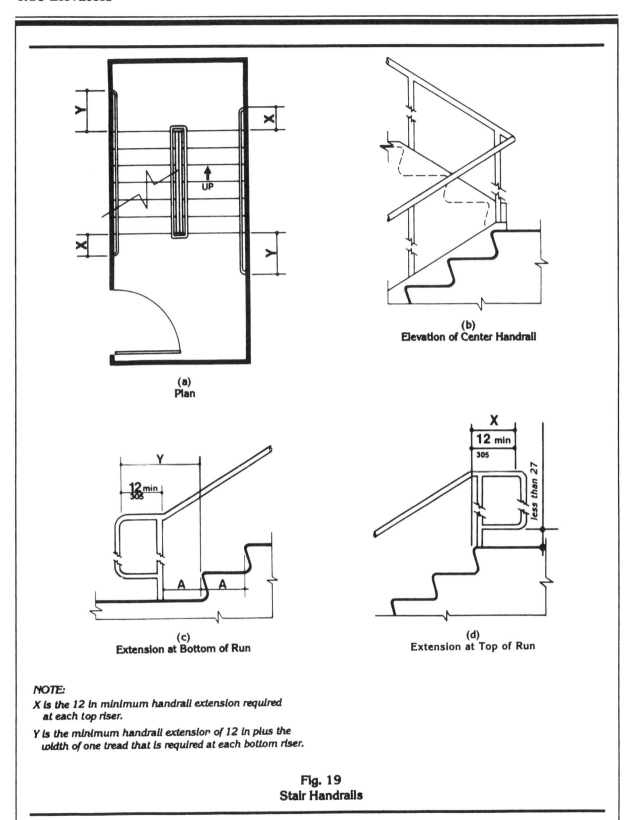

(a)
Plan

(b)
Elevation of Center Handrail

(c)
Extension at Bottom of Run

(d)
Extension at Top of Run

NOTE:

X is the 12 in minimum handrail extension required at each top riser.

Y is the minimum handrail extension of 12 in plus the width of one tread that is required at each bottom riser.

Fig. 19
Stair Handrails

32

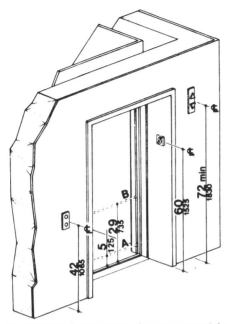

NOTE: The automatic door reopening device is activated if an object passes through either line A or line B. Line A and line B represent the vertical locations of the door reopening device not requiring contact.

Fig. 20
Hoistway and Elevator Entrances

4.10.4 Hall Lanterns. A visible and audible signal shall be provided at each hoistway entrance to indicate which car is answering a call. Audible signals shall sound once for the up direction and twice for the down direction or shall have verbal annunciators that say "up" or "down." Visible signals shall have the following features:

(1) Hall lantern fixtures shall be mounted so that their centerline is at least 72 in (1830 mm) above the lobby floor. (See Fig. 20.)

(2) Visual elements shall be at least 2-1/2 in (64 mm) in the smallest dimension.

(3) Signals shall be visible from the vicinity of the hall call button (see Fig. 20). In-car lanterns located in cars, visible from the vicinity of hall call buttons, and conforming to the above requirements, shall be acceptable.

4.10.5 Raised and Braille Characters on Hoistway Entrances. All elevator hoistway entrances shall have *raised and Braille* floor designations provided on both jambs. The centerline of the characters shall be 60 in (1525 mm) *above finish* floor. Such characters shall be 2 in (50 mm) high and shall comply with 4.30.4. Permanently applied plates are acceptable if they are permanently fixed to the jambs. (See Fig. 20).

4.10.6* Door Protective and Reopening Device. Elevator doors shall open and close automatically. They shall be provided with a reopening device that will stop and reopen a car door and hoistway door automatically if the door becomes obstructed by an object or person. The device shall be capable of completing these operations without requiring contact for an obstruction passing through the opening at heights of 5 in and 29 in (125 mm and 735 mm) above finish floor (see Fig. 20). Door reopening devices shall remain effective for at least 20 seconds. After such an interval, doors may close in accordance with the requirements of *ASME A17.1-1990.*

4.10.7* Door and Signal Timing for Hall Calls. The minimum acceptable time from notification that a car is answering a call until the doors of that car start to close shall be calculated from the following equation:

$$T = D/(1.5 \text{ ft/s}) \text{ or } T = D/(445 \text{ mm/s})$$

where T total time in seconds and D distance (in feet or millimeters) from a point in the lobby or corridor 60 in (1525 mm) directly in front of the farthest call button controlling that car to the centerline of its hoistway door (see Fig. 21). For cars with in-car lanterns, T begins when the lantern is visible from the vicinity of hall call buttons and an audible signal is sounded. *The minimum acceptable notification time shall be 5 seconds.*

4.10.8 Door Delay for Car Calls. The minimum time for elevator doors to remain fully open in response to a car call shall be 3 seconds.

4.10.9 Floor Plan of Elevator Cars. The floor area of elevator cars shall provide space for wheelchair users to enter the car, maneuver

33

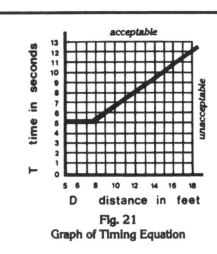

Fig. 21
Graph of Timing Equation

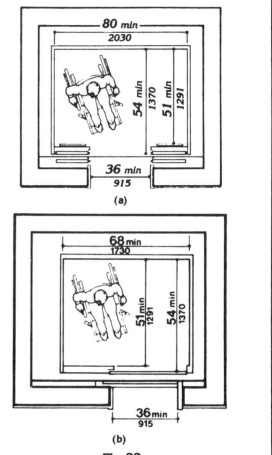

(a)

(b)

Fig. 22
Minimum Dimensions of Elevator Cars

within reach of controls, and exit from the car. Acceptable door opening and inside dimensions shall be as shown in Fig. 22. The clearance between the car platform sill and the edge of any hoistway landing shall be no greater than 1-1/4 in (32 mm).

4.10.10 Floor Surfaces. Floor surfaces shall comply with 4.5.

4.10.11 Illumination Levels. The level of illumination at the car controls, platform, and car threshold and landing sill shall be at least 5 footcandles (53.8 lux).

4.10.12* Car Controls. Elevator control panels shall have the following features:

(1) Buttons. All control buttons shall be at least 3/4 in (19 mm) in their smallest dimension. They *shall* be *raised* or flush.

(2) Tactile, *Braille*, and Visual Control Indicators. All control buttons shall be designated by *Braille and by raised* standard alphabet characters for letters, arabic characters for numerals, or standard symbols as shown in Fig. 23(a), and as required in *ASME A17.1-1990. Raised and Braille* characters and symbols shall comply with 4.30. The call button for the main entry floor shall be designated by a *raised* star at the left of the floor designation (see Fig. 23(a)). All raised designations for control buttons shall be placed immediately to the left of the button to which they apply. Applied plates,

permanently attached, are an acceptable means to provide raised control designations. Floor buttons shall be provided with visual indicators to show when each call is registered. The visual indicators shall be extinguished when each call is answered.

(3) Height. All floor buttons shall be no higher than 54 in (1370 mm) above the *finish floor for side approach and 48 in (1220 mm) for front approach.* Emergency controls, including the emergency alarm and emergency stop, shall be grouped at the bottom of the panel and shall have their centerlines no less than 35 in (890 mm) above the finish floor (see Fig. 23(a) and (b)).

34

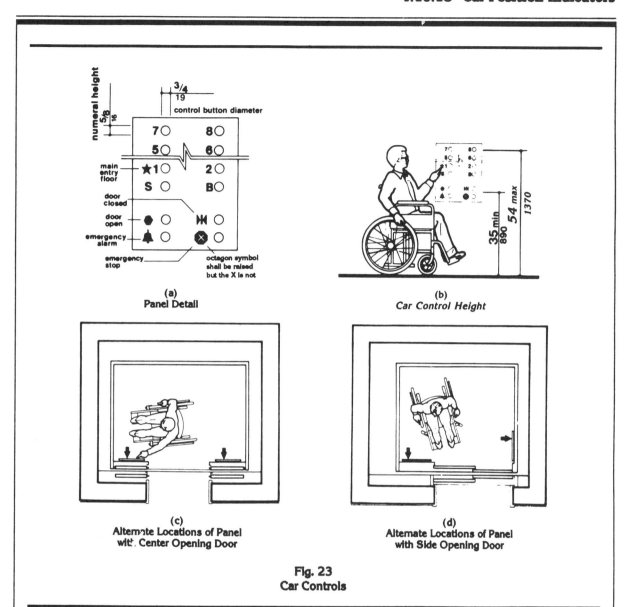

(a)
Panel Detail

(b)
Car Control Height

(c)
Alternate Locations of Panel with Center Opening Door

(d)
Alternate Locations of Panel with Side Opening Door

Fig. 23
Car Controls

(4) Location. Controls shall be located on a front wall if cars have center opening doors, and at the side wall or at the front wall next to the door if cars have side opening doors (see Fig. 23(c) and (d)).

4.10.13* Car Position Indicators. In elevator cars, a visual car position indicator shall be provided above the car control panel or over the door to show the position of the elevator in the hoistway. As the car passes or stops at a floor served by the elevators, the corresponding numerals shall illuminate,

and an audible signal shall sound. Numerals shall be a minimum of 1/2 in (13 mm) high. The audible signal shall be no less than 20 decibels with a frequency no higher than 1500 Hz. An automatic verbal announcement of the floor number at which a car stops or which a car passes may be substituted for the audible signal.

4.10.14* Emergency Communications. If provided, emergency two-way communication systems between the elevator and a point outside the hoistway shall comply with *ASME*

A17.1-1990. The highest operable part of a two-way communication system shall be a maximum of *48 in (1220 mm)* from the floor of the car. It shall be identified by a raised symbol and lettering complying with 4.30 and located adjacent to the device. If the system uses a handset then the length of the cord from the panel to the handset shall be at least 29 in (735 mm). *If the system is located in a closed compartment the compartment door hardware shall conform to 4.27, Controls and Operating Mechanisms. The emergency inter-communication system shall not require voice communication.*

4.11 Platform Lifts (Wheelchair Lifts).

4.11.1 Location. *Platform lifts (wheelchair lifts) permitted by 4.1 shall comply with the requirements of 4.11.*

4.11.2* Other Requirements. If platform lifts *(wheelchair lifts)* are used, they shall comply with 4.2.4, 4.5, 4.27, and *ASME A17.1 Safety Code for Elevators and Escalators, Section XX, 1990.*

4.11.3 Entrance. *If platform lifts are used then they shall facilitate unassisted entry, operation, and exit from the lift in compliance with 4.11.2.*

4.12 Windows.

4.12.1* General. *(Reserved).*

4.12.2* Window Hardware. *(Reserved).*

4.13 Doors.

4.13.1 General. *Doors required to be accessible by 4.1 shall comply with the requirements of 4.13.*

4.13.2 Revolving Doors and Turnstiles. Revolving doors or turnstiles shall not be the only means of passage at an accessible entrance or along an accessible route. *An accessible gate or door shall be provided adjacent to the turnstile or revolving door and shall be so designed as to facilitate the same use pattern.*

4.13.3 Gates. Gates, including ticket gates, shall meet all applicable specifications of 4.13.

4.13.4 Double-Leaf Doorways. If doorways have two *independently operated* door leaves, then at least one leaf shall meet the specifications in 4.13.5 and 4.13.6. That leaf shall be an active leaf.

4.13.5 Clear Width. Doorways shall have a minimum clear opening of 32 in (815 mm) with the door open 90 degrees, measured between the face of the door and the *opposite* stop (see Fig. 24(a), (b), (c), and (d)). Openings more than 24 in (610 mm) in depth shall comply with 4.2.1 and 4.3.3 (see Fig. 24(e)).

EXCEPTION: Doors not requiring full user passage, such as shallow closets, may have the clear opening reduced to 20 in (510 mm) minimum.

4.13.6 Maneuvering Clearances at Doors. Minimum maneuvering clearances at doors that are not automatic or power-assisted shall be as shown in Fig. 25. The floor or ground area within the required clearances shall be level and clear.

EXCEPTION: Entry doors to acute care hospital bedrooms for in-patients shall be exempted from the requirement for space at the latch side of the door (see dimension "x" in Fig. 25) if the door is at least 44 in (1120 mm) wide.

4.13.7 Two Doors in Series. The minimum space between two hinged or pivoted doors in series shall be 48 in (1220 mm) plus the width of any door swinging into the space. Doors in series shall swing either in the same direction or away from the space between the doors (see Fig. 26).

4.13.8* Thresholds at Doorways. Thresholds at doorways shall not exceed 3/4 in (19 mm) in height for exterior sliding doors or 1/2 in (13 mm) for other types of doors. Raised thresholds and floor level changes at accessible doorways shall be beveled with a slope no greater than 1:2 (see 4.5.2).

4.13.9* Door Hardware. Handles, pulls, latches, locks, and other operating devices on accessible doors shall have a shape that is easy

36

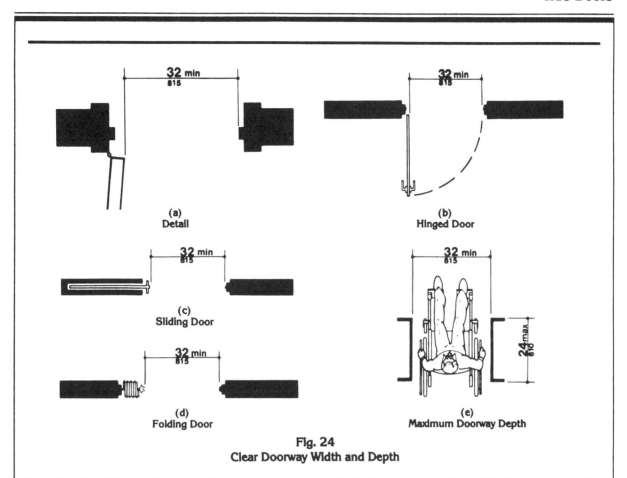

Fig. 24
Clear Doorway Width and Depth

to grasp with one hand and does not require tight grasping, tight pinching, or twisting of the wrist to operate. Lever-operated mechanisms, push-type mechanisms, and U-shaped handles are acceptable designs. When sliding doors are fully open, operating hardware shall be exposed and usable from both sides. *Hardware required for accessible door passage shall be mounted no higher than 48 in (1220 mm) above finished floor.*

4.13.10* Door Closers. If a door has a closer, then the sweep period of the closer shall be adjusted so that from an open position of 70 degrees, the door will take at least 3 seconds to move to a point 3 in (75 mm) from the latch, measured to the leading edge of the door.

4.13.11* Door Opening Force. The maximum force for pushing or pulling open a door shall be as follows:

(1) Fire doors shall have the minimum opening force allowable by the appropriate administrative authority.

(2) Other doors.

(a) exterior hinged doors: *(Reserved).*

(b) interior hinged doors: 5 lbf (22.2N)

(c) sliding or folding doors: 5 lbf (22.2N)

These forces do not apply to the force required to retract latch bolts or disengage other devices that may hold the door in a closed position.

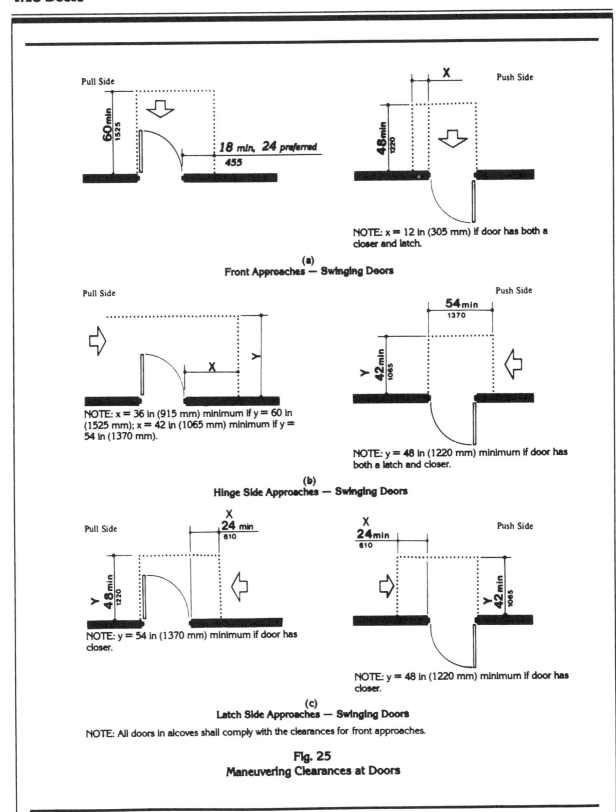

Pull Side

60 min 1525

18 min, 24 preferred 455

X Push Side

48 min 1220

NOTE: x = 12 in (305 mm) if door has both a closer and latch.

(a)
Front Approaches — Swinging Doors

Pull Side

X Y

NOTE: x = 36 in (915 mm) minimum if y = 60 in (1525 mm); x = 42 in (1065 mm) minimum if y = 54 in (1370 mm).

Push Side

54 min 1370

Y 42 min 1065

NOTE: y = 48 in (1220 mm) minimum if door has both a latch and closer.

(b)
Hinge Side Approaches — Swinging Doors

Pull Side

X 24 min 610

Y 48 min 1220

NOTE: y = 54 in (1370 mm) minimum if door has closer.

X 24 min 610

Push Side

Y 42 min 1065

NOTE: y = 48 in (1220 mm) minimum if door has closer.

(c)
Latch Side Approaches — Swinging Doors

NOTE: All doors in alcoves shall comply with the clearances for front approaches.

Fig. 25
Maneuvering Clearances at Doors

38

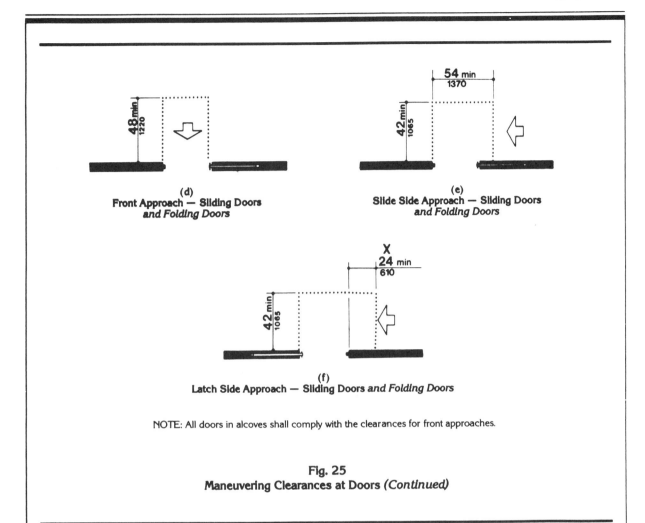

(d)
Front Approach — Sliding Doors
and Folding Doors

(e)
Slide Side Approach — Sliding Doors
and Folding Doors

(f)
Latch Side Approach — Sliding Doors and Folding Doors

NOTE: All doors in alcoves shall comply with the clearances for front approaches.

Fig. 25
Maneuvering Clearances at Doors (*Continued*)

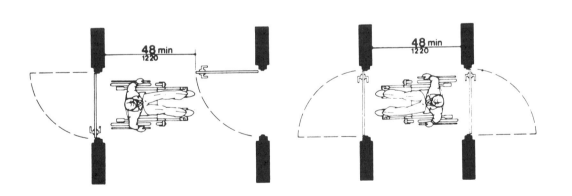

Fig. 26
Two Hinged Doors in Series

39

4.13.12* Automatic Doors and Power-Assisted Doors. If an automatic door is used, then it shall comply with *ANSI/BHMA A156.10-1985.* Slowly opening, low-powered, automatic doors shall *comply with ANSI A156.19-1984.* Such doors shall not open to back check faster than 3 seconds and shall require no more than 15 lbf (66.6N) to stop door movement. If a power-assisted door is used, its door-opening force shall comply with 4.13.11 and its closing shall conform to the requirements in *ANSI A156.19-1984.*

4.14 Entrances.

4.14.1 Minimum Number. *Entrances required to be accessible by 4.1* shall be part of an accessible route complying with 4.3. Such entrances shall be connected by an accessible route to public transportation stops, to accessible parking and passenger loading zones, and to public streets or sidewalks if available (see 4.3.2(1)). They shall also be connected by an accessible route to all accessible spaces or elements within the building or facility.

4.14.2 Service Entrances. A service entrance shall not be the sole accessible entrance unless it is the only entrance to a building or facility (for example, in a factory or garage).

4.15 Drinking Fountains and Water Coolers.

4.15.1 Minimum Number. *Drinking fountains or water coolers required to be accessible by 4.1* shall comply with 4.15.

4.15.2* Spout Height. Spouts shall be no higher than 36 in (915 mm), measured from the floor or ground surfaces to the spout outlet (see Fig. 27(a)).

4.15.3 Spout Location. The spouts of drinking fountains and water coolers shall be at the front of the unit and shall direct the water flow in a trajectory that is parallel or nearly parallel to the front of the unit. The spout shall provide a flow of water at least 4 in (100 mm) high so as to allow the insertion of a cup or glass under the flow of water. *On an accessible drinking fountain with a round or oval bowl, the spout must be positioned so the flow of water is within 3 in (75 mm) of the front edge of the fountain.*

4.15.4 Controls. Controls shall comply with 4.27.4. *Unit controls shall be front mounted or side mounted near the front edge.*

4.15.5 Clearances.

(1) Wall- and post-mounted cantilevered units shall have a clear knee space between the bottom of the apron and the floor or ground at least 27 in (685 mm) high, 30 in (760 mm) wide, and 17 in to 19 in (430 mm to 485 mm) deep (see Fig. 27(a) and (b)). Such units shall also have a minimum clear floor space 30 in by 48 in (760 mm by 1220 mm) to allow a person in a wheelchair to approach the unit facing forward.

(2) Free-standing or built-in units not having a clear space under them shall have a clear floor space at least 30 in by 48 in (760 mm by 1220 mm) that allows a person in a wheelchair to make a parallel approach to the unit (see Fig. 27(c) and (d)). This clear floor space shall comply with 4.2.4.

4.16 Water Closets.

4.16.1 General. Accessible water closets shall comply with 4.16.

4.16.2 Clear Floor Space. Clear floor space for water closets not in stalls shall comply with Fig. 28. Clear floor space may be arranged to allow either a left-handed or right-handed approach.

4.16.3* Height. The height of water closets shall be 17 in to 19 in (430 mm to 485 mm), measured to the top of the toilet seat (see Fig. 29(b)). *Seats shall not be sprung to return to a lifted position.*

4.16.4* Grab Bars. Grab bars for water closets not located in stalls shall comply with 4.26 and Fig. 29. *The grab bar behind the water closet shall be 36 in (915 mm) minimum.*

4.16.5* Flush Controls. Flush controls shall be hand operated *or automatic* and shall comply with 4.27.4. Controls for flush valves

40

shall be mounted on the wide side of toilet areas no more than 44 in (1120 mm) above the floor.

4.16.6 Dispensers. Toilet paper dispensers shall be installed within reach, as shown in Fig. 29(b). *Dispensers that control delivery, or that do not permit continuous paper flow, shall not be used.*

4.17 Toilet Stalls.

4.17.1 Location. Accessible toilet stalls shall be on an accessible route and shall meet the requirements of 4.17.

4.17.2 Water Closets. Water closets in accessible stalls shall comply with 4.16.

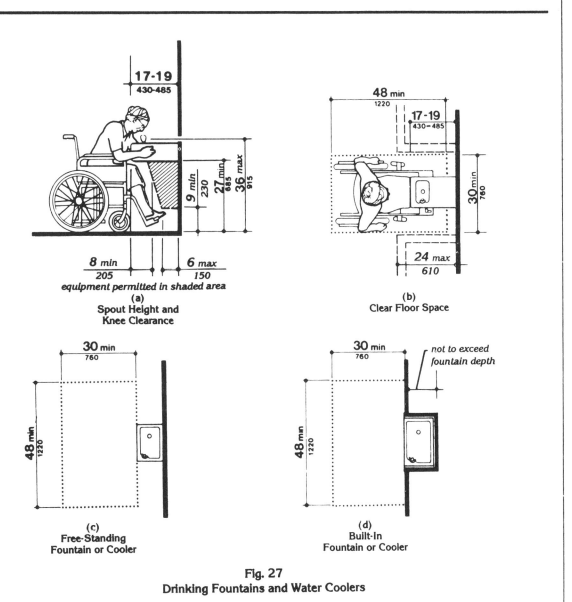

(a)
Spout Height and
Knee Clearance

(b)
Clear Floor Space

(c)
Free-Standing
Fountain or Cooler

(d)
Built-In
Fountain or Cooler

Fig. 27
Drinking Fountains and Water Coolers

41

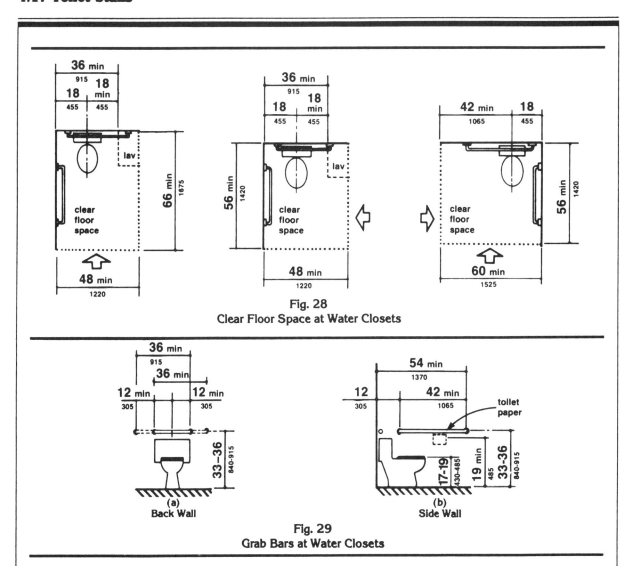

Fig. 28
Clear Floor Space at Water Closets

Fig. 29
Grab Bars at Water Closets

4.17.3* Size and Arrangement. The size and arrangement of the standard toilet stall shall comply with Fig. 30(a), *Standard Stall.* Standard toilet stalls with a minimum depth of 56 in (1420 mm) (see Fig. 30(a)) shall have wall-mounted water closets. If the depth of a standard toilet stall is increased at least 3 in (75 mm), then a floor-mounted water closet may be used. Arrangements shown for standard toilet stalls may be reversed to allow either a left- or right-hand approach. Additional stalls shall be provided in conformance with 4.22.4.

EXCEPTION: In instances of alteration work where provision of a standard stall (Fig. 30(a))

is technically infeasible or where plumbing code requirements prevent combining existing stalls to provide space, either alternate stall (Fig. 30(b)) may be provided in lieu of the standard stall.

4.17.4 Toe Clearances. In standard stalls, the front partition and at least one side partition shall provide a toe clearance of at least 9 in (230 mm) above the floor. If the depth of the stall is greater than 60 in (1525 mm), then the toe clearance is not required.

4.17.5* Doors. Toilet stall doors, *including door hardware,* shall comply with 4.13. *If toilet stall approach is from the latch side of the stall door, clearance between the door side of the*

42

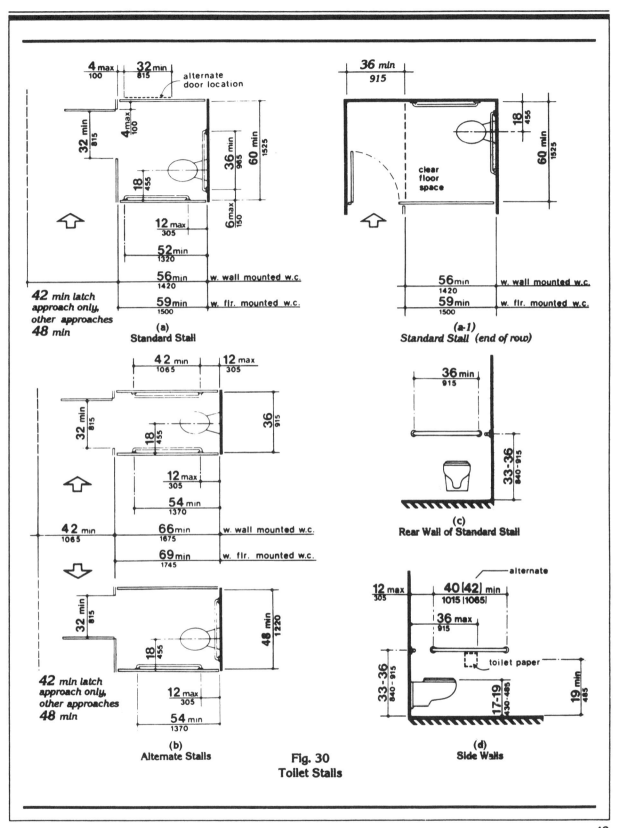

Fig. 30
Toilet Stalls

(a)
Standard Stall

42 min latch approach only, other approaches 48 min

(a-1)
Standard Stall (end of row)

(b)
Alternate Stalls

42 min latch approach only, other approaches 48 min

(c)
Rear Wall of Standard Stall

(d)
Side Walls

stall and any obstruction may be reduced to a minimum of 42 in (1065 mm) (Fig. 30).

4.17.6 Grab Bars. Grab bars complying with the length and positioning shown in Fig. 30(a), (b), (c), and (d) shall be provided. Grab bars may be mounted with any desired method as long as they have a gripping surface at the locations shown and do not obstruct the required clear floor area. Grab bars shall comply with 4.26.

4.18 Urinals.

4.18.1 General. Accessible urinals shall comply with 4.18.

4.18.2 Height. Urinals shall be stall-type or wall-hung with an elongated rim at a maximum of 17 in (430 mm) above the finish floor.

4.18.3 Clear Floor Space. A clear floor space 30 in by 48 in (760 mm by 1220 mm) shall be provided in front of urinals to allow forward approach. This clear space shall adjoin or overlap an accessible route and shall comply with 4.2.4. *Urinal shields that do not extend beyond the front edge of the urinal rim may be provided with 29 in (735 mm) clearance between them.*

4.18.4 Flush Controls. Flush controls shall be hand operated or automatic, and shall comply with 4.27.4, and shall be mounted no more than 44 in (1120 mm) above the finish floor.

4.19 Lavatories and Mirrors.

4.19.1 General. The requirements of 4.19 shall apply to lavatory fixtures, vanities, and built-in lavatories.

4.19.2 Height and Clearances. Lavatories shall be mounted with *the rim or counter surface no higher than 34 in (865 mm) above the finish floor.* Provide a clearance of at least 29 in (735 mm) above the finish floor to the bottom of the apron. Knee and toe clearance shall comply with Fig. 31.

4.19.3 Clear Floor Space. A clear floor space 30 in by 48 in (760 mm by 1220 mm) complying with 4.2.4 shall be provided in front of a lavatory to allow forward approach. Such

clear floor space shall adjoin or overlap an accessible route and shall extend a maximum of 19 in (485 mm) underneath the lavatory (see Fig. 32).

4.19.4 Exposed Pipes and Surfaces. Hot water and drain pipes under lavatories shall be insulated or otherwise *configured to protect against contact.* There shall be no sharp or abrasive surfaces under lavatories.

4.19.5 Faucets. Faucets shall comply with 4.27.4. Lever-operated, push-type, and electronically controlled mechanisms are examples of acceptable designs. *If self-closing valves are*

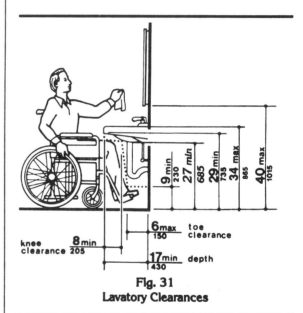

Fig. 31
Lavatory Clearances

Fig. 32
Clear Floor Space at Lavatories

44

used the faucet *shall remain* open for at least 10 seconds.

4.19.6* Mirrors. Mirrors shall be mounted with the bottom edge *of the reflecting surface* no higher than 40 in (1015 mm) *above the finish* floor (see Fig. 31).

4.20 Bathtubs.

4.20.1 General. Accessible bathtubs shall comply with 4.20.

4.20.2 Floor Space. Clear floor space in front of bathtubs shall be as shown in Fig. 33.

4.20.3 Seat. An in-tub seat or a seat at the head end of the tub shall be provided as shown in Fig. 33 and 34. The structural strength of seats and their attachments shall comply with 4.26.3. Seats shall be mounted securely and shall not slip during use.

4.20.4 Grab Bars. Grab bars complying with 4.26 shall be provided as shown in Fig. 33 and 34.

4.20.5 Controls. Faucets and other controls complying with 4.27.4 shall be located as shown in Fig. 34.

4.20.6 Shower Unit. A shower spray unit with a hose at least 60 in (1525 mm) long that can be used *both* as a fixed shower head *and* as a hand-held shower shall be provided.

4.20.7 Bathtub Enclosures. If provided, enclosures for bathtubs shall not obstruct controls or transfer from wheelchairs onto bathtub seats or into tubs. Enclosures on bathtubs shall not have tracks mounted on their rims.

4.21 Shower Stalls.

4.21.1* General. Accessible shower stalls shall comply with 4.21.

4.21.2 Size and Clearances. Except as specified in 9.1.2, shower stall size and clear floor space shall comply with Fig. 35(a) or (b). The shower stall in Fig. 35(a) shall be 36 in by 36 in (915 mm by 915 mm). Shower stalls required by 9.1.2 shall comply with Fig. 57(a)

or (b). The shower stall in Fig. 35(b) will fit into the space required for a bathtub.

4.21.3 Seat. A seat shall be provided in shower stalls 36 in by 36 in (915 mm by 915 mm) and shall be as shown in Fig. 36. The seat shall be mounted 17 in to 19 in (430 mm to 485 mm) from the bathroom floor and shall extend the full depth of the stall. In a 36 in by 36 in (915 mm by 915 mm) shower stall, the seat shall be on the wall opposite the controls. *Where a fixed seat is provided in a 30 in by 60 in minimum (760 mm by 1525 mm) shower stall, it shall be a folding type and shall be mounted on the wall adjacent to the controls as shown in Fig. 57.* The structural strength of seats and their attachments shall comply with 4.26.3.

4.21.4 Grab Bars. Grab bars complying with 4.26 shall be provided as shown in Fig. 37.

4.21.5 Controls. Faucets and other controls complying with 4.27.4 shall be located as shown in Fig. 37. In shower stalls 36 in by 36 in (915 mm by 915 mm), all controls, faucets, and the shower unit shall be mounted on the side wall opposite the seat.

4.21.6 Shower Unit. A shower spray unit with a hose at least 60 in (1525 mm) long that can be used *both* as a fixed shower head *and* as a hand-held shower shall be provided.

EXCEPTION: In unmonitored facilities where vandalism is a consideration, a fixed shower head mounted at 48 in (1220 mm) above the shower floor may be used in lieu of a hand-held shower head.

4.21.7 Curbs. If provided, curbs in shower stalls 36 in by 36 in (915 mm by 915 mm) shall be no higher than *1/2 in (13 mm)*. Shower stalls that are 30 in by 60 in (760 mm by 1525 mm) minimum shall not have curbs.

4.21.8 Shower Enclosures. If provided, enclosures for shower stalls shall not obstruct controls or obstruct transfer from wheelchairs onto shower seats.

4.22 Toilet Rooms.

4.22.1 Minimum Number. *Toilet facilities required to be accessible by 4.1 shall comply*

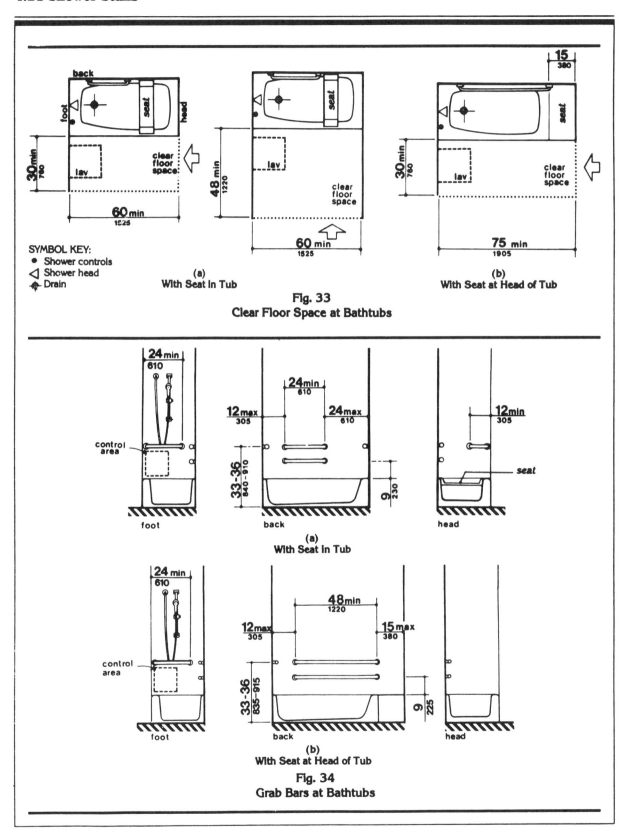

SYMBOL KEY:
- Shower controls
- Shower head
- Drain

(a)
With Seat in Tub

(b)
With Seat at Head of Tub

Fig. 33
Clear Floor Space at Bathtubs

(a)
With Seat in Tub

(b)
With Seat at Head of Tub

Fig. 34
Grab Bars at Bathtubs

46

with 4.22. Accessible toilet rooms shall be on an accessible route.

4.22.2 Doors. All doors to accessible toilet rooms shall comply with 4.13. Doors shall not swing into the clear floor space required for any fixture.

4.22.3* Clear Floor Space. The accessible fixtures and controls required in 4.22.4, 4.22.5, 4.22.6, and 4.22.7 shall be on an accessible route. An unobstructed turning space complying with 4.2.3 shall be provided within an accessible toilet room. The clear floor space at fixtures and controls, the accessible route, and the turning space may overlap.

4.22.4 Water Closets. If toilet stalls are provided, then at least one shall be a standard toilet stall complying with 4.17; *where 6 or more stalls are provided, in addition to the stall complying with 4.17.3, at least one stall 36 in (915 mm) wide with an outward swinging, self-closing door and parallel grab bars complying with Fig. 30(d) and 4.26 shall be provided. Water closets in such stalls shall comply with 4.16. If water closets are not in stalls, then at least one shall comply with 4.16.*

4.22.5 Urinals. If urinals are provided, *then* at least one shall comply with 4.18.

4.22.6 Lavatories and Mirrors. If lavatories and mirrors are provided, *then* at least one of each shall comply with 4.19.

4.22.7 Controls and Dispensers.
If controls, dispensers, receptacles, or other

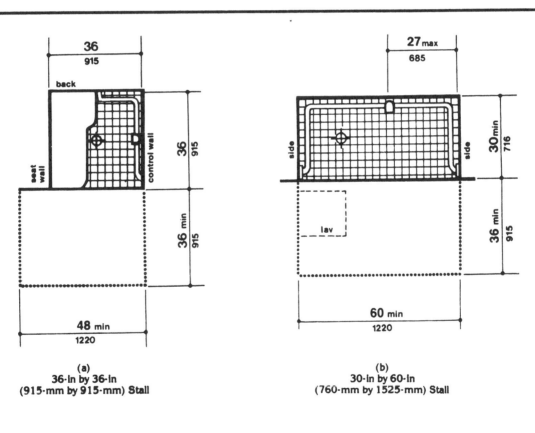

(a)
36-in by 36-in
(915-mm by 915-mm) Stall

(b)
30-in by 60-in
(760-mm by 1525-mm) Stall

Fig. 35
Shower Size and Clearances

47

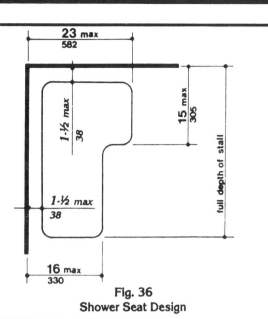

Fig. 36
Shower Seat Design

equipment are provided, *then* at least one of each shall be on an accessible route and shall comply with 4.27.

4.23 Bathrooms, Bathing Facilities, and Shower Rooms.

4.23.1 Minimum Number. Bathrooms, bathing facilities, or shower rooms *required to be accessible by 4.1* shall comply with 4.23 and shall be on an accessible route.

4.23.2 Doors. Doors to accessible bathrooms shall comply with 4.13. Doors shall not swing into the floor space required for any fixture.

4.23.3* Clear Floor Space. The accessible fixtures and controls required in 4.23.4, 4.23.5, 4.23.6, 4.23.7, 4.23.8, and 4.23.9 shall be on an accessible route. An unobstructed turning

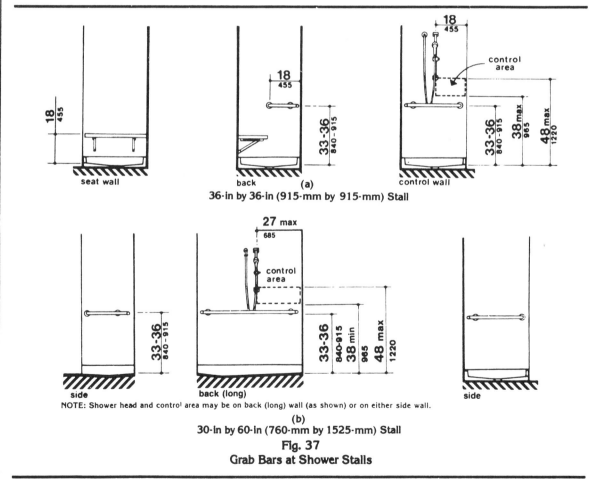

NOTE: Shower head and control area may be on back (long) wall (as shown) or on either side wall.

(b)
30-in by 60-in (760-mm by 1525-mm) Stall

Fig. 37
Grab Bars at Shower Stalls

48

space complying with 4.2.3 shall be provided within an accessible bathroom. The clear floor spaces at fixtures and controls, the accessible route, and the turning space may overlap.

4.23.4 Water Closets. If toilet stalls are provided, then at least one shall be a standard toilet stall complying with 4.17; *where 6 or more stalls are provided, in addition to the stall complying with 4.17.3, at least one stall 36 in (915 mm) wide with an outward swinging, self-closing door and parallel grab bars complying with Fig. 30(d) and 4.26 shall be provided.* Water closets in such stalls shall comply with 4.16. If water closets are not in stalls, then at least one shall comply with 4.16.

4.23.5 Urinals. If urinals are provided, then at least one shall comply with 4.18.

4.23.6 Lavatories and Mirrors. If lavatories and mirrors are provided, then at least one of each shall comply with 4.19.

4.23.7 Controls and Dispensers. If controls, dispensers, receptacles, or other equipment *are* provided, *then* at least one of each shall be on an accessible route and shall comply with 4.27.

4.23.8 Bathing and Shower Facilities. If tubs or showers are provided, then at least one accessible tub that complies with 4.20 or at least one accessible shower that complies with 4.21 shall be provided.

4.23.9* Medicine Cabinets. If medicine cabinets are provided, at least one shall be located with a usable shelf no higher than 44 in (1120 mm) above the floor space. The floor space shall comply with 4.2.4.

4.24 Sinks.

4.24.1 General. Sinks *required to be accessible by 4.1* shall comply with 4.24.

4.24.2 Height. Sinks shall be mounted with the counter or rim no higher than 34 in (865 mm) *above the finish* floor.

4.24.3 Knee Clearance. Knee clearance that is at least 27 in (685 mm) high, 30 in (760 mm) wide, and 19 in (485 mm) deep shall be pro-

vided underneath sinks.

4.24.4 Depth. Each sink shall be a maximum of 6-1/2 in (165 mm) deep.

4.24.5 Clear Floor Space. A clear floor space at least 30 in by 48 in (760 mm by 1220 mm) complying with 4.2.4 shall be provided in front of a sink to allow forward approach. The clear floor space shall be on an accessible route and shall extend a maximum of 19 in (485 mm) underneath the sink (see Fig. 32).

4.24.6 Exposed Pipes and Surfaces. Hot water and drain pipes exposed under sinks shall be insulated or otherwise *configured so as to protect against contact.* There shall be no sharp or abrasive surfaces under sinks.

4.24.7 Faucets. Faucets shall comply with 4.27.4. Lever-operated, push-type, touch-type, or electronically controlled mechanisms are acceptable designs.

4.25 Storage.

4.25.1 General. *Fixed* storage facilities such as cabinets, shelves, closets, and drawers *required to be accessible by 4.1* shall comply with 4.25.

4.25.2 Clear Floor Space. A clear floor space at least 30 in by 48 in (760 mm by 1220 mm) complying with 4.2.4 that allows either a forward or parallel approach by a person using a wheelchair shall be provided at accessible storage facilities.

4.25.3 Height. Accessible storage spaces shall be within at least one of the reach ranges specified in 4.2.5 and 4.2.6 *(see Fig. 5 and Fig. 6).* Clothes rods or shelves shall be a maximum of 54 in (1370 mm) *above the finish floor for a side approach. Where the distance from the wheelchair to the clothes rod or shelf exceeds 10 in (255 mm) (as in closets without accessible doors) the height and depth to the rod or shelf shall comply with Fig. 38(a) and Fig. 38(b).*

4.25.4 Hardware. Hardware for accessible storage facilities shall comply with 4.27.4. Touch latches and U-shaped pulls are acceptable.

49

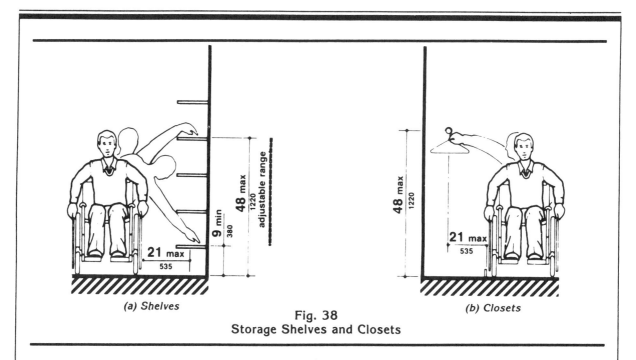

(a) Shelves

Fig. 38
Storage Shelves and Closets

(b) Closets

4.26 Handrails, Grab Bars, and Tub and Shower Seats.

4.26.1* General. All handrails, grab bars, and tub and shower seats *required to be accessible by 4.1, 4.8, 4.9, 4.16, 4.17, 4.20 or 4.21* shall comply with 4.26.

4.26.2* Size and Spacing of Grab Bars and Handrails. The diameter or width of the gripping surfaces of a handrail or grab bar shall be 1-1/4 in to 1-1/2 in (32 mm to 38 mm), or the shape shall provide an equivalent gripping surface. If handrails or grab bars are mounted adjacent to a wall, the space between the wall and the grab bar shall be 1-1/2 in (38 mm) (see Fig. 39(a), (b), (c), and *(e)*). Handrails may be located in a recess if the recess is a maximum of 3 in (75 mm) deep and extends at least 18 in (455 mm) above the top of the rail (see Fig. 39(d)).

4.26.3 Structural Strength. The structural strength of grab bars, tub and shower seats, fasteners, and mounting devices shall meet the following specification:

(1) Bending stress in a grab bar or seat induced by the maximum bending moment from the application of 250 lbf (1112N) shall be less than the allowable stress for the material of the grab bar or seat.

(2) Shear stress induced in a grab bar or seat by the application of 250 lbf (1112N) shall be less than the allowable shear stress for the material of the grab bar or seat. If the connection between the grab bar or seat and its mounting bracket or other support is considered to be fully restrained, then direct and torsional shear stresses shall be totaled for the combined shear stress, which shall not exceed the allowable shear stress.

(3) Shear force induced in a fastener or mounting device from the application of 250 lbf (1112N) shall be less than the allowable lateral load of either the fastener or mounting device or the supporting structure, whichever is the smaller allowable load.

(4) Tensile force induced in a fastener by a direct tension force of 250 lbf (1112N) plus the maximum moment from the application of 250 lbf (1112N) shall be less than the allowable withdrawal load between the fastener and the supporting structure.

(5) Grab bars shall not rotate within their fittings.

50

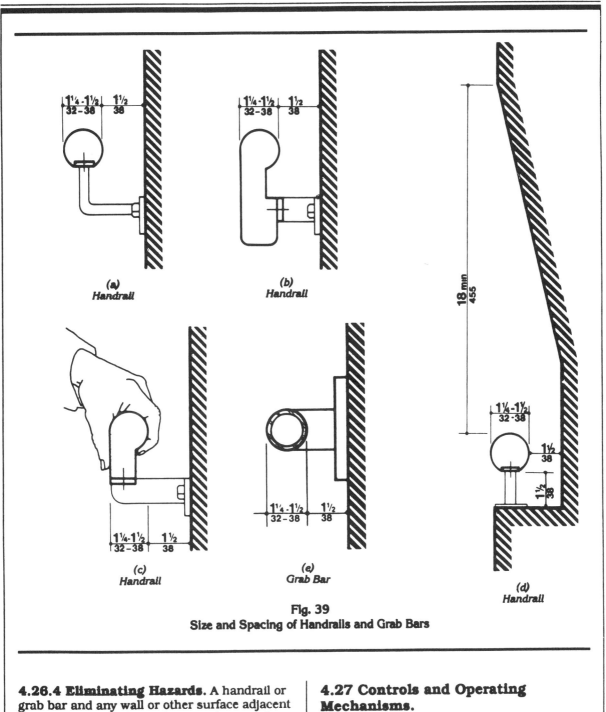

Fig. 39
Size and Spacing of Handrails and Grab Bars

4.26.4 Eliminating Hazards. A handrail or grab bar and any wall or other surface adjacent to it shall be free of any sharp or abrasive elements. Edges shall have a minimum radius of 1/8 in (3.2 mm).

4.27 Controls and Operating Mechanisms.

4.27.1 General. Controls and operating mechanisms *required to be accessible by 4.1* shall comply with 4.27.

51

4.27.2 Clear Floor Space. Clear floor space complying with 4.2.4 that allows a forward or a parallel approach by a person using a wheelchair shall be provided at controls, dispensers, receptacles, and other operable equipment.

4.27.3* Height. The highest operable part of controls, dispensers, receptacles, and other operable equipment shall be placed within at least one of the reach ranges specified in 4.2.5 and 4.2.6. Electrical and communications system receptacles on walls shall be mounted no less than 15 in (380 mm) above the floor.

EXCEPTION: These requirements do not apply where the use of special equipment dictates otherwise or where electrical and communications systems receptacles are not normally intended for use by building occupants.

4.27.4 Operation. Controls and operating mechanisms shall be operable with one hand and shall not require tight grasping, pinching, or twisting of the wrist. The force required to activate controls shall be no greater than 5 lbf (22.2 N).

4.28 Alarms.

4.28.1 General. *Alarm systems required to be accessible by 4.1 shall comply with 4.28. At a minimum, visual signal appliances shall be provided in buildings and facilities in each of the following areas: restrooms and any other general usage areas (e.g., meeting rooms), hallways, lobbies, and any other area for common use.*

4.28.2* Audible Alarms. If provided, audible emergency alarms shall produce a sound that exceeds the prevailing equivalent sound level in the room or space by at least 15 dbA or exceeds any maximum sound level with a duration of 60 seconds by 5 dbA, whichever is louder. Sound levels for alarm signals shall not exceed 120 dbA.

4.28.3* Visual Alarms. *Visual alarm signal appliances shall be integrated into the building or facility alarm system. If single station audible alarms are provided then single station visual alarm signals shall be provided. Visual alarm signals shall have the following minimum photometric and location features:*

(1) The lamp shall be a xenon strobe type or equivalent.

(2) The color shall be clear or nominal white (i.e., unfiltered or clear filtered white light).

(3) The maximum pulse duration shall be two-tenths of one second (0.2 sec) with a maximum duty cycle of 40 percent. The pulse duration is defined as the time interval between initial and final points of 10 percent of maximum signal.

(4) The intensity shall be a minimum of 75 candela.

(5) The flash rate shall be a minimum of 1 Hz and a maximum of 3 Hz.

(6) The appliance shall be placed 80 in (2030 mm) above the highest floor level within the space or 6 in (152 mm) below the ceiling, whichever is lower.

(7) In general, no place in any room or space required to have a visual signal appliance shall be more than 50 ft (15 m) from the signal (in the horizontal plane). In large rooms and spaces exceeding 100 ft (30 m) across, without obstructions 6 ft (2 m) above the finish floor, such as auditoriums, devices may be placed around the perimeter, spaced a maximum 100 ft (30 m) apart, in lieu of suspending appliances from the ceiling.

(8) No place in common corridors or hallways in which visual alarm signalling appliances are required shall be more than 50 ft (15 m) from the signal.

4.28.4* Auxiliary Alarms. *Units and sleeping accommodations shall have a visual alarm connected to the building emergency alarm system or shall have a standard 110-volt electrical receptacle into which such an alarm can be connected and a means by which a signal from the building emergency alarm system can trigger such an auxiliary alarm. When visual alarms are in place the signal shall be visible in all areas of the unit or room. Instructions for use of the auxiliary alarm or receptacle shall be provided.*

52

4.29 Detectable Warnings.

4.29.1 General. *Detectable* warnings *required by 4.1 and 4.7 shall comply with 4.29.*

4.29.2* Detectable Warnings on Walking Surfaces. *Detectable* warnings shall consist of raised truncated domes with a diameter of nominal 0.9 in (23 mm), a height of nominal 0.2 in (5 mm) and a center-to-center spacing of nominal 2.35 in (60 mm) and shall contrast visually with *adjoining surfaces, either light-on-dark, or dark-on-light.*

The material used to provide contrast shall be an integral part of the walking surface. Detectable warnings used on interior surfaces shall differ from adjoining walking surfaces in resiliency or sound-on-cane contact.

4.29.3 Detectable Warnings on Doors To Hazardous Areas. *(Reserved).*

4.29.4 Detectable Warnings at Stairs. *(Reserved).*

4.29.5 Detectable Warnings at Hazardous Vehicular Areas. If a walk crosses or adjoins a vehicular way, *and the walking surfaces are not separated by* curbs, railings, or other elements *between the pedestrian areas and vehicular areas*, the boundary between the areas shall be defined by a continuous *detectable* warning *which is* 36 in (915 mm) wide, complying with 4.29.2.

4.29.6 Detectable Warnings at Reflecting Pools. The edges of reflecting pools shall be protected by railings, walls, curbs, or *detectable* warnings complying with 4.29.2.

4.29.7 Standardization. *(Reserved).*

4.30 Signage.

4.30.1* General. Signage *required to be accessible by 4.1 shall comply with the applicable provisions of 4.30.*

4.30.2* Character Proportion. Letters and numbers on signs shall have a width-to-height ratio between 3:5 and 1:1 and a stroke-width-to-height ratio between 1:5 and 1:10.

4.30.3 Character Height. *Characters and numbers on signs shall be sized according to the viewing distance from which they are to be read. The minimum height is measured using an upper case X. Lower case characters are permitted.*

Height Above Finished Floor	*Minimum Character Height*
Suspended or Projected Overhead in compliance with 4.4.2	*3 in. (75 mm) minimum*

4.30.4* Raised and Brailled Characters and Pictorial Symbol Signs (Pictograms). Letters and numerals shall be raised 1/32 in, upper case, sans serif or simple serif type and shall be accompanied with Grade 2 Braille. Raised characters shall be at least 5/8 in (16 mm) high, but no higher than 2 in (50 mm). *Pictograms shall be accompanied by the equivalent verbal description placed directly below the pictogram. The border dimension of the pictogram shall be 6 in (152 mm) minimum in height.*

4.30.5* Finish and Contrast. *The characters and background of signs shall be eggshell, matte, or other non-glare finish.* Characters and symbols shall contrast with their background — either light characters on a dark background or dark characters on a light background.

4.30.6 Mounting Location and Height. *Where permanent identification is provided for rooms and spaces, signs shall be installed on the wall adjacent to the latch side of the door. Where there is no wall space to the latch side of the door, including at double leaf doors, signs shall be placed on the nearest adjacent wall. Mounting height shall be 60 in (1525 mm) above the finish floor to the centerline of the sign. Mounting location for such signage shall be so that a person may approach within 3 in (76 mm) of signage without encountering protruding objects or standing within the swing of a door.*

4.30.7* Symbols of Accessibility.

(1) Facilities and elements required to be identified as accessible by 4.1 shall use the international symbol of accessibility. The

53

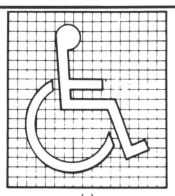

(a)
Proportions
International Symbol of Accessibility

(b)
Display Conditions
International Symbol of Accessibility

(c)
International TDD Symbol

(d)
International Symbol of Access for Hearing Loss

Fig. 43
International Symbols

symbol shall be displayed as shown in Fig. 43*(a)* and *(b)*.

(2) Volume Control Telephones. Telephones required to have a volume control by 4.1.3(17)(b) shall be identified by a sign containing a depiction of a telephone handset with radiating sound waves.

(3) Text Telephones. Text telephones required by 4.1.3 (17)(c) shall be identified by the international TDD symbol (Fig 43(c)). In addition, if a facility has a public text telephone, directional signage indicating the location of the nearest text telephone shall be placed adjacent to all banks of telephones which do not contain a text telephone. Such directional signage shall include the international TDD symbol. If a facility has no banks of telephones, the directional signage shall be provided at the entrance (e.g., in a building directory).

(4) Assistive Listening Systems. In assembly areas where permanently installed assistive listening systems are required by 4.1.3(19)(b) the availability of such systems shall be identified with signage that includes the international symbol of access for hearing loss (Fig 43(d)).

4.30.8* Illumination Levels. *(Reserved).*

4.31 Telephones.

4.31.1 General. Public telephones *required to be accessible by 4.1* shall comply with 4.31.

4.31.2 Clear Floor or Ground Space. A clear floor or ground space at least 30 in by 48 in (760 mm by 1220 mm) that allows either a forward or parallel approach by a person using a wheelchair shall be provided at telephones (see Fig. 44). The clear floor or ground space shall comply with 4.2.4. Bases, enclosures, and fixed seats shall not impede approaches to telephones by people who use wheelchairs.

4.31.3* Mounting Height. The highest operable part of the telephone shall be within the reach ranges specified in 4.2.5 or 4.2.6.

4.31.4 Protruding Objects. *Telephones shall comply with 4.4.*

54

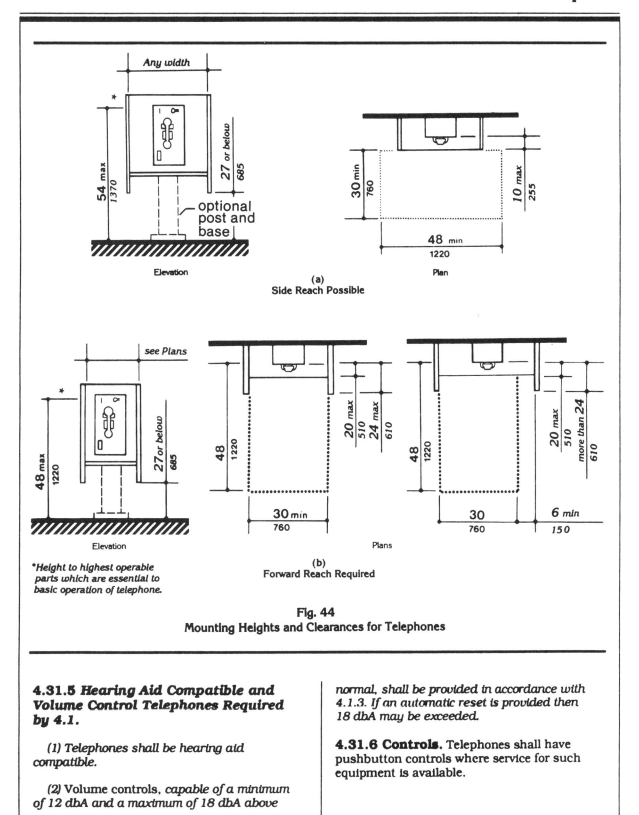

**Fig. 44
Mounting Heights and Clearances for Telephones**

4.31.5 Hearing Aid Compatible and Volume Control Telephones Required by 4.1.

(1) Telephones shall be hearing aid compatible.

(2) Volume controls, *capable of a minimum of 12 dbA and a maximum of 18 dbA above* normal, shall be provided in accordance with 4.1.3. If an automatic reset is provided then 18 dbA may be exceeded.

4.31.6 Controls. Telephones shall have pushbutton controls where service for such equipment is available.

55

4.31.7 Telephone Books. Telephone books, if provided, shall be located *in a position that complies with the reach ranges specified in 4.2.5 and 4.2.6.*

4.31.8 Cord Length. The cord from the telephone to the handset shall be at least 29 in (735 mm) long.

4.31.9* Text Telephones Required by 4.1.

(1) Text telephones used with a pay telephone shall be permanently affixed within, or adjacent to, the telephone enclosure. If an acoustic coupler is used, the telephone cord shall be sufficiently long to allow connection of the text telephone and the telephone receiver.

(2) Pay telephones designed to accommodate a portable text telephone shall be equipped with a shelf and an electrical outlet within or adjacent to the telephone enclosure. The telephone handset shall be capable of being placed flush on the surface of the shelf. The shelf shall be capable of accommodating a text telephone and shall have 6 in (152 mm) minimum vertical clearance in the area where the text telephone is to be placed.

(3) Equivalent facilitation may be provided. For example, a portable text telephone may be made available in a hotel at the registration desk if it is available on a 24-hour basis for use with nearby public pay telephones. In this instance, at least one pay telephone shall comply with paragraph 2 of this section. In addition, if an acoustic coupler is used, the telephone handset cord shall be sufficiently long so as to allow connection of the text telephone and the telephone receiver. Directional signage shall be provided and shall comply with 4.30.7.

4.32 Fixed or Built-in Seating and Tables.

4.32.1 Minimum Number. Fixed or built-in seating or tables *required to be accessible by 4.1* shall comply with 4.32.

4.32.2 Seating. If seating spaces for people in wheelchairs are provided at *fixed* tables or counters, clear floor space complying with 4.2.4 shall be provided. Such clear floor space

shall not overlap knee space by more than 19 in (485 mm) (see Fig. 45).

4.32.3 Knee Clearances. If seating for people in wheelchairs is provided at tables *or* counters, knee spaces at least 27 in (685 mm) high, 30 in (760 mm) wide, and 19 in (485 mm) deep shall be provided (see Fig. 45).

4.32.4* Height of Tables or Counters. The tops of *accessible* tables and *counters* shall be from 28 in to 34 in (710 mm to 865 mm) *above the finish* floor or ground.

4.33 Assembly Areas.

4.33.1 Minimum Number. Assembly *and associated* areas *required to be accessible by 4.1 shall comply with 4.33.*

4.33.2* Size of Wheelchair Locations. Each wheelchair location shall provide minimum clear ground or floor spaces as shown in Fig. 46.

4.33.3* Placement of Wheelchair Locations. Wheelchair areas shall be an integral part of any fixed seating plan and shall be *provided so as to provide people with physical disabilities a choice of admission prices and lines of sight comparable to those for members of the general public.* They shall adjoin an accessible route that also serves as a means of egress in case of emergency. *At least one companion fixed seat shall be provided next to each wheelchair seating area. When the seating capacity exceeds 300, wheelchair spaces shall be provided in more than one location. Readily removable seats may be installed in wheelchair spaces when the spaces are not required to accommodate wheelchair users.*

EXCEPTION: Accessible viewing positions may be clustered for bleachers, balconies, and other areas having sight lines that require slopes of greater than 5 percent. Equivalent accessible viewing positions may be located on levels having accessible egress.

4.33.4 Surfaces. The ground or floor at wheelchair locations shall be level and shall comply with 4.5.

56

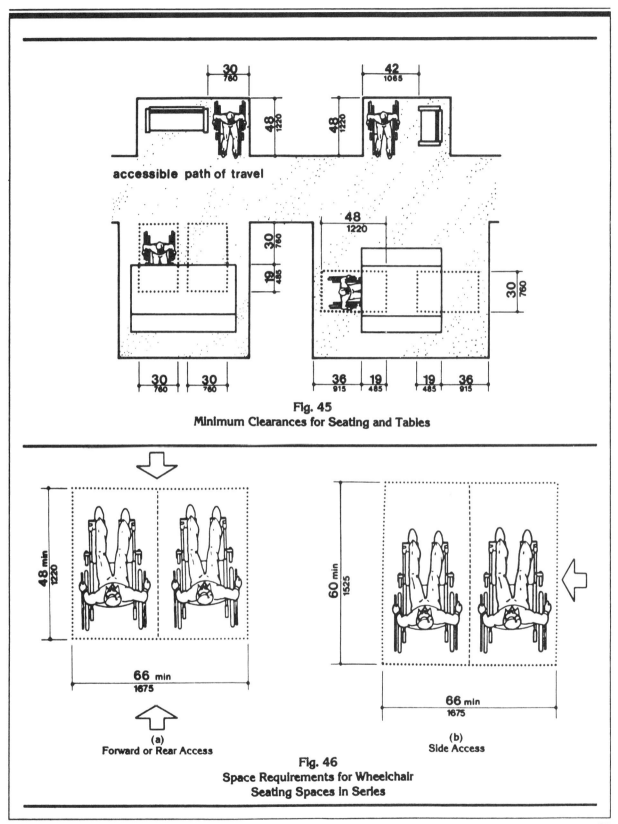

Fig. 45
Minimum Clearances for Seating and Tables

accessible path of travel

(a)
Forward or Rear Access

(b)
Side Access

Fig. 46
Space Requirements for Wheelchair
Seating Spaces in Series

57

4.33.5 Access to Performing Areas.
An accessible route shall connect wheelchair seating locations with performing areas, including stages, arena floors, dressing rooms, locker rooms, and other spaces used by performers.

4.33.6* Placement of Listening Systems.
If the listening system provided serves individual fixed seats, then such seats shall be located within a 50 ft (15 m) viewing distance of the stage or playing area and shall have a complete view of the stage or playing area.

4.33.7* Types of Listening Systems.
Assistive listening systems (ALS) are intended to augment standard public address and audio systems by providing signals which can be received directly by persons with special receivers or their own hearing aids and which eliminate or filter background noise. The type of assistive listening system appropriate for a particular application depends on the characteristics of the setting, the nature of the program, and the intended audience. Magnetic induction loops, infra-red and radio frequency systems are types of listening systems which are appropriate for various applications.

4.34 Automated Teller Machines.

4.34.1 General.
Each machine required to be accessible by 4.1.3 shall be on an accessible route and shall comply with 4.34.

4.34.2 Controls.
Controls for user activation shall comply with the requirements of 4.27.

4.34.3 Clearances and Reach Range.
Free standing or built-in units not having a clear space under them shall comply with 4.27.2 and 4.27.3 and provide for a parallel approach and both a forward and side reach to the unit allowing a person in a wheelchair to access the controls and dispensers.

4.34.4 Equipment for Persons with Vision Impairments.
Instructions and all information for use shall be made accessible to and independently usable by persons with vision impairments.

4.35 Dressing and Fitting Rooms.

4.35.1 General.
Dressing and fitting rooms required to be accessible by 4.1 shall comply with 4.35 and shall be on an accessible route.

4.35.2 Clear Floor Space.
A clear floor space allowing a person using a wheelchair to make a 180-degree turn shall be provided in every accessible dressing room entered through a swinging or sliding door. No door shall swing into any part of the turning space. Turning space shall not be required in a private dressing room entered through a curtained opening at least 32 in (815 mm) wide if clear floor space complying with section 4.2 renders the dressing room usable by a person using a wheelchair.

4.35.3 Doors.
All doors to accessible dressing rooms shall be in compliance with section 4.13.

4.35.4 Bench.
Every accessible dressing room shall have a 24 in by 48 in (610 mm by 1220 mm) bench fixed to the wall along the longer dimension. The bench shall be mounted 17 in to 19 in (430 mm to 485 mm) above the finish floor. Clear floor space shall be provided alongside the bench to allow a person using a wheelchair to make a parallel transfer onto the bench. The structural strength of the bench and attachments shall comply with 4.26.3. Where installed in conjunction with showers, swimming pools, or other wet locations, water shall not accumulate upon the surface of the bench and the bench shall have a slip-resistant surface.

4.35.5 Mirror.
Where mirrors are provided in dressing rooms of the same use, then in an accessible dressing room, a full-length mirror, measuring at least 18 in wide by 54 in high (460 mm by 1370 mm), shall be mounted in a position affording a view to a person on the bench as well as to a person in a standing position.

NOTE: Sections 4.1.1 through 4.1.7 and sections 5 through 10 are different from ANSI A117.1 in their entirety and are printed in standard type.

5. RESTAURANTS AND CAFETERIAS.

5.1* General.
Except as specified or modified in this section, restaurants and cafeterias shall comply with the requirements of 4.1 to 4.35. Where fixed tables (or dining counters where food is consumed but there is no service) are provided, at least 5 percent, but not less than one, of the fixed tables (or a portion of the dining counter) shall be accessible and shall comply with 4.32 as required in 4.1.3(18). In establishments where separate areas are designated for smoking and non-smoking patrons, the required number of accessible fixed tables (or counters) shall be proportionally distributed between the smoking and non-smoking areas. In new construction, and where practicable in alterations, accessible fixed tables (or counters) shall be distributed throughout the space or facility.

5.2 Counters and Bars.
Where food or drink is served at counters exceeding 34 in (865 mm) in height for consumption by customers seated on stools or standing at the counter, a portion of the main counter which is 60 in (1525 mm) in length minimum shall be provided in compliance with 4.32 or service shall be available at accessible tables within the same area.

5.3 Access Aisles.
All accessible fixed tables shall be accessible by means of an access aisle at least 36 in (915 mm) clear between parallel edges of tables or between a wall and the table edges.

5.4 Dining Areas.
In new construction, all dining areas, including raised or sunken dining areas, loggias, and outdoor seating areas, shall be accessible. In non-elevator buildings, an accessible means of vertical access to the mezzanine is not required under the following conditions: 1) the area of mezzanine seating measures no more than 33 percent of the area of the total accessible seating area; 2) the same services and decor are provided in an accessible space usable by the general public; and, 3) the accessible areas are not restricted to use by people with disabilities. In alterations, accessibility to raised or sunken dining areas, or to all parts of outdoor seating areas is not required provided that the same services and decor are provided in an accessible space usable by the general public and are not restricted to use by people with disabilities.

5.5 Food Service Lines.
Food service lines shall have a minimum clear width of 36 in (915 mm), with a preferred clear width of 42 in (1065 mm) to allow passage around a person using a wheelchair. Tray slides shall be mounted no higher than 34 in (865 mm) above the floor (see Fig. 53). If self-service shelves

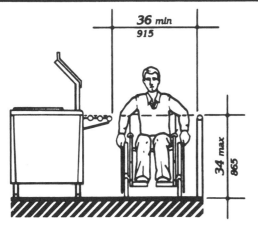

Fig. 53
Food Service Lines

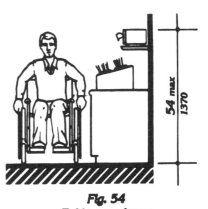

Fig. 54
Tableware Areas

59

are provided, at least 50 percent of each type must be within reach ranges specified in 4.2.5 and 4.2.6.

5.6 Tableware and Condiment Areas.
Self-service shelves and dispensing devices for tableware, dishware, condiments, food and beverages shall be installed to comply with 4.2 (see Fig. 54).

5.7 Raised Platforms.
In banquet rooms or spaces where a head table or speaker's lectern is located on a raised platform, the platform shall be accessible in compliance with 4.8 or 4.11. Open edges of a raised platform shall be protected by placement of tables or by a curb.

5.8 Vending Machines and Other Equipment.
Spaces for vending machines and other equipment shall comply with 4.2 and shall be located on an accessible route.

5.9 Quiet Areas.
(Reserved).

6. | MEDICAL CARE FACILITIES.

6.1 General. Medical care facilities included in this section are those in which people receive physical or medical treatment or care and where persons may need assistance in responding to an emergency and where the period of stay may exceed twenty-four hours. In addition to the requirements of 4.1 through 4.35, medical care facilities and buildings shall comply with 6.

(1) Hospitals - general purpose hospitals, psychiatric facilities, detoxification facilities — At least 10 percent of patient bedrooms and toilets, and all public use and common use areas are required to be designed and constructed to be accessible.

(2) Hospitals and rehabilitation facilities that specialize in treating conditions that affect mobility, or units within either that specialize in treating conditions that affect mobility — All patient bedrooms and toilets, and all public use and common use areas are required to be designed and constructed to be accessible.

(3) Long term care facilities, nursing homes — At least 50 percent of patient bedrooms and toilets, and all public use and common use areas are required to be designed and constructed to be accessible.

(4) Alterations to patient bedrooms.

(a) When patient bedrooms are being added or altered as part of a planned renovation of an entire wing, a department, or other discrete area of an existing medical facility, a percentage of the patient bedrooms that are being added or altered shall comply with 6.3. The percentage of accessible rooms provided shall be consistent with the percentage of rooms required to be accessible by the applicable requirements of 6.1(1), 6.1(2), or 6.1(3), until the number of accessible patient bedrooms in the facility equals the overall number that would be required if the facility were newly constructed. (For example, if 20 patient bedrooms are being altered in the obstetrics department of a hospital, 2 of the altered rooms must be made accessible. If, within the same hospital, 20 patient bedrooms are being altered in a unit that specializes in treating mobility impairments, all of the altered rooms must be made accessible.) Where toilet/bath rooms are part of patient bedrooms which are added or altered and required to be accessible, each such patient toilet/bathroom shall comply with 6.4.

(b) When patient bedrooms are being added or altered individually, and not as part of an alteration of the entire area, the altered patient bedrooms shall comply with 6.3, unless either: a) the number of accessible rooms provided in the department or area containing the altered patient bedroom equals the number of accessible patient bedrooms that would be required if the percentage requirements of 6.1(1), 6.1(2), or 6.1(3) were applied to that department or area; or b) the number of accessible patient bedrooms in the facility equals the overall number that would be required if the facility were newly constructed. Where toilet/bathrooms are part of patient bedrooms which are added or altered and required to be accessible, each such toilet/bathroom shall comply with 6.4.

60

6.2 Entrances. At least one accessible entrance that complies with 4.14 shall be protected from the weather by canopy or roof overhang. Such entrances shall incorporate a passenger loading zone that complies with 4.6.6.

6.3 Patient Bedrooms. Provide accessible patient bedrooms in compliance with 4.1 through 4.35. Accessible patient bedrooms shall comply with the following:

(1) Each bedroom shall have a door that complies with 4.13.

EXCEPTION: Entry doors to acute care hospital bedrooms for in-patients shall be exempted from the requirement in 4.13.6 for maneuvering space at the latch side of the door if the door is at least 44 in (1120 mm) wide.

(2) Each bedroom shall have adequate space to provide a maneuvering space that complies with 4.2.3. In rooms with 2 beds, it is preferable that this space be located between beds.

(3) Each bedroom shall have adequate space to provide a minimum clear floor space of 36 in (915 mm) along each side of the bed and to provide an accessible route complying with 4.3.3 to each side of each bed.

6.4 Patient Toilet Rooms. Where toilet/bath rooms are provided as a part of a patient bedroom, each patient bedroom that is required to be accessible shall have an accessible toilet/bath room that complies with 4.22 or 4.23 and shall be on an accessible route.

7. | BUSINESS AND MERCANTILE.

7.1 General. In addition to the requirements of 4.1 to 4.35, the design of all areas used for business transactions with the public shall comply with 7.

7.2 Sales and Service Counters, Teller Windows, Information Counters.

(1) In department stores and miscellaneous retail stores where counters have cash registers and are provided for sales or distribution of goods or services to the public, at least one of each type shall have a portion of the counter which is at least 36 in (915 mm) in length with a maximum height of 36 in (915 mm) above the finish floor. It shall be on an accessible route complying with 4.3. The accessible counters must be dispersed throughout the building or facility. In alterations where it is technically infeasible to provide an accessible counter, an auxiliary counter meeting these requirements may be provided.

(2) At ticketing counters, teller stations in a bank, registration counters in hotels and motels, box office ticket counters, and other counters that may not have a cash register but at which goods or services are sold or distributed, either:

(i) a portion of the main counter which is a minimum of 36 in (915 mm) in length shall be provided with a maximum height of 36 in (915 mm); or

(ii) an auxiliary counter with a maximum height of 36 in (915 mm) in close proximity to the main counter shall be provided; or

(iii) equivalent facilitation shall be provided (e.g., at a hotel registration counter, equivalent facilitation might consist of: (1) provision of a folding shelf attached to the main counter on which an individual with disabilities can write, and (2) use of the space on the side of the counter or at the concierge desk, for handing materials back and forth).

All accessible sales and service counters shall be on an accessible route complying with 4.3.

(3)* Assistive Listening Devices. (Reserved)

61

7.3* Check-out Aisles.

(1) In new construction, accessible check-out aisles shall be provided in conformance with the table below:

Total Check-out Aisles of Each Design	Minimum Number of Accessible Check-out Aisles (of each design)
1 – 4	1
5 – 8	2
8 – 15	3
over 15	3, plus 20% of additional aisles

EXCEPTION: In new construction, where the selling space is under 5000 square feet, only one check-out aisle is required to be accessible.

EXCEPTION: In alterations, at least one check-out aisle shall be accessible in facilities under 5000 square feet of selling space. In facilities of 5000 or more square feet of selling space, at least one of each design of check-out aisle shall be made accessible when altered until the number of accessible check-out aisles of each design equals the number required in new construction.

Examples of check-out aisles of different "design" include those which are specifically designed to serve different functions. Different "design" includes but is not limited to the following features - length of belt or no belt; or permanent signage designating the aisle as an express lane.

(2) Clear aisle width for accessible check-out aisles shall comply with 4.2.1 and maximum adjoining counter height shall not exceed 38 in (965 mm) above the finish floor. The top of the lip shall not exceed 40 in (1015 mm) above the finish floor.

(3) Signage identifying accessible check-out aisles shall comply with 4.30.7 and shall be mounted above the check-out aisle in the same location where the check-out number or type of check-out is displayed.

7.4 Security Bollards.

Any device used to prevent the removal of shopping carts from store premises shall not prevent access or egress to people in wheelchairs. An alternate entry that is equally convenient to that provided for the ambulatory population is acceptable.

8. | LIBRARIES.

8.1 General. In addition to the requirements of 4.1 to 4.35, the design of all public areas of a library shall comply with 8, including reading and study areas, stacks, reference rooms, reserve areas, and special facilities or collections.

8.2 Reading and Study Areas. At least 5 percent or a minimum of one of each element of fixed seating, tables, or study carrels shall comply with 4.2 and 4.32. Clearances between fixed accessible tables and between study carrels shall comply with 4.3.

8.3 Check-Out Areas. At least one lane at each check-out area shall comply with 7.2(1). Any traffic control or book security gates or turnstiles shall comply with 4.13.

8.4 Card Catalogs and Magazine Displays. Minimum clear aisle space at card catalogs and magazine displays shall comply with Fig. 55. Maximum reach height shall comply with 4.2, with a height of 48 in (1220 mm) preferred irrespective of approach allowed.

8.5 Stacks. Minimum clear aisle width between stacks shall comply with 4.3, with a minimum clear aisle width of 42 in (1065 mm) preferred where possible. Shelf height in stack areas is unrestricted (see Fig. 56).

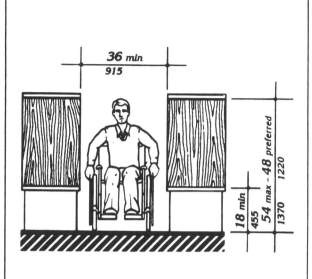

Fig. 55
Card Catalog

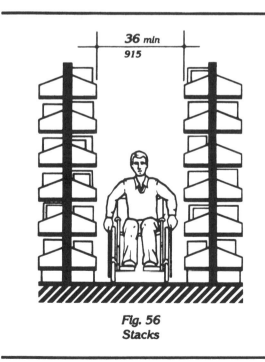

Fig. 56
Stacks

9. ACCESSIBLE TRANSIENT LODGING.

(1) Except as specified in the special technical provisions of this section, accessible transient lodging shall comply with the applicable requirements of 4.1 through 4.35. Transient lodging includes facilities or portions thereof used for sleeping accommodations, when not classed as a medical care facility.

9.1 Hotels, Motels, Inns, Boarding Houses, Dormitories, Resorts and Other Similar Places of Transient Lodging.

9.1.1 General. All public use and common use areas are required to be designed and constructed to comply with section 4 (Accessible Elements and Spaces: Scope and Technical Requirements).

EXCEPTION: Sections 9.1 through 9.4 do not apply to an establishment located within a building that contains not more than five rooms for rent or hire and that is actually occupied by the proprietor of such establishment as the residence of such proprietor.

9.1.2 Accessible Units, Sleeping Rooms, and Suites. Accessible sleeping rooms or suites that comply with the requirements of 9.2 (Requirements for Accessible Units, Sleeping Rooms, and Suites) shall be provided in conformance with the table below. In addition, in hotels, of 50 or more sleeping rooms or suites, additional accessible sleeping rooms or suites that include a roll-in shower shall also be provided in conformance with the table below. Such accommodations shall comply with the requirements of 9.2, 4.21, and Figure 57(a) or (b).

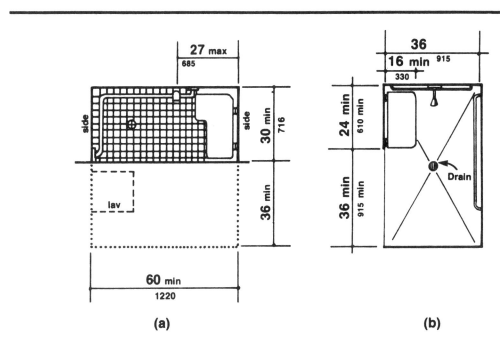

Fig. 57
Roll-in Shower with Folding Seat

Number of Rooms	Accessible Rooms	Rooms with Roll-in Showers
1 to 25	1	
26 to 50	2	
51 to 75	3	1
76 to 100	4	1
101 to 150	5	2
151 to 200	6	2
201 to 300	7	3
301 to 400	8	4
401 to 500	9	4 plus one for each additional 100 over 400
501 to 1000	2% of total	
1001 and over	20 plus 1 for each 100 over 1000	

9.1.3 Sleeping Accommodations for Persons with Hearing Impairments.
In addition to those accessible sleeping rooms and suites required by 9.1.2, sleeping rooms and suites that comply with 9.3 (Visual Alarms, Notification Devices, and Telephones) shall be provided in conformance with the following table:

Number of Elements	Accessible Elements
1 to 25	1
26 to 50	2
51 to 75	3
76 to 100	4
101 to 150	5
151 to 200	6
201 to 300	7
301 to 400	8
401 to 500	9
501 to 1000	2% of total
1001 and over	20 plus 1 for each 100 over 1000

64

9.1.4 Classes of Sleeping Accommodations.

(1) In order to provide persons with disabilities a range of options equivalent to those available to other persons served by the facility, sleeping rooms and suites required to be accessible by 9.1.2 shall be dispersed among the various classes of sleeping accommodations available to patrons of the place of transient lodging. Factors to be considered include room size, cost, amenities provided, and the number of beds provided.

(2) Equivalent Facilitation. For purposes of this section, it shall be deemed equivalent facilitation if the operator of a facility elects to limit construction of accessible rooms to those intended for multiple occupancy, provided that such rooms are made available at the cost of a single-occupancy room to an individual with disabilities who requests a single-occupancy room.

9.1.5. Alterations to Accessible Units, Sleeping Rooms, and Suites.
When sleeping rooms are being altered in an existing facility, or portion thereof, subject to the requirements of this section, at least one sleeping room or suite that complies with the requirements of 9.2 (Requirements for Accessible Units, Sleeping Rooms, and Suites) shall be provided for each 25 sleeping rooms, or fraction thereof, of rooms being altered until the number of such rooms provided equals the number required to be accessible with 9.1.2. In addition, at least one sleeping room or suite that complies with the requirements of 9.3 (Visual Alarms, Notification Devices, and Telephones) shall be provided for each 25 sleeping rooms, or fraction thereof, of rooms being altered until the number of such rooms equals the number required to be accessible by 9.1.3.

9.2 Requirements for Accessible Units, Sleeping Rooms and Suites.

9.2.1 General.
Units, sleeping rooms, and suites required to be accessible by 9.1 shall comply with 9.2.

9.2.2 Minimum Requirements.
An accessible unit, sleeping room or suite shall be on an accessible route complying with 4.3 and have the following accessible elements and spaces.

(1) Accessible sleeping rooms shall have a 36 in (915 mm) clear width maneuvering space located along both sides of a bed, except that where two beds are provided, this requirement can be met by providing a 36 in (915 mm) wide maneuvering space located between the two beds.

(2) An accessible route complying with 4.3 shall connect all accessible spaces and elements, including telephones, within the unit, sleeping room, or suite. This is not intended to require an elevator in multi-story units as long as the spaces identified in 9.2.2(6) and (7) are on accessible levels and the accessible sleeping area is suitable for dual occupancy.

(3) Doors and doorways designed to allow passage into and within all sleeping rooms, suites or other covered units shall comply with 4.13.

(4) If fixed or built-in storage facilities such as cabinets, shelves, closets, and drawers are provided in accessible spaces, at least one of each type provided shall contain storage space complying with 4.25. Additional storage may be provided outside of the dimensions required by 4.25.

(5) All controls in accessible units, sleeping rooms, and suites shall comply with 4.27.

(6) Where provided as part of an accessible unit, sleeping room, or suite, the following spaces shall be accessible and shall be on an accessible route:

    (a) the living area.

    (b) the dining area.

    (c) at least one sleeping area.

    (d) patios, terraces, or balconies.

EXCEPTION: The requirements of 4.13.8 and 4.3.8 do not apply where it is necessary to utilize a higher door threshold or a change in level to protect the integrity of the unit from wind/water damage. Where this exception results in patios, terraces or balconies that are not at an accessible level, equivalent facilitation shall be provided. (E.g., equivalent facilitation at a hotel patio or balcony might consist of providing raised decking or a ramp to provide accessibility.)

(e) at least one full bathroom (i.e., one with a water closet, a lavatory, and a bathtub or shower).

(f) if only half baths are provided, at least one half bath.

(g) carports, garages or parking spaces.

(7) Kitchens, Kitchenettes, or Wet Bars. When provided as accessory to a sleeping room or suite, kitchens, kitchenettes, wet bars, or similar amenities shall be accessible. Clear floor space for a front or parallel approach to cabinets, counters, sinks, and appliances shall be provided to comply with 4.2.4. Countertops and sinks shall be mounted at a maximum height of 34 in (865 mm) above the floor. At least fifty percent of shelf space in cabinets or refrigerator/freezers shall be within the reach ranges of 4.2.5 or 4.2.6 and space shall be designed to allow for the operation of cabinet and/or appliance doors so that all cabinets and appliances are accessible and usable. Controls and operating mechanisms shall comply with 4.27.

(8) Sleeping room accommodations for persons with hearing impairments required by 9.1 and complying with 9.3 shall be provided in the accessible sleeping room or suite.

9.3 Visual Alarms, Notification Devices and Telephones.

9.3.1 General. In sleeping rooms required to comply with this section, auxiliary visual alarms shall be provided and shall comply with 4.28.4. Visual notification devices shall also be provided in units, sleeping rooms and suites to alert room occupants of incoming telephone calls and a door knock or bell. Notification devices shall **not** be connected to auxiliary visual alarm signal appliances. Permanently installed telephones shall have volume controls complying with 4.31.5; an accessible electrical outlet within 4 ft (1220 mm) of a telephone connection shall be provided to facilitate the use of a text telephone.

9.3.2 Equivalent Facilitation. For purposes of this section, equivalent facilitation shall include the installation of electrical outlets (including outlets connected to a facility's central alarm system) and telephone wiring in sleeping rooms and suites to enable persons with hearing impairments to utilize portable visual alarms and communication devices provided by the operator of the facility.

9.4 Other Sleeping Rooms and Suites.
Doors and doorways designed to allow passage into and within all sleeping units or other covered units shall comply with 4.13.5.

9.5 Transient Lodging in Homeless Shelters, Halfway Houses, Transient Group Homes, and Other Social Service Establishments.

9.5.1 New Construction. In new construction all public use and common use areas are required to be designed and constructed to comply with section 4. At least one of each type of amenity (such as washers, dryers and similar equipment installed for the use of occupants) in each common area shall be accessible and shall be located on an accessible route to any accessible unit or sleeping accommodation.

EXCEPTION: Where elevators are not provided as allowed in 4.1.3(5), accessible amenities are not required on inaccessible floors as long as one of each type is provided in common areas on accessible floors.

9.5.2 Alterations.

(1) Social service establishments which are not homeless shelters:

(a) The provisions of 9.5.3 and 9.1.5 shall apply to sleeping rooms and beds.

(b) Alteration of other areas shall be consistent with the new construction provisions of 9.5.1.

(2) Homeless shelters. If the following elements are altered, the following requirements apply:

66

(a) at least one public entrance shall allow a person with mobility impairments to approach, enter and exit including a minimum clear door width of 32 in (815 mm).

(b) sleeping space for homeless persons as provided in the scoping provisions of 9.1.2 shall include doors to the sleeping area with a minimum clear width of 32 in (815 mm) and maneuvering space around the beds for persons with mobility impairments complying with 9.2.2(1).

(c) at least one toilet room for each gender or one unisex toilet room shall have a minimum clear door width of 32 in (815 mm), minimum turning space complying with 4.2.3, one water closet complying with 4.16, one lavatory complying with 4.19 and the door shall have a privacy latch; and, if provided, at least one tub or shower shall comply with 4.20 or 4.21, respectively.

(d) at least one common area which a person with mobility impairments can approach, enter and exit including a minimum clear door width of 32 in (815 mm).

(e) at least one route connecting elements (a), (b), (c) and (d) which a person with mobility impairments can use including minimum clear width of 36 in (915 mm), passing space complying with 4.3.4, turning space complying with 4.2.3 and changes in levels complying with 4.3.8.

(f) homeless shelters can comply with the provisions of (a)-(e) by providing the above elements on one accessible floor.

9.5.3. Accessible Sleeping Accommodations in New Construction.
Accessible sleeping rooms shall be provided in conformance with the table in 9.1.2 and shall comply with 9.2 Accessible Units, Sleeping Rooms and Suites (where the items are provided). Additional sleeping rooms that comply with 9.3 Sleeping Accommodations for Persons with Hearing Impairments shall be provided in conformance with the table provided in 9.1.3.

In facilities with multi-bed rooms or spaces, a percentage of the beds equal to the table provided in 9.1.2 shall comply with 9.2.2(1).

10. TRANSPORTATION FACILITIES. (Reserved).

67

APPENDIX

This appendix contains *materials of an advisory nature* and provides additional information that should help the reader to understand the minimum requirements of the *guidelines* or to design buildings or facilities for greater accessibility. The paragraph numbers correspond to the sections or paragraphs of the *guideline* to which the material relates and are therefore not consecutive (for example, A4.2.1 contains additional information relevant to 4.2.1). Sections *of the guidelines* for which additional material appears in this appendix have been indicated by an asterisk. *Nothing in this appendix shall in any way obviate any obligation to comply with the requirements of the guidelines itself.*

A2.2 Equivalent Facilitation. *Specific examples of equivalent facilitation are found in the following sections:*

4.1.6(3)(c)	*Elevators in Alterations*
4.31.9	*Text Telephones*
7.2	*Sales and Service Counters, Teller Windows, Information Counters*
9.1.4	*Classes of Sleeping Accommodations*
9.2.2(6)(d)	*Requirements for Accessible Units, Sleeping Rooms, and Suites*

A4.1.1 Application.

A4.1.1(3) Areas Used Only by Employees as Work Areas. *Where there are a series of individual work stations of the same type (e.g., laboratories, service counters, ticket booths), 5%, but not less than one, of each type of work station should be constructed so that an individual with disabilities can maneuver within the work stations. Rooms housing individual offices in a typical office building must meet the requirements of the guidelines concerning doors, accessible routes, etc. but do not need to allow for maneuvering space around individual desks. Modifications required to permit maneuvering within the work area may be accomplished as a reasonable accommodation to individual employees with disabilities under Title I of the ADA. Consideration should also be given to placing shelves in employee work areas at a* convenient height for accessibility or installing commercially available shelving that is adjustable so that reasonable accommodations can be made in the future.

If work stations are made accessible they should comply with the applicable provisions of 4.2 through 4.35.

A4.1.2 Accessible Sites and Exterior Facilities: New Construction.

A4.1.2(5)(e) Valet Parking. *Valet parking is not always usable by individuals with disabilities. For instance, an individual may use a type of vehicle controls that render the regular controls inoperable or the driver's seat in a van may be removed. In these situations, another person cannot park the vehicle. It is recommended that some self-parking spaces be provided at valet parking facilities for individuals whose vehicles cannot be parked by another person and that such spaces be located on an accessible route to the entrance of the facility.*

A4.1.3 Accessible Buildings: New Construction.

A4.1.3(5) *Only full passenger elevators are covered by the accessibility provisions of 4.10. Materials and equipment hoists, freight elevators not intended for passenger use, dumbwaiters, and construction elevators are not covered by these guidelines. If a building is exempt from the elevator requirement, it is not necessary to provide a platform lift or other means of vertical access in lieu of an elevator.*

Under Exception 4, platform lifts are allowed where existing conditions make it impractical to install a ramp or elevator. Such conditions generally occur where it is essential to provide access to small raised or lowered areas where space may not be available for a ramp. Examples include, but are not limited to, raised pharmacy platforms, commercial offices raised above a sales floor, or radio and news booths.

A4.1.3(9) *Supervised automatic sprinkler systems have built in signals for monitoring features of the system such as the opening and closing of water control valves, the power supplies for needed pumps, water tank levels, and for indicating conditions that will impair the satisfactory operation of the sprinkler system.*

A1

Because of these monitoring features, supervised automatic sprinkler systems have a high level of satisfactory performance and response to fire conditions.

A4.1.3(10) *If an odd number of drinking fountains is provided on a floor, the requirement in 4.1.3(10)(b) may be met by rounding down the odd number to an even number and calculating 50% of the even number. When more than one drinking fountain on a floor is required to comply with 4.15, those fountains should be dispersed to allow wheelchair users convenient. access. For example, in a large facility such as a convention center that has water fountains at several locations on a floor, the accessible water fountains should be located so that wheelchair users do not have to travel a greater distance than other people to use a drinking fountain.*

A4.1.3(17)(b) *In addition to the requirements of section 4.1.3(17)(b), the installation of additional volume controls is encouraged. Volume controls may be installed on any telephone.*

A4.1.3(19)(a) *Readily removable or folding seating units may be installed in lieu of providing an open space for wheelchair users. Folding seating units are usually two fixed seats that can be easily folded into a fixed center bar to allow for one or two open spaces for wheelchair users when necessary. These units are more easily adapted than removable seats which generally require the seat to be removed in advance by the facility management.*

Either a sign or a marker placed on seating with removable or folding arm rests is required by this section. Consideration should be given for ensuring identification of such seats in a darkened theater. For example, a marker which contrasts (light on dark or dark on light) and which also reflects light could be placed on the side of such seating so as to be visible in a lighted auditorium and also to reflect light from a flashlight.

A4.1.6 Accessible Buildings: Alterations.

A4.1.6(1)(h) *When an entrance is being altered, it is preferable that those entrances being altered be made accessible to the extent feasible.*

A4.2 Space Allowances and Reach Ranges.

A4.2.1 Wheelchair Passage Width.

(1) Space Requirements for Wheelchairs. Many persons who use wheelchairs need a 30 in (760 mm) clear opening width for doorways, gates, and the like, when the latter are entered head-on. If the *person* is unfamiliar with a building, if competing traffic is heavy, if sudden or frequent movements are needed, or if the wheelchair must be turned at an opening, then greater clear widths are needed. For most situations, the addition of an inch of leeway on either side is sufficient. Thus, a minimum clear width of 32 in (815 mm) will provide adequate clearance. However, when an opening or a restriction in a passageway is more than 24 in (610 mm) long, it is essentially a passageway and must be at least 36 in (915 mm) wide.

(2) Space Requirements for Use of Walking Aids. Although people who use walking aids can maneuver through clear width openings of 32 in (815 mm), they need 36 in (915 mm) wide passageways and walks for comfortable gaits. Crutch tips, often extending down at a wide angle, are a hazard in narrow passageways where they might not be seen by other pedestrians. Thus, the 36 in (915 mm) width provides a safety allowance both for the person *with a disability* and for others.

(3) Space Requirements for Passing. Ablebodied *persons* in winter clothing, walking

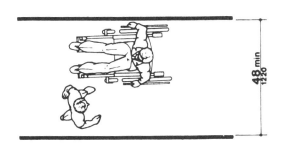

Fig. A1
Minimum Passage Width for One Wheelchair and One Ambulatory Person

A2

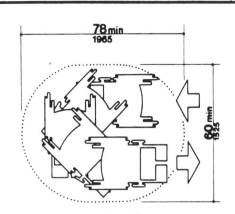

Fig. A2
Space Needed for Smooth U-Turn in a Wheelchair

straight ahead with arms swinging, need 32 in (815 mm) of width, which includes 2 in (50 mm) on either side for sway, and another 1 in (25 mm) tolerance on either side for clearing nearby objects or other pedestrians. Almost all wheelchair users and those who use walking aids can also manage within this 32 in (815 mm) width for short distances. Thus, two streams of traffic can pass in 64 in (1625 mm) in a comfortable flow. Sixty inches (1525 mm) provides a minimum width for a somewhat more restricted flow. If the clear width is less than 60 in (1525 mm), two wheelchair users will not be able to pass but will have to seek a wider place for passing. Forty-eight inches (1220 mm) is the minimum width needed for an ambulatory person to pass a nonambulatory or semi-ambulatory person. Within this 48 in (1220 mm) width, the ambulatory person will have to twist to pass a wheelchair user, a person with a *service animal*, or a

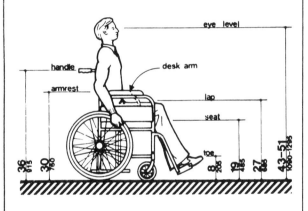

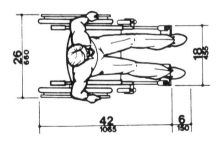

NOTE: Footrests may extend further for tall people

Fig. A3
Dimensions of Adult-Sized Wheelchairs

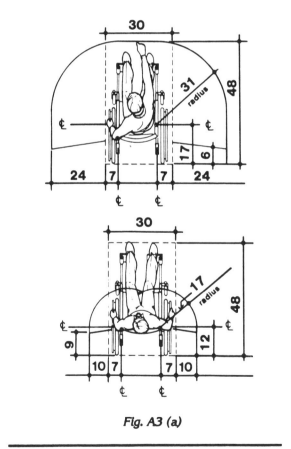

Fig. A3 (a)

A3

semi-ambulatory person. There will be little leeway for swaying or missteps (see Fig. A1).

A4.2.3 Wheelchair Turning Space.
These guidelines specify a minimum space of 60 in (1525 mm) diameter *or a 60 in by 60 in (1525 mm by 1525 mm) T-shaped space* for a pivoting 180-degree turn of a wheelchair. This space is usually satisfactory for turning around, but many people will not be able to turn without repeated tries and bumping into surrounding objects. The space shown in Fig. A2 will allow most wheelchair users to complete U-turns without difficulty.

A4.2.4 Clear Floor or Ground Space for Wheelchairs.
The wheelchair and user shown in Fig. A3 represent typical dimensions for a large adult male. The space requirements in this *guideline* are based upon maneuvering clearances that will accommodate most wheelchairs. Fig. A3 provides a uniform reference for design not covered by this *guideline*.

A4.2.5 & A4.2.6 Reach.
Reach ranges for persons seated in wheelchairs may be further clarified by Fig. A3(a). These drawings approximate in the plan view the information shown in Fig. 4, 5, and 6.

A4.3 Accessible Route.

A4.3.1 General.

(1) Travel Distances. Many people with mobility impairments can move at only very slow speeds; for many, traveling 200 ft (61 m) could take about 2 minutes. This assumes a rate of about 1.5 ft/s (455 mm/s) on level ground. It also assumes that the traveler would move continuously. However, on trips over 100 ft (30 m), disabled people are apt to rest frequently, which substantially increases their trip times. Resting periods of 2 minutes for every 100 ft (30 m) can be used to estimate travel times for people with severely limited stamina. In inclement weather, slow progress and resting can greatly increase a disabled person's exposure to the elements.

(2) Sites. Level, indirect routes or those with running slopes lower than 1:20 can sometimes provide more convenience than direct routes with maximum allowable slopes or with ramps.

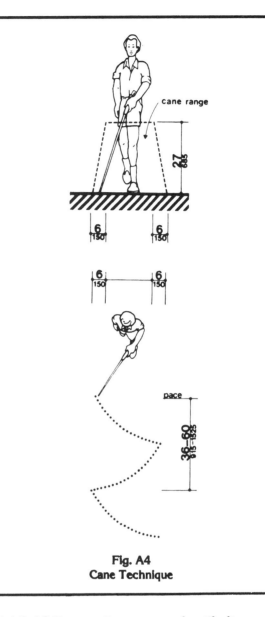

cane range

**Fig. A4
Cane Technique**

A4.3.10 Egress.
Because people with disabilities may visit, be employed or be a resident in any building, emergency management plans with specific provisions to ensure their safe evacuation also play an essential role in fire safety and life safety.

A4.3.11.3 Stairway Width.
A 48 inch (1220 mm) wide exit stairway is needed to allow assisted evacuation (e.g., carrying a person in a wheelchair) without encroaching on the exit path for ambulatory persons.

A4

A4.3.11.4 Two-way Communication. *It is essential that emergency communication not be dependent on voice communications alone because the safety of people with hearing or speech impairments could be jeopardized. The visible signal requirement could be satisfied with something as simple as a button in the area of rescue assistance that lights, indicating that help is on the way, when the message is answered at the point of entry.*

A4.4 Protruding Objects.

A4.4.1 General. *Service animals* are trained to recognize and avoid hazards. However, most people with severe impairments of vision use the long cane as an aid to mobility. The two principal cane techniques are the touch technique, where the cane arcs from side to side and touches points outside both shoulders; and the diagonal technique, where the cane is held in a stationary position diagonally across the body with the cane tip touching or just above the ground at a point outside one shoulder and the handle or grip extending to a point outside the other shoulder. The touch technique is used primarily in uncontrolled areas, while the diagonal technique is used primarily in certain limited, controlled, and familiar environments. Cane users are often trained to use both techniques.

Potential hazardous objects are noticed only if they fall within the detection range of canes (see Fig. A4). Visually impaired people walking toward an object can detect an overhang if its lowest surface is not higher than 27 in (685 mm). When walking alongside *protruding* objects, they cannot detect overhangs. Since proper cane and *service animal* techniques keep people away from the edge of a path or from walls, a slight overhang of no more than 4 in (100 mm) is not hazardous.

A4.5 Ground and Floor Surfaces.

A4.5.1 General. *People who have difficulty walking or* maintaining balance *or who use* crutches, canes, *or walkers,* and those with restricted gaits are particularly sensitive to slipping and tripping hazards. For such people, a stable and regular surface is necessary for safe walking, particularly on stairs. Wheelchairs can be propelled most easily on surfaces that are hard, stable, and regular. Soft loose surfaces such as shag carpet, loose sand or gravel, wet clay, and irregular surfaces such as cobblestones can significantly impede wheelchair movement.

Slip resistance is based on the frictional force necessary to keep a shoe heel or crutch tip from slipping on a walking surface under conditions likely to be found on the surface. *While the* <u>*dynamic*</u> *coefficient of friction during walking varies in a complex and non-uniform way, the* <u>*static*</u> *coefficient of friction, which can be measured in several ways, provides a close approximation of the slip resistance of a surface. Contrary to popular belief, some slippage is* <u>*necessary*</u> *to walking, especially for persons with restricted gaits; a truly "non-slip" surface could not be negotiated.*

The Occupational Safety and Health Administration recommends that walking surfaces have a static coefficient of friction of 0.5. A research project sponsored by the Architectural and Transportation Barriers Compliance Board (Access Board) conducted tests with persons with disabilities and concluded that a higher coefficient of friction was needed by such persons. A static coefficient of friction of 0.6 is recommended for accessible routes and 0.8 for ramps.

It is recognized that the coefficient of friction varies considerably due to the presence of contaminants, water, floor finishes, and other factors not under the control of the designer or builder and not subject to design and construction guidelines and that compliance would be difficult to measure on the building site. Nevertheless, many common building materials suitable for flooring are now labeled with information on the static coefficient of friction. While it may not be possible to compare one product directly with another, or to guarantee a constant measure, builders and designers are encouraged to specify materials with appropriate values. As more products include information on slip resistance, improved uniformity in measurement and specification is likely. The Access Board's advisory guidelines on Slip Resistant Surfaces provides additional information on this subject.

Cross slopes on walks and ground or floor surfaces can cause considerable difficulty in propelling a wheelchair in a straight line.

A5

A4.5.3 Carpet.

Much more needs to be done in developing both quantitative and qualitative criteria for carpeting (i.e., problems associated with texture and weave need to be studied). However, certain functional characteristics are well established. When both carpet and padding are used, it is desirable to have minimum movement (preferably none) between the floor and the pad and the pad and the carpet which would allow the carpet to hump or warp. In heavily trafficked areas, a thick, soft (plush) pad or cushion, particularly in combination with long carpet pile, makes it difficult for individuals in wheelchairs and those with other ambulatory disabilities to get about. Firm carpeting can be achieved through proper selection and combination of pad and carpet, sometimes with the elimination of the pad or cushion, and with proper installation. *Carpeting designed with a weave that causes a zig-zag effect when wheeled across is strongly discouraged.*

A4.6 Parking and Passenger Loading Zones.

A4.6.3 Parking Spaces.

The increasing use of vans with side-mounted lifts or ramps by persons with disabilities has necessitated some revisions in specifications for parking spaces and adjacent access aisles. The typical accessible parking space is 96 in (2440 mm) wide with an adjacent 60 in (1525 mm) access aisle. However, this aisle does not permit lifts or ramps to be deployed and still leave room for a person using a wheelchair or other mobility aid to exit the lift platform or ramp. In tests conducted with actual lift/van/wheelchair combinations, (under a Board-sponsored Accessible Parking and Loading Zones Project) researchers found that a space and aisle totaling almost 204 in (5180 mm) wide was needed to deploy a lift and exit conveniently. The "van accessible" parking space required by these guidelines provides a 96 in (2440 mm) wide space with a 96 in (2440 mm) adjacent access aisle which is just wide enough to maneuver and exit from a side mounted lift. If a 96 in (2440 mm) access aisle is placed between two spaces, two "van accessible" spaces are created. Alternatively, if the wide access aisle is provided at the end of a row (an area often unused), it may be possible to provide the wide access aisle without additional space (see Fig. A5(a)).

A sign is needed to alert van users to the presence of the wider aisle, but the space is not intended to be restricted only to vans.

"Universal" Parking Space Design. An alternative to the provision of a percentage of spaces with a wide aisle, and the associated need to include additional signage, is the use of what has been called the "universal" parking space design. Under this design, all accessible spaces are 132 in (3350 mm) wide with a 60 in (1525 mm) access aisle (see Fig. A5(b)). One

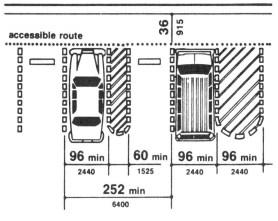

(a)
Van Accessible Space at End Row

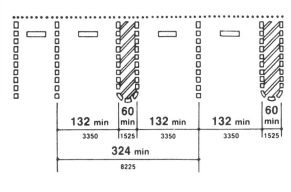

(b)
Universal Parking Space Design

Fig. A5
Parking Space Alternatives

A6

advantage to this design is that no additional signage is needed because all spaces can accommodate a van with a side-mounted lift or ramp. Also, there is no competition between cars and vans for spaces since all spaces can accommodate either. Furthermore, the wider space permits vehicles to park to one side or the other within the 132 in (3350 mm) space to allow persons to exit and enter the vehicle on either the driver or passenger side, although, in some cases, this would require exiting or entering without a marked access aisle.

An essential consideration for any design is having the access aisle level with the parking space. Since a person with a disability, using a lift or ramp, must maneuver within the access aisle, the aisle cannot include a ramp or sloped area. The access aisle must be connected to an accessible route to the appropriate accessible entrance of a building or facility. The parking access aisle must either blend with the accessible route or have a curb ramp complying with 4.7. Such a curb ramp opening must be located within the access aisle boundaries, not within the parking space boundaries. Unfortunately, many facilities are designed with a ramp that is blocked when any vehicle parks in the accessible space. Also, the required dimensions of the access aisle cannot be restricted by planters, curbs or wheel stops.

A4.6.4 Signage. Signs designating parking places for disabled people can be seen from a driver's seat if the signs are mounted high enough above the ground and located at the front of a parking space.

A4.6.5 Vertical Clearance. High-top vans, which disabled people or transportation services often use, require higher clearances in parking garages than automobiles.

A4.8 Ramps.

A4.8.1 General. Ramps are essential for wheelchair users if elevators or lifts are not available to connect different levels. However, some people who use walking aids have difficulty with ramps and prefer stairs.

A4.8.2 Slope and Rise. *Ramp slopes between 1:16 and 1:20 are preferred.* The ability to manage an incline is related to both its slope and its length. Wheelchair users with

disabilities affecting *their* arms or with low stamina have serious difficulty using inclines. Most ambulatory people and most people who use wheelchairs can manage a slope of 1:16. Many people cannot manage a slope of 1:12 for 30 ft (9 m).

A4.8.4 Landings. *Level landings are essential toward maintaining an aggregate slope that complies with these guidelines. A ramp landing that is not level causes individuals using wheelchairs to tip backward or bottom out when the ramp is approached.*

A4.8.5 Handrails. The requirements for stair and ramp handrails in this *guideline* are for adults. When children are principal users in a building or facility, a second set of handrails at an appropriate height can assist them and aid in preventing accidents.

A4.9 Stairs.

A4.9.1 Minimum Number. *Only interior and exterior stairs connecting levels that are not connected by an elevator, ramp, or other accessible means of vertical access have to comply with 4.9.*

A4.10 Elevators.

A4.10.6 Door Protective and Reopening Device. The required door reopening device would hold the door open for 20 seconds if the doorway remains obstructed. After 20 seconds, the door may begin to close. However, if designed in accordance with *ASME A17.1-1990*, the door closing movement could still be stopped if a person or object exerts sufficient force at any point on the door edge.

A4.10.7 Door and Signal Timing for Hall Calls. This paragraph allows variation in the location of call buttons, advance time for warning signals, and the door-holding period used to meet the time requirement.

A4.10.12 Car Controls. Industry-wide standardization of elevator control panel design would make all elevators significantly more convenient for use by people with severe visual impairments. In many cases, it will be possible to locate the highest control on elevator panels within 48 in (1220 mm) from the floor.

A7

A4.10.13 Car Position Indicators. A special button may be provided that would activate the audible signal within the given elevator only for the desired trip, rather than maintaining the audible signal in constant operation.

A4.10.14 Emergency Communications. A device that requires no handset is easier to use by people who have difficulty reaching. *Also, small handles on handset compartment doors are not usable by people who have difficulty grasping.*

Ideally, emergency two-way communication systems should provide both voice and visual display intercommunication so that persons with hearing impairments and persons with vision impairments can receive information regarding the status of a rescue. A voice intercommunication system cannot be the only means of communication because it is not accessible to people with speech and hearing impairments. While a voice intercommunication system is not required, at a minimum, the system should provide both an audio and visual indication that a rescue is on the way.

A4.11 Platform Lifts (Wheelchair Lifts).

A4.11.2 Other Requirements. *Inclined stairway chairlifts, and inclined and vertical platform lifts (wheelchair lifts) are available* for short-distance, vertical transportation of people with disabilities. Care should be taken in selecting lifts *as some lifts are not equally suitable for use by both wheelchair users and semi-ambulatory individuals.*

A4.12 Windows.

A4.12.1 General. *Windows intended to be operated by occupants in accessible spaces should comply with 4.12.*

A4.12.2 Window Hardware. *Windows requiring pushing, pulling, or lifting to open (for example, double-hung, sliding, or casement and awning units without cranks) should require no more than 5 lbf (22.2 N) to open or close. Locks, cranks, and other window hardware should comply with 4.27.*

A4.13 Doors.

A4.13.8 Thresholds at Doorways. Thresholds and surface height changes in doorways are particularly inconvenient for wheelchair users who also have low stamina or restrictions in arm movement because complex maneuvering is required to get over the level change while operating the door.

A4.13.9 Door Hardware. Some disabled persons must push against a door with their chair or walker to open it. Applied kickplates on doors with closers can reduce required maintenance by withstanding abuse from wheelchairs and canes. To be effective, they should cover the door width, less approximately 2 in (51 mm), up to a height of 16 in (405 mm) from its bottom edge and be centered across the *width of the door.*

A4.13.10 Door Closers. Closers with delayed action features give a person more time to maneuver through doorways. They are particularly useful on frequently used interior doors such as entrances to toilet rooms.

A4.13.11 Door Opening Force. Although most people with disabilities can exert at least 5 lbf (22.2N), both pushing and pulling from a stationary position, a few people with severe disabilities cannot exert 3 lbf (13.13N). Although some people cannot manage the allowable forces in this guideline and many others have difficulty, door closers must have certain minimum closing forces to close doors satisfactorily. Forces for pushing or pulling doors open are measured with a push-pull scale under the following conditions:

(1) Hinged doors: Force applied perpendicular to the door at the door opener or 30 in (760 mm) from the hinged side, whichever is farther from the hinge.

(2) Sliding or folding doors: Force applied parallel to the door at the door pull or latch.

(3) Application of force: Apply force gradually so that the applied force does not exceed the resistance of the door. In high-rise buildings, air-pressure differentials may require a modification of this specification in order to meet the functional intent.

A4.13.12 Automatic Doors and Power-Assisted Doors. Sliding automatic doors do not need guard rails and are more convenient for wheelchair users and visually impaired people to use. If slowly opening automatic doors can be reactivated before their closing cycle is completed, they will be more convenient in busy doorways.

A4.15 Drinking Fountains and Water Coolers.

A4.15.2 Spout Height. *Two drinking fountains, mounted side by side or on a single post, are usable by people with disabilities and people who find it difficult to bend over.*

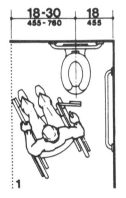

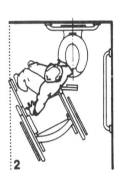

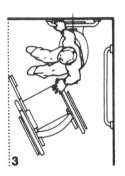

1 Takes transfer position, swings footrest out of the way, sets brakes.

2 Removes armrest, transfers.

3 Moves wheelchair out of the way, changes position (some people fold chair or pivot it 90° to the toilet).

4 Positions on toilet, releases brake.

**(a)
Diagonal Approach**

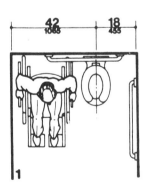

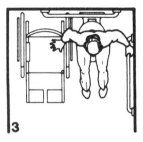

1 Takes transfer position, removes armrest, sets brakes.

2 Transfers.

3 Positions on toilet.

**(b)
Side Approach**

**Fig. A6
Wheelchair Transfers**

A9

A4.16 Water Closets.

A4.16.3 Height. Height preferences for toilet seats vary considerably among disabled people. Higher seat heights may be an advantage to some ambulatory disabled people, but are often a disadvantage for wheelchair users and others. Toilet seats 18 in (455 mm) high seem to be a reasonable compromise. Thick seats and filler rings are available to adapt standard fixtures to these requirements.

A4.16.4 Grab Bars. Fig. A6(a) and (b) show the diagonal and side approaches most commonly used to transfer from a wheelchair to a water closet. Some wheelchair users can transfer from the front of the toilet while others use a 90-degree approach. Most people who use the two additional approaches can also use either the diagonal approach or the side approach.

A4.16.5 Flush Controls. Flush valves and related plumbing can be located behind walls or to the side of the toilet, or a toilet seat lid can be provided if plumbing fittings are directly behind the toilet seat. Such designs reduce the chance of injury and imbalance caused by leaning back against the fittings. Flush controls for tank-type toilets have a standardized mounting location on the left side of the tank (facing the tank). Tanks can be obtained by special order with controls mounted on the right side. If administrative authorities require flush controls for flush valves to be located in a position that conflicts with the location of the rear grab bar, then that bar may be split or shifted toward the wide side of the toilet area.

A4.17 Toilet Stalls.

A4.17.3 Size and Arrangement. This section requires use of the 60 in (1525 mm) standard stall (Figure 30(a)) and permits the 36 in (915 mm) or 48 in (1220 mm) wide alternate stall (Figure 30(b)) only in alterations where provision of the standard stall is technically infeasible or where local plumbing codes prohibit reduction in the number of fixtures. A standard stall provides a clear space on one side of the water closet to enable persons who use wheelchairs to perform a side or diagonal transfer from the wheelchair to the water closet. However, some persons with disabilities who use mobility aids such as walkers, canes or crutches are better able to use the two parallel grab bars in the 36 in (915 mm) wide alternate stall to achieve a standing position.

In large toilet rooms, where six or more toilet stalls are provided, it is therefore required that a 36 in (915 mm) wide stall with parallel grab bars be provided in addition to the standard stall required in new construction. The 36 in (915 mm) width is necessary to achieve proper use of the grab bars; wider stalls would position the grab bars too far apart to be easily used and narrower stalls would position the grab bars too close to the water closet. Since the stall is primarily intended for use by persons using canes, crutches and walkers, rather than wheelchairs, the length of the stall could be conventional. The door, however, must swing outward to ensure a usable space for people who use crutches or walkers.

A4.17.5 Doors. To make it easier for wheelchair users to close toilet stall doors, doors can be provided with closers, spring hinges, or a pull bar mounted on the inside surface of the door near the hinge side.

A4.19 Lavatories and Mirrors.

A4.19.6 Mirrors. If mirrors are to be used by both ambulatory people and wheelchair users, then they must be at least 74 in (1880 mm) high at their topmost edge. A single full length mirror can accommodate all people, including children.

A4.21 Shower Stalls.

A4.21.1 General. Shower stalls that are 36 in by 36 in (915 mm by 915 mm) wide provide additional safety to people who have difficulty maintaining balance because all grab bars and walls are within easy reach. Seated people use the walls of 36 in by 36 in (915 mm by 915 mm) showers for back support. Shower stalls that are 60 in (1525 mm) wide and have no curb may increase usability of a bathroom by wheelchair users because the shower area provides additional maneuvering space.

A4.22 Toilet Rooms.

A4.22.3 Clear Floor Space. In many small facilities, single-user restrooms may be the only facilities provided for all building users. In addition, the guidelines allow the use of "unisex" or "family" accessible toilet rooms in alterations when technical infeasibility can be demonstrated. Experience has shown that the provision of accessible "unisex" or single-user restrooms is a reasonable way to provide access for wheelchair users and any attendants, especially when attendants are of the opposite sex. Since these facilities have proven so useful, it is often considered advantageous to install a "unisex" toilet room in new facilities in addition to making the multi-stall restrooms accessible, especially in shopping malls, large auditoriums, and convention centers.

Figure 28 (section 4.16) provides minimum clear floor space dimensions for toilets in accessible "unisex" toilet rooms. The dotted lines designate the minimum clear floor space, depending on the direction of approach, required for wheelchair users to transfer onto the water closet. The dimensions of 48 in (1220 mm) and 60 in (1525 mm), respectively, correspond to the space required for the two common transfer approaches utilized by wheelchair users (see Fig. A6). It is important to keep in mind that the placement of the lavatory to the immediate side of the water closet will preclude the side approach transfer illustrated in Figure A6(b).

To accommodate the side transfer, the space adjacent to the water closet must remain clear of obstruction for 42 in (1065 mm) from the centerline of the toilet (Figure 28) and the lavatory must not be located within this clear space. A turning circle or T-turn, the clear floor space at the lavatory, and maneuvering space at the door must be considered when determining the possible wall locations. A privacy latch or other accessible means of ensuring privacy during use should be provided at the door.

RECOMMENDATIONS:

1. In new construction, accessible single-user restrooms may be desirable in some situations because they can accommodate a wide variety of building users. However, they cannot be used in lieu of making the multi-stall toilet rooms accessible as required.

2. Where strict compliance to the guidelines for accessible toilet facilities is technically infeasible in the alteration of existing facilities, accessible "unisex" toilets are a reasonable alternative.

3. In designing accessible single-user restrooms, the provisions of adequate space to allow a side transfer will provide accommodation to the largest number of wheelchair users.

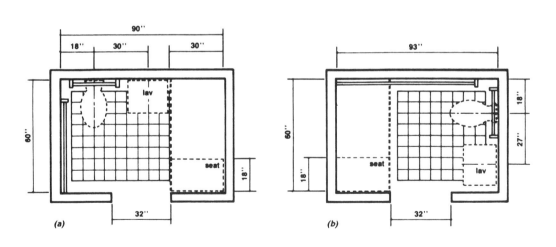

Fig. A7

A11

A4.23 Bathrooms, Bathing Facilities, and Shower Rooms.

A4.23.3 Clear Floor Space. *Figure A7 shows two possible configurations of a toilet room with a roll-in shower. The specific shower shown is designed to fit exactly within the dimensions of a standard bathtub. Since the shower does not have a lip, the floor space can be used for required maneuvering space. This would permit a toilet room to be smaller than would be permitted with a bathtub and still provide enough floor space to be considered accessible. This design can provide accessibility in facilities where space is at a premium (i.e., hotels and medical care facilities). The alternate roll-in shower (Fig. 57b) also provides sufficient room for the "T-turn" and does not require plumbing to be on more than one wall.*

A4.23.9 Medicine Cabinets. Other alternatives for storing medical and personal care items are very useful to disabled people. Shelves, drawers, and floor-mounted cabinets can be provided within the reach ranges of disabled people.

A4.26 Handrails, Grab Bars, and Tub and Shower Seats.

A4.26.1 General. Many disabled people rely heavily upon grab bars and handrails to maintain balance and prevent serious falls. Many people brace their forearms between supports and walls to give them more leverage and stability in maintaining balance or for lifting. The grab bar clearance of 1-1/2 in (38 mm) required in this guideline is a safety clearance to prevent injuries resulting from arms slipping through the openings. It also provides adequate gripping room.

A4.26.2 Size and Spacing of Grab Bars and Handrails. This specification allows for alternate shapes of handrails as long as they allow an opposing grip similar to that provided by a circular section of 1-1/4 in to 1-1/2 in (32 mm to 38 mm).

A4.27 Controls and Operating Mechanisms.

A4.27.3 Height. *Fig. A8 further illustrates*

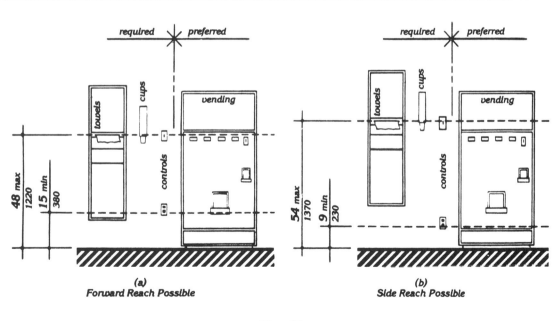

(a)
Forward Reach Possible

(b)
Side Reach Possible

Fig. A8
Control Reach Limitations

A12

mandatory and advisory control mounting height provisions for typical equipment.

Electrical receptacles installed to serve individual appliances and not intended for regular or frequent use by building occupants are not required to be mounted within the specified reach ranges. Examples would be receptacles installed specifically for wall-mounted clocks, refrigerators, and microwave ovens.

A4.28 Alarms.

A4.28.2 Audible Alarms. Audible emergency signals must have an intensity and frequency that can attract the attention of individuals who have partial hearing loss. People over 60 years of age generally have difficulty perceiving frequencies higher than 10,000 Hz. *An alarm signal which has a periodic element to its signal, such as single stroke bells (clang-pause-clang-pause), hi-low (up-down-up-down) and fast whoop (on-off-on-off) are best. Avoid continuous or reverberating tones. Select a signal which has a sound characterized by three or four clear tones without a great deal of "noise" in between.*

A4.28.3 Visual Alarms. The specifications in this section do not preclude the use of zoned or coded alarm systems.

A4.28.4 Auxiliary Alarms. Locating visual emergency alarms in rooms where persons who are deaf may work or reside alone can ensure that they will always be warned when an emergency alarm is activated. To be effective, such devices must be located and oriented so that they will spread signals and reflections throughout a space or raise the overall light level sharply. *However, visual alarms alone are not necessarily the best means to alert sleepers. A study conducted by Underwriters Laboratory (UL) concluded that a flashing light more than seven times brighter was required (110 candela v. 15 candela, at the same distance) to awaken sleepers as was needed to alert awake subjects in a normal daytime illuminated room.*

For hotel and other rooms where people are likely to be asleep, a signal-activated vibrator placed between mattress and box spring or under a pillow was found by UL to be much more effective in alerting sleepers. Many readily available devices are sound-activated so that they could respond to an alarm clock, clock

radio, wake-up telephone call or room smoke detector. Activation by a building alarm system can either be accomplished by a separate circuit activating an auditory alarm which would, in turn, trigger the vibrator or by a signal transmitted through the ordinary 110-volt outlet. Transmission of signals through the power line is relatively simple and is the basis of common, inexpensive remote light control systems sold in many department and electronic stores for home use. So-called "wireless" intercoms operate on the same principal.

A4.29 *Detectable Warnings.*

A4.29.2 *Detectable Warnings on Walking Surfaces.* *The material used to provide contrast should contrast by at least 70%. Contrast in percent is determined by:*

$$Contrast = [(B_1 - B_2)/B_1] \times 100$$

*where B_1 = light reflectance value (LRV) of the lighter area
and B_2 = light reflectance value (LRV) of the darker area.*

Note that in any application both white and black are never absolute; thus, B_1 never equals 100 and B_2 is always greater than 0.

A4.30 Signage.

A4.30.1 General. In building complexes where finding locations independently on a routine basis may be a necessity (for example, college campuses), tactile maps or prerecorded instructions can be very helpful to visually impaired people. Several maps and auditory instructions have been developed and tested for specific applications. The type of map or instructions used must be based on the information to be communicated, which depends highly on the type of buildings or users.

Landmarks that can easily be distinguished by visually impaired individuals are useful as orientation cues. Such cues include changes in illumination level, bright colors, unique patterns, wall murals, location of special equipment or other architectural features.

Many people with disabilities have limitations in movement of their heads and reduced peripheral vision. Thus, signage positioned

A13

perpendicular to the path of travel is easiest for them to notice. People can generally distinguish signage within an angle of 30 degrees to either side of the centerlines of their faces without moving their heads.

A4.30.2 Character Proportion. The legibility of printed characters is a function of the viewing distance, character height, the ratio of the stroke width to the height of the character, the contrast of color between character and background, and print font. The size of characters must be based upon the intended viewing distance. A severely nearsighted person may have to be much closer to recognize a character of a given size than a person with normal visual acuity.

A4.30.4 Raised and Brailled Characters and Pictorial Symbol Signs (Pictograms). *The standard dimensions for literary Braille are as follows:*

Dot diameter	*.059 in.*
Inter-dot spacing	*.090 in.*
Horizontal separation between cells	*.241 in.*
Vertical separation between cells	*.395 in.*

Raised borders around *signs containing* raised characters may make them confusing to read unless the border is set far away from the characters. *Accessible signage with descriptive materials about public buildings, monuments, and objects of cultural interest may not provide sufficiently detailed and meaningful information. Interpretive guides, audio tape devices, or other methods may be more effective in presenting such information.*

A4.30.5 Finish and Contrast. *An eggshell finish (11 to 19 degree gloss on 60 degree glossimeter) is recommended. Research indicates that signs are more legible for persons with low vision when characters contrast with their background by at least 70 percent. Contrast in percent shall be determined by:*

$$Contrast = [(B_1 - B_2)/B_1] \times 100$$

where B_1 = light reflectance value (LRV) of the lighter area
and B_2 = light reflectance value (LRV) of the darker area.

Note that in any application both white and black are never absolute; thus, B_1 never equals 100 and B_2 is always greater than 0.

The greatest readability is usually achieved through the use of light-colored characters or symbols on a dark background.

A4.30.7 Symbols of Accessibility for Different Types of Listening Systems. *Paragraph 4 of this section requires signage indicating the availability of an assistive listening system. An appropriate message should be displayed with the international symbol of access for hearing loss since this symbol conveys general accessibility for people with hearing loss. Some suggestions are:*

INFRARED
ASSISTIVE LISTENING SYSTEM
AVAILABLE
——PLEASE ASK——

AUDIO LOOP IN USE
TURN T-SWITCH FOR
BETTER HEARING
——OR ASK FOR HELP——

FM
ASSISTIVE LISTENING
SYSTEM AVAILABLE
——PLEASE ASK——

The symbol may be used to notify persons of the availability of other auxiliary aids and services such as: real time captioning, captioned note taking, sign language interpreters, and oral interpreters.

A4.30.8 Illumination Levels. *Illumination levels on the sign surface shall be in the 100 to 300 lux range (10 to 30 footcandles) and shall be uniform over the sign surface. Signs shall be located such that the illumination level on the surface of the sign is not significantly exceeded by the ambient light or visible bright lighting source behind or in front of the sign.*

A14

A4.31 Telephones.

A4.31.3 Mounting Height. In localities where the dial-tone first system is in operation, calls can be placed at a coin telephone through the operator without inserting coins. The operator button is located at a height of 46 in (1170 mm) if the coin slot of the telephone is at 54 in (1370 mm). A generally available public telephone with a coin slot mounted lower on the equipment would allow universal installation of telephones at a height of 48 in (1220 mm) or less to all operable parts.

A4.31.9 Text Telephones. A public text telephone may be an integrated text telephone pay phone unit or a conventional portable text telephone that is permanently affixed within, or adjacent to, the telephone enclosure. In order to be usable with a pay phone, a text telephone which is not a single integrated text telephone pay phone unit will require a shelf large enough (10 in (255mm) wide by 10 in (255 mm) deep with a 6 in (150 mm) vertical clearance minimum) to accommodate the device, an electrical outlet, and a power cord. Movable or portable text telephones may be used to provide equivalent facilitation. A text telephone should be readily available so that a person using it may access the text telephone easily and conveniently. As currently designed pocket-type text telephones for personal use do not accommodate a wide range of users. Such devices would not be considered substantially equivalent to conventional text telephones. However, in the future as technology develops this could change.

A4.32 Fixed or Built-in Seating and Tables.

A4.32.4 Height of Tables or Counters. Different types of work require different *table or counter* heights for comfort and optimal performance. Light detailed work such as writing requires a *table or counter* close to elbow height for a standing person. Heavy manual work such as rolling dough requires *a counter or table* height about 10 in (255 mm) below elbow height for a standing person. This principle of *high/low table or counter heights* also applies for seated persons; however, the limiting condition for seated manual work is clearance under the *table or counter.*

Table A1 shows convenient *counter heights* for seated persons. The great variety of heights for comfort and optimal performance indicates a need for alternatives or a compromise in height if people who stand and people who sit will be using the same counter area.

Table A1
Convenient Heights of Tables and Counters for Seated People[1]

Conditions of Use	Short Women in	mm	Tall Men in	mm
Seated in a wheelchair:				
Manual work–				
Desk or removeable armrests	26	660	30	760
Fixed, full-size armrests[2]	32[3]	815	32[3]	815
Light detailed work:				
Desk or removable armrests	29	735	34	865
Fixed, full-size armrests[2]	32[3]	815	34	865
Seated in a 16-in. (405-mm)				
High chair:				
Manual work	26	660	27	685
Light detailed work	28	710	31	785

[1] All dimensions are based on a work-surface thickness of 1 1/2 in (38 mm) and a clearance of 1 1/2 in (38 mm) between legs and the underside of a work surface.

[2] This type of wheelchair arm does not interfere with the positioning of a wheelchair under a work surface.

[3] This dimension is limited by the height of the armrests: a lower height would be preferable. Some people in this group prefer lower work surfaces, which require positioning the wheelchair back from the edge of the counter.

A4.33 Assembly Areas.

A4.33.2 Size of Wheelchair Locations. Spaces large enough for two wheelchairs allow people who are coming to a performance together to sit together.

A4.33.3 Placement of Wheelchair Locations. The location of wheelchair areas can be planned so that a variety of positions within the seating area are provided. This will allow choice in viewing and price categories.

Building/life safety codes set minimum distances between rows of fixed seats with consideration of the number of seats in a row, the exit aisle width and arrangement, and the location of exit doors. "Continental" seating, with a greater number of seats per row and a

commensurate increase in row spacing and exit doors, facilitates emergency egress for all people and increases ease of access to mid-row seats especially for people who walk with difficulty. Consideration of this positive attribute of "continental" seating should be included along with all other factors in the design of fixed seating areas.

Table A2. Summary of Assistive Listening Devices

System	Advantages	Disadvantages	Typical Applications
Induction Loop Transmitter: Transducer wired to induction loop around listening area. Receiver: Self-contained induction receiver or personal hearing aid with telecoil.	Cost-Effective Low Maintenance Easy to use Unobtrusive May be possible to integrate into existing public address system. Some hearing aids can function as receivers.	Signal spills over to adjacent rooms. Susceptible to electrical interference. Limited portability Inconsistent signal strength. Head position affects signal strength. Lack of standards for induction coil performance.	Meeting areas Theaters Churches and Temples Conference rooms Classrooms TV viewing
FM Transmitter: Flashlight-sized worn by speaker. Receiver: With personal hearing aid via DAI or induction neck-loop and telecoil; or self-contained with earphone(s).	Highly portable Different channels allow use by different groups within the same room. High user mobility Variable for large range of hearing losses.	High cost of receivers Equipment fragile Equipment obtrusive High maintenance Expensive to maintain Custom fitting to individual user may be required	Classrooms Tour groups Meeting areas Outdoor events One-on-one
Infrared Transmitter: Emitter in line-of-sight with receiver. Receiver: Self-contained. Or with personal hearing aid via DAI or induction neckloop and telecoil.	Easy to use Insures privacy or confidentiality Moderate cost Can often be integrated into existing public address system.	Line-of-sight required between emitter and receiver. Ineffective outdoors Limited portability Requires installation	Theaters Churches and Temples Auditoriums Meetings requiring confidentiality TV viewing

Source: Rehab Brief, National Institute on Disability and Rehabilitation Research, Washington, DC, Vol. XII, No. 10, (1990).

A4.33.6 Placement of Listening Systems.
A distance of 50 ft (15 m) allows a person to distinguish performers' facial expressions.

A4.33.7 Types of Listening Systems.
An assistive listening system appropriate for an assembly area for a group of persons or where the specific individuals are not known in advance, such as a playhouse, lecture hall or movie theater, may be different from the system appropriate for a particular individual provided as an auxiliary aid or as part of a reasonable accommodation. The appropriate device for an individual is the type that individual can use, whereas the appropriate system for an assembly area will necessarily be geared toward the "average" or aggregate needs of various individuals. A listening system that can be used from any seat in a seating area is the most flexible way to meet this specification. Earphone jacks with variable volume controls can benefit only people who have slight hearing loss and do not help people who use hearing aids. At the present time, *magnetic induction* loops are the most feasible type of listening system for people who use hearing aids *equipped with "T-coils,"* but people without hearing aids or those with hearing aids not equipped with inductive pick-ups cannot use them *without special receivers.* Radio frequency systems can be extremely effective and inexpensive. People without hearing aids can use them, but people with hearing aids need a special receiver to use them as they are presently designed. If hearing aids had a jack to allow a by-pass of microphones, then radio frequency systems would be suitable for people with and without hearing aids. Some listening systems may be subject to interference from other equipment and feedback from hearing aids of people who are using the systems. Such interference can be controlled by careful engineering design that anticipates feedback sources in the surrounding area.

Table A2, reprinted from a National Institute of Disability and Rehabilitation Research "Rehab Brief," shows some of the advantages and disadvantages of different types of assistive listening systems. In addition, the Architectural and Transportation Barriers Compliance Board (Access Board) has published a pamphlet on Assistive Listening Systems which lists demonstration centers across the country where technical assistance can be obtained in selecting and installing appropriate systems. The state of New York has also adopted a detailed technical specification which may be useful.

A5.0 Restaurants and Cafeterias.

A5.1 General.
Dining counters (where there is no service) are typically found in small carry-out restaurants, bakeries, or coffee shops and may only be a narrow eating surface attached to a wall. This section requires that where such a dining counter is provided, a portion of the counter shall be at the required accessible height.

A7.0 Business and Mercantile.

A7.2(3) Assistive Listening Devices.
At all sales and service counters, teller windows, box offices, and information kiosks where a physical barrier separates service personnel and customers, it is recommended that at least one permanently installed assistive listening device complying with 4.33 be provided at each location or series. Where assistive listening devices are installed, signage should be provided identifying those stations which are so equipped.

A7.3 Check-out Aisles.
Section 7.2 refers to counters without aisles; section 7.3 concerns check-out aisles. A counter without an aisle (7.2) can be approached from more than one direction such as in a convenience store. In order to use a check-out aisle (7.3), customers must enter a defined area (an aisle) at a particular point, pay for goods, and exit at a particular point.

UNITED STATES ARCHITECTURAL AND TRANSPORTATION BARRIERS COMPLIANCE BOARD

"Committed to enhancing the quality of life by ensuring accessibility and broadening the public awareness that access makes economic and practical sense for all."

What Accessibility Is

Accessibility means a building, facility or mode of transportation which can be approached, entered and used independently by *all* people. It means common design features like ramps, easy to use door handles and sink hardware, curb ramps, lowered water fountains and light switches, restrooms with maneuvering space and wider stalls, doors which require little pressure to open, accessible elevator control panels with raised letters and buttons, visual fire alarms and telecommunication devices (TDD).

Accessibility Benefits All Americans

- According to a recent survey, 43 million Americans or more than one in every six, have some type of disability.

- As Americans live longer, the likelihood increases as we grow older, that we will experience a disability. Today, of all adults 55-64 years of age, one in three has a limitation of some degree; nearly one in two of those 65-69; more than half of those 70 - 74 years old; and nearly three-fourths of those 75 years of age and older.

- When we add temporarily disabled persons, such as those persons injured in auto, recreational or other accidents, these figures grow even higher.

- Millions of non-disabled Americans benefit from access features everyday. Parents who often push their children around in strollers, persons carrying groceries or luggage, and the families, friends, and associates of persons with physical disabilities know firsthand the benefits of accessibility.

Accessible Design Makes Economic and Practical Sense

- In spite of the fact that thousands of disabled persons desire gainful employment, persons with disabilities comprise the largest unemployed minority. Almost 73% of the disabled population is unemployed; only 18.2% are employed full-time; 8.9% are employed part-time. Accessibility to transportation systems and to the workplace will provide employers with a new source of employees who are willing and eager to work.

- A recent survey indicates that 88% of accommodations for the disabled that are made in the workplace cost the company under $1000; 1% of the accommodations may be made at no cost; 19% at a cost of less than $50; and 19% at a cost of between $50 and $500 dollars.

- Costs of accessibility in new construction are minimal and in existing buildings costs of alterations can be kept to a minimum with careful design. In retail businesses, this cost is offset by the increase in patronage for a restaurant, theatre or other business establishment.

By providing barrier-free facilities, the freedom to use transportation systems, and the ability to communicate, accessible design features make economic and practical sense for *all* Americans.

GSA DC-89110020010

The Architectural and Transportation Barriers Compliance Board

The Architectural and Transportation Barriers Compliance Board (Board) is an independent Federal agency charged with ensuring that the requirements of the Architectural Barriers Act (Public Law 90-480) are met. This Act requires that certain facilities designed, constructed, leased or altered with Federal funds are accessible to and usable by persons with disabilities. The Board's mandate also includes providing technical assistance and proposing alternative solutions to barriers disabled individuals face in housing, transportation, communication, education, recreation and attitudes.

The Board serves as a lead agency in promoting accessibility throughout all segments of society and is a major resource for accessibility solutions, materials and information.

How Can The Architectural and Transportation Barriers Compliance Board Assist You?

- The Board has a trained and experienced staff of architects, lawyers and accessibility and compliance specialists to assist you.
- The Board provides informational and technical manuals and publications on architectural, transportation and communication access.
- The Board's Office of Technical and Information Services maintains minimum guidelines and requirements for accessibility and provides government agencies, public and private organizations, and individuals with technical guidance, interpretation of design standards and training on the elimination of architectural, transportation, communication and attitudinal barriers.
- The Office of Compliance and Enforcement investigates written complaints regarding the accessibility of certain federally-funded facilities. Complaints are received from the general public and include those referred by Congressional offices on behalf of their constituents.

For further information or assistance, please contact (voice or TDD):

Mr. Lawrence Roffee (202) 653-7834
Executive Director

Ms. Elizabeth Stewart (202) 653-7834
Congressional Liaison; Office of General Counsel

Ms. Ruth Lusher (202) 653-7848
Director, Office of Technical and Information Services

Ms. Judith Newton (202) 653-7951
Director, Office of Compliance and Enforcement

<u>Address:</u>
1111 18th Street NW, Suite 501
Washington, D.C. 20036-3894
Fax (202) 653-7863

Chapter Ten
CODES AND NEW LEGISLATION

This chapter attempts to clarify what the new Americans with Disabilities Act really means and how it will impact on our society. Changes will be felt in the business community and in the real estate and construction industries. It will have an effect on homebuilders, general contractors, interior designers, landscape contractors, manufacturers of the products used in the home, and the entire design profession.

The full impact of this legislation has not yet been felt, but there are signs now appearing in the industry that its impact will be great. The media is now starting to pay attention to the problems that face the disabled and the elderly. The physically challenged themselves are now becoming more aware of their civil rights, and their voices will be heard even more now that their requirements have become the law. One such example is the law enacted in July 1992, which specifies that companies with more than 25 employees must provide access for the physically challenged.

There is a growing awareness of the needs of the disabled and the elderly; these substantial numbers of the population have the right to live their lives as independently as they want to.

Many states have adopted the federal guidelines for making facilities accessible and usable for the physically disabled. The code identified as ANSI A117.1 is used almost in its entirety. The federal guidelines refer to this code of standards in the sections that pertain to accessibility. This code makes it necessary for employees to do a status report of their facility and determine what barriers exist there. The survey forms in this book will help to identify these barriers and the guidelines included herein will help to understand what the requirements for access are. Always check your own state and local building codes and your local building code officials to ascertain which laws pertain to your locale.

You can also query your local professional engineering and architectural groups and your occupational therapist and rehabilitation groups about additional information on what is required for accessibility in the private, commercial, and public sectors of your community.

It is very sad that these laws provide no help for persons in single-family residences, or persons living in a duplex or any unit that contains less than four units. A unified voice complaining about this lack of standards will someday cause enough of an uproar to legislate accessibility provisions for this large and rapidly growing segment of our society.

ABBREVIATIONS YOU SHOULD KNOW

Below is a list of abbreviations with which anyone interested in barrier-free housing or other facilities should become familiar:

ADA	Americans with Disability Act
ATBCB	Architectural and Transportation Barriers Compliance Board
DOJ	Department of Justice
DOT	Department of Transportation
EEOC	Equal Employment Opportunity Commission
FCC	Federal Communications Commission
MGRAD	Minimum Guidelines and Requirements for Accessible Design
UFAS	Uniform Federal Accessibility Standards

NONDISCRIMINATION ON THE BASIS OF DISABILITY IN PUBLIC ACCOMMODATIONS AND IN COMMERCIAL PRACTICE

This rule implements Title III of the Americans with Disabilities Act, Pub. L. 101-336, which prohibits discrimination on the basis of disability by private entities in places of public accommodation. It further requires that all new places of public accommodation and commercial facilities be designed and constructed so as to be readily accessible to and usable by persons with disabilities, and requires that examinations or courses related to licensing or certification for professional and trade purposes be accessible to persons with disabilities. (Preamble of the opening summary of the final rule for the Department of Justice, July 17, 1991.)

I must quote another part of the law in its entirety, to readily explain the continuation for the rights of people:

The Americans with Disabilities Act gives to individuals with disabilities civil rights protections with respect to discrimination that are parallel to those provided to individuals on the basis of race, color, national origin, sex, and religion. It combines in its own unique formula elements drawn principally from two key civil rights statutes—the Civil Rights Act of 1964 and Title V of the Rehabilitation Act 1973. The ADA generally employs the framework of Titles II (42 U.S.C. 2000a to 2000a-6) and Title VII (42 U.S.C. 2000e to 2000e-16) of the Civil Rights Act of 1964 for coverage and enforcement, and the terms and concepts of Section 504 of the Rehabilitation Act 11973 (29 U.S.C. 794) for what constitutes discrimination. (Dept of Justice, Office of the Attorney General, 28CFR, Part 36, dated July 17, 1991.)

The new standard guidelines set forth on July 17, 1991, and published as ADA Accessibility Guidelines for Buildings and Facilities (ADAAG) should now be consulted to determine accessibility requirements.

ADAGA consists of nine main sections and a separate appendix. Sections 1 through 3 contain general provisions and definitions. Section 4 contains scoping provisions and technical specifications applicable to all covered buildings and facilities. The scoping provisions are listed separately for new construction of sites and exterior facilities; new construction of buildings; additions; alterations; and alterations to historical

*properties. Sections 5 through 9 of the guidelines are special-applica-
tion sections and contain additional requirements for restaurants and
cafeterias, medical care facilities, business and mercantile facilities,
libraries, and transient lodging.*

Many of the sketches used in this book came from two basic sources.
One was the *American National Standard for Buildings and Facilities—
Providing Accessibility and Usability for Physically Handicapped People,*
(ANSI A117.1 1986). The second source was data and sketches from
the *North Carolina State Building Code, Volume I-C; Making Buildings
and Facilities Accessible to and Usable by the Physically Handicapped,*
April 1, 1991.

Chapter Eleven
RESOURCES

In this chapter I have listed some publications I recommend very highly. Some of them are free publications from the U.S. Architectural and Transportation Barriers Compliance Board (ATBCB), and other organizations. Those that are free are so noted.

I have also compiled a recommended list of products and accommodations that are convenient for the disabled. To keep the list short, I have limited the number of recommended sources, but there are many more.

At the end of this chapter is a complete copy of the ATBCB Publications Checklist showing many more publications that are available for the asking.

RECOMMENDED READING MATERIAL AND GUIDEBOOKS

Access for the Handicapped
Peter S. Hopf, AIA, and John A. Raeber, AIA
Van Nostrand Reinhold
Division of Thompson Publishing
7625 Empire Drive
Florence, KY 41042
(606) 525-6600

Adaptable Housing
Barrier Free Environments Inc.
Raleigh, NC, for
The U.S. Department of Housing and Urban Development
Office of Policy Development and Research
Washington, DC

Design for Hospitality, Planning for Accessible Hotels and Motels
Thomas D. Davies, AIA, and Kim A. Beasley, AIA
Paralyzed Veterans of America
American Hotel & Motel Association
Paralyzed Veterans of America
801 18th Street NW
Washington, DC 20006

The following Associations have free booklets that will help in the understanding of a barrier free environment.

General Electric Co.
Division of Consumer Affairs
4706 Almond Ave.,
Dept. WDS
Louisville, KY 20209

AARP
P.O. Box 2246
Long Beach, CA 90801

Accent on Living
Buyers Guide
P.O. Box 77
Bloomington, IL 61701

RECOMMENDED PRODUCTS

Portable Ramps

Alumi Ramp by Lakeshore Products
  855 West Chicago
  Quincy, MI 49082

Handi-Ramp, Inc.
  P.O. Box 745
  Mundelein, IL 60060

Door Hardware, Lever Handles

Russwin Division
  Emhart Hardware Group
  225 Episcopal Road
  P.O. Box 4004
  Berlin, CT 86037

Schlage Lock Co.
  P.O. Box 3324
  San Francisco, CA 94119

Power Door Openers

Gyro Tech, Inc.
  S82,W18717 Gemini Drive
  P.O. Box 906
  Muskego, WI 53150

Power Access Corp.
  Bridge Street
  P.O. Box 235
  Collinsville, CT 06022

Electronically Controlled Faucets

Continental Systems
  1330 West Olympic Blvd.
  Los Angeles, CA 90015

Water Temperature Controls

Memry Plumbing Products Corp.
  83 Keeler Ave.
  Norwalk, CT 06854

Grab Bars

Bradley Corp.
  P.O. Box 309
  Menomonie Falls, WI 53051

Mc Kinney Parker
  1591 Indiana Street
  San Francisco, CA 94104

Hewi, Inc.
  6 Pearl Ct.
  Allendale, NJ 07401

Safety Technologies
  P.O. Box 23
  Melbourne, FL 32902

Roll-in Shower Units

Kohler
  Kohler, WI 53044

Universal-Rundle Corp.
  303 North Street
  New Castle, PA 16103

Shower Seats

Franklin Brass Mfg.
  P.O. Box 5226
  Culver City, CA 90231

Tubular Specialties Mfg, Inc.
  13011 South Spring Street
  Los Angeles, CA 90061

Hand-Held Shower Units

Gemini Bath & Kitchen Products
  4733 East Broadway Blvd.
  Tucson, AZ 85713

Teldyne Water Pic
  1730 East Prospect Street
  Fort Collins, CO 80524

Bathroom Accessories

Bobrick Washroom Equipment
  1161 Hart Street
  North Hollywood, CA 91605

Bathroom Fixtures

Kohler
  Kohler, WI 53044

Lasco
  3255 E. Miraloma Ave.
  Anaheim, CA 92806

Aqua Glass Corp.
  P.O. Box 412
  Industrial Park
  Adamsville, TN 38310

PUBLICATIONS CHECKLIST
U.S. ARCHITECTURAL AND TRANSPORTATION BARRIERS COMPLIANCE BOARD
Suite 501, 1111 18th Street, NW, Washington, DC 20036-3894

The ATBCB (Access Board) produces or distributes a variety of publications, available at no cost. To request copies, write the quantity you want beside each publication and clearly write your name and address in the space provided. If you want more than ten (10) copies of any single publication, send a letter explaining the planned distribution (e.g., conference for planners) and the anticipated audience.

The ATBCB is committed to providing, where feasible, these materials in formats for readers to use independently. Some are already available in a variety of alternative formats: B (Braille), LT (large type), CST (cassette), DIS (5¼" floppy disc in ACSII). Circle the format(s) you wish. Publications not marked will be reproduced soon in as many forms as possible, given their original formats. Priority is given to requests.

General Publications

_____ (G2)   *Access America* newsletter. Published quarterly to provide information about the Access Board and its activities. To be added to the newsletter mailing list, check here _____ . B, CST, DIS, LT

_____ (G3)   *Access America: The Architectural Barriers Act and You.* Describes the Access Board and how to file complaints about inaccessible federally funded buildings and facilities. B, CST, DIS, LT

_____ (G12)   *The Americans with Disabilities Act: ADA in Brief.* Gives brief overview of the act's provisions on employment, public services, public accommodations, and telecommunications. The act was signed into law by President Bush on July 26, 1990. B, DIS, LT

_____ (G4)   *Annual Report to the President and Congress.* Report on Access Board activities for the previous fiscal year. B, CST, DIS, LT

_____ (G5)   *Laws Concerning the ATBCB.* Contains the Architectural Barriers Act of 1968 (Public Law 90-480) and sections 502 (which established the ATBCB), 506, and 507 of the Rehabilitation Act of 1973. B. CST, DIS, LT

_____ (G11)   *Symposium Presentation to the 20th Anniversary Celebration of the Architectural Barriers Act of 1968.* Report on symposium hosted by Disabled American Veterans in Washington, D.C., in August 1988. B, DIS, LT

_____ (G10)   *Toward an Accessible Environment: Effective Research.* Describes seven exemplary federally funded research projects on environmental accessibility. B, CST, LT

Architectural Access

_____ (A20)   *Design Standards for Accessible Single-Toilet Rest Rooms.* To be used with the Uniform Federal Accessibility Standards, this design bulletin #1 provides recommendations for single toilet rest rooms to increase usability by those who make side transfers. B, DIS, LT

_____ (A12)   *Ground and Floor Surface Treatments.* Describes characteristics of five interior and exterior surfaces that may pose hazards for persons with disabilities. B, CST, DIS, LT

_____ (A13)   *Hand Anthropometrics.* The full report, including methodology and data, of a project to examine the use of various controls and operating mechanisms by individuals with arm, hand, and finger limitations (for recommendations from this project, order the publication below). CST

_____ (A26)   *Hands-On Architecture.* Contains the Executive Summary and recommendations from the above project with suggested standards for specifying controls and operating mechanisms. B, DIS, LT

_____ (A15)   *Orientation and Wayfinding.* Examines how pedestrians, like people with disabilities, experience problems and needs in wayfinding. CST

_____ (A25)   *Transit Facility Design for Persons with Visual Impairments.* Combines recommendations from several research reports on signage, platform edge cuing, lighting, and slip resistant surfaces geared toward transit stations but partly applicable to other facility types. B, CST, LT

_____ (A22)   *Visual Alarms.* Gives detailed recommendations on alarms for alerting persons with hearing impairment to emergencies, including flash rate, intensity, placement and cost estimates. B, CST, DIS, LT

_____ (S4)   *Uniform Federal Accessibility Standards* (UFAS). Design, construction and alteration standards for access to federally funded facilities (based on the ATBCB *Minimum Guidelines and Requirements for Accessible Design*). CST

Communication Access

_____ (C1)   *Assistive Listening Systems.* Describes commercially available devices and systems for making public address and other types of communication systems more accessible to persons with hearing impairments. B, CST, DIS, LT

_____ (C3)   *TDD: Final Report.* Describes a study of the needs of users of Telecommunication Devices for Deaf persons (TDD) for communication with and within the federal government. CST

_____ (C4)   *TDD: Appendix.* Appendix to the above report includes data on available equipment, a list of interviewees, discussion of methodology, and bibliography. (Included on cassette with *TDD: Final Report.*)

Transportation Access

_____ (T4)   *Air Carrier Policies on Transport of Battery-Powered Wheelchairs.* Describes policies of major air carriers for transporting battery-powered wheelchairs, the section of the operating manual where it is codified, and constraints imposed by different types of aircraft. B, DIS, LT

_____ (T19)   *Aircraft Stowage Procedures for Battery-Powered Wheelchairs.* Contains a detailed description of a procedure for safely stowing battery-powered wheelchairs on aircraft in conformance with Hazardous Materials regulations, based on successful practices of several domestic and foreign air carriers. B, DIS, LT

_____ (T10)   *Guidelines for Aircraft Boarding Chairs.* Provides guidance to purchasers, designers, and manufacturers of boarding chairs, for the design or purchase of safer and more effective devices; also identifies elements of a proper training program. B, DIS, LT

_____ (T13)   *Lifts and Wheelchair Securement.* Assists transportation providers and potential patrons plan services and select equipment to meet the needs of disabled persons; supplements UMTA-sponsored model safety specifications for lifts, ramps, and wheelchair securement on buses and paratransit vehicles. B, DIS, LT

_____ (T17)   *Mobility Aids Stowage.* Intended to help air carriers develop effective policies, procedures, and practices for safe stowage and return of mobility aids; synthesized from a broad cross-section of air carriers; the appendix contains a detailed procedure for stowing power wheelchairs and mobility aids which is available as a separate brochure, T19, described above). B, CST, DIS, LT

Name _____

Organization _____

Address _____

City _____ State _____ Zip _____

_____ (G8)   *Publications Checklist.* Additional copies of this order form can be obtained from: ATBCB, 1111 18th Street, NW, Suite 501, Washington, DC 20036-3894; or call (202) 653-7834 (voice or TDD). (This list may be duplicated or reproduced). B, DIS, LT

Chapter Twelve
SITE SURVEY CHECKLISTS

This chapter will offer you the opportunity to perform your own site survey to determine, in a very brief time, what barriers for the elderly and disabled exist in your home. I have also included a preliminary questionnaire to help you determine whether some action should be taken soon. You will also find a second survey form, designed to be used in commercial environments; it will be helpful in identifying any barriers that may exist in retail establishments and the workplace.

Figure 12-1 should be used to determine what changes you anticipate having made to make your environment accessible to the elderly and/or disabled.

Feel free to make as many copies as you require of this questionnaire.

HOME ACCESSIBILITY SURVEY

Figure 12-2 is designed to be used by homeowners for surveying their homes to identify architectural barriers. Answer each question and comment as necessary to clarify the current situation or condition in your home. This will help to make the barriers easier to identify. When the survey is complete, you will have a brief list of barriers you have identified. You can then bring this list to an architect or general contractor for a cost estimate on removing the barriers.

Figure 12-3 (p. 165) is a checklist of suggested improvements to your kitchen for making it barrier-free.

USING THE COMMERCIAL ACCESSIBILITY SURVEY FORM

Figure 12-4, the commercial accessibility survey form, is designed to be used by the owner, contractor, or any other professional, such as an architect or engineer. It will be helpful in determining what architectural barriers there may be in a facility. These surveys have been adjusted to take into account some of the new ADAAG guidelines for the requirements of the disabled.

When this survey is completed, it will be easier to recognize some of the most pressing problems for the disabled. If the existing problems go beyond what has been identified in the form, I recommend that a design professional be called in to further examine the facility. Then a decision can be made about what exactly needs to be done to comply with current regulations.

Again, call on your local building inspection official for information on what is required in your own city or state. When making a study of the workplace, remember that wheelchair-bound people need a direct, obstruction-free route to work. Be sure to make note of any existing barriers for all physically challenged people, including the blind, the hearing-impaired, or any others. Removing these barriers is one of the requirements of this civil rights bill (ADA).

Of course, identifying the barriers is the first step in the process of removal and compliance!

---

1. Is there someone in the household who is elderly or has a physical impairment?

_____ yes _____ no

2. Are you considering having someone who is elderly or disabled come to live with you?

_____ yes _____ no

3. Are you considering making some changes to your home to allow someone elderly or disabled to come and live with you?

_____ yes _____ no

4. Do you plan to use the services of a professional architect, engineer, or interior designer?

_____ yes _____ no

5. Do you plan to use the services of a general contractor, or a contractor who specializes in remodeling?

_____ yes _____ no

6. Are there special conditions required in your home in order to accommodate the elderly or disabled?

_____ yes _____ no

7. Can the physical changes you require be performed only by a licensed plumber?

_____ yes _____ no

8. Do the physical changes you require have to be performed by a licensed electrical contractor?

_____ yes _____ no

9. Have you used the services of a rehabilitation office recently?

_____ yes _____ no

10. Have you required the services of an occupational therapist recently?

_____ yes _____ no

Figure 12-1 Questionnaire

Parking

1. Is there off-street parking close to your home?
   Comments _____ Y ☐   N ☐
2. Is there a specified handicapped parking space close to your front door?
   Comments _____ Y ☐   N ☐
3. Are the spaces designated at least 12-ft 6-in. wide and do they have a 48" space next to them?
   Comments _____ Y ☐   N ☐
4. Does the parking space have a sign designating it as reserved for the handicapped?
   Comments _____ Y ☐   N ☐
5. Is the parking area surface firm and smooth? If it is not, what kind of surface does it have?
   Comments _____ Y ☐   N ☐
6. Can a person travel from the parking area to the front door without having to go over any steps? Is the walk very steep? Does it have more than a 1 in 20 slope?
   Comments _____ Y ☐   N ☐
7. Is the walkway at least 48-in. wide, and is it smooth and firm?
   Comments _____ Y   N
8. Are there any other hazards that may interfere with the travel of a wheelchair?
   Comments _____ Y ☐   N ☐

Entrances

1. Is there an entrance door at least 36-in. wide that provides a clearance of 32 in.?
   Comments _____ Y ☐   N ☐
2. Are there any steps that one must climb to get to the front door? How wide and how long is the front stoop at this entrance?
   Comments _____ Y ☐   N ☐
   Size of stoop _____
3. Is the threshold at the front door more than ¾-in. high?
   Comments _____ Y ☐   N ☐
4. Does the front door have a lever handle opener? If not, what kind of opener does it have?
   Comments _____ Y ☐   N ☐
5. Is the front door easy to open? Does it take a lot of pulling? Is it extra heavy?
   Comments _____ Y ☐   N ☐
6. Is there carpet on the floor at the inside entrance to the home? What kind of floor surface is there?
   Comments _____ Y ☐   N ☐
7. Is the floor slippery? Are there loose rugs on the floor?
   Comments _____ Y ☐   N ☐
8. Is there enough space in the foyer to move around? Is there at least a 5-ft diameter circle of space?
   Comments _____ Y ☐   N ☐
9. Is there enough light at the entrance to satisfy safety requirements?
   Comments _____ Y ☐   N ☐

Figure 12-2 Home Accessibility Survey Form

Interior

1. Is the entire home on one floor? If not, are there a number of steps to climb to another floor?
   Comments _____ Y ☐   N ☐
2. Are all halls at least 3-ft wide?
   Comments _____ Y ☐   N ☐
3. Are there any objects that protrude into the hall? Identify them.
   Comments _____ Y ☐   N ☐
4. Are there any thresholds in the home that are more than ¾ in. high?
   Comments _____ Y ☐   N ☐
5. Is there any surface or flooring inside your home that is loose, slippery, or has a deep pile carpet?
   Comments _____ Y ☐   N ☐
6. Is there any furniture that is in the way of travel in a wheelchair?
   Comments _____ Y ☐   N ☐
7. Do all the doorways to all the rooms have at least a 32-in.-wide clearance between the frames?
   Comments _____ Y ☐   N ☐

Kitchen

1. How much space is there between the kitchen cabinets? Are there at least 48 in.? Is there any object in the kitchen that prevents free movement?
   Comments _____ Y ☐   N ☐
2. What is the height from the floor of storage shelving?
   Comments and Size _____
3. Can we reach all appliances from a sitting position? Is there difficulty in reaching the oven? The microwave? Other appliances stored on the counter?
   Comments _____ Y ☐   N ☐
4. Can the sink be reached from a wheelchair? Can the faucet be turned on and off?
   Comments _____ Y ☐   N ☐
5. Is there a pantry or are there other storage areas?
   Comments _____ Y ☐   N ☐
6. Are there at least 30 in. of counter space on both sides of the cooktop? Is there space on either side of the sink? How much is there?
   Comments _____ Y ☐   N ☐
7. Is there a minimum of 12 sq ft of countertop? If not, how much space does it have?
   Comments _____ Y ☐   N ☐
8. Are the wall receptacles easy to reach? Are there enough wall outlets for our appliances? Can we get to all wall switches? Are all the receptacles grounded?
   Comments _____ Y ☐   N ☐
9. Is the floor slippery? Does it often get wet?
   Comments _____ Y ☐   N ☐
10. Are the washing machine and/or the dryer in the kitchen?
    Comments _____ Y ☐   N ☐

Figure 12-2 Home Accessibility Survey Form (*Continued*)

11. Are the controls for the washer and dryer easy to reach?
    Comments _____ Y □   N □
12. Is there enough space to fold your clothes when you get them from the dryer? How much space is there?
    Comments _____ Y □   N □
13. Is the floor of the laundry area susceptible to getting wet?
    Comments _____ Y □   N □
14. Is there enough space around the bed to move about? How much space do you have from the bed to the wall on every side?
    Comments _____ Y □   N □
15. Is there adjustable shelving in your bedroom closets? Can you reach all parts of your closets?
    Comments _____ Y □   N □

Bathroom
 1. Does the doorway to the bathroom have at least 32-in. clear space?
    Comments _____ Y □   N □
 2. What is the amount of space between the floor and the vanity or lavatory? Is there enough space for the wheelchair to slide under? Enough room to move about?
    Comments _____ Y □   N □
 3. Can a person reach the sink faucets while in a seated position?
    Comments _____ Y □   N □
 4. Is the bottom edge of the mirror 40 in. from the floor? If not, at what height is it? Is there a shelf at the same height?
    Comments _____ Y □   N □
 5. Is there a clear path of 36-in. wide to the commode?
    Comments _____ Y □   N □
 6. Is there a clear space of 32 in. × 48 in. of floor space adjacent to the commode?
    Comments _____ Y □   N □
 7. Is the rim of the commode (seat) at least 19 in. from the floor?
    Comments _____ Y □   N □
 8. Is there a grab bar at least 42-in. long on one side of the commode? Is there a grab bar at least 24 in. long on the rear wall of the commode?
    Comments _____ Y □   N □
 9. Are the heights of these grab bars between 33 in. minimum and 36 in. maximum?
    Comments _____ Y □   N □
10. Is there a minimum space of 1-1/2 in. between the wall and the grab bar?
    Comments _____ Y □   N □
11. Are the grab bars at least 1-1/4 in. minimum to 1-1/2 in. maximum in diameter?
    Comments _____ Y □   N □

Figure 12-2 Home Accessibility Survey Form (*Continued*)

12. Is there a grab bar at the control side of the tub? Is it at least 24 ft long?
    Comments _____ Y ☐   N ☐
13. Is the grab bar on the side of tub (without seat) at least 24 in., and is it between a 25-in. minimum and a 27-in. maximum height?
    Comments _____ Y ☐   N ☐
14. Is the grab bar at least 42-in. long (with built-in seat) and set between a 25-in. minimum and 27-in. maximum height?
    Comments _____ Y ☐   N ☐
15. Is there a 12-in. × 1-1/4-in. diameter grab bar set at the head of the tub (required only if a built-in seat is provided)?
    Comments _____ Y ☐   N ☐
16. Is the floor of the tub slippery?
    Comments _____ Y ☐   N ☐
17. Is there some provision for built-in seats or a portable seat in the bathtub?
    Comments _____ Y ☐   N ☐
18. Is there a hand-held shower-control spray in the tub? If there is, does it comply with Fig. 6-25?
    Comments _____ Y ☐   N ☐
19. Is there a separate temperature control unit?
    Comments _____ Y ☐   N ☐
20. Is there a roll-in shower unit that is designed for a wheelchair? Does it comply with Fig. 6-30?
    Comments _____ Y ☐   N ☐
21. Is there a regular shower-stall unit in place? Is the doorway at least 32 in. clear? Is there a curb?
    Comments _____ Y ☐   N ☐
22. Is the floor of the shower unit slippery?
    Comments _____ Y ☐   N ☐
23. Are the shower controls in compliance with the requirements shown in Fig. 6-30?
    Comments _____ Y ☐   N ☐
24. Is there a built-in seat inside the shower unit?
    Comments _____ Y ☐   N ☐
25. Is the towel bar set at a height of 36 in.?
    Comments _____ Y ☐   N ☐

Outdoors
1. Is there a threshold higher than ¾ in. at the exit door to the outside?
   Comments _____ Y ☐   N ☐
2. Does the doorway provide at least a 32-in.-wide clearance?
   Comments _____ Y   N
3. Is there a firm and solid surface at this exit door? If not, what kind of surface is it?
   Comments _____ Y ☐   N ☐
4. Are there any benches, chairs, or other types of seats outside?
   Comments _____ Y ☐   N ☐
5. Is there any protection from rain or sun? Is any kind of shelter provided in the yard?
   Comments _____ Y ☐   N ☐

Figure 12-2 Home Accessibility Survey Form (*Continued*)

6. Is the telephone in close proximity to the outside area? Is there a portable telephone you can use?
   Comments _____ Y ☐   N ☐
7. Is there an adequate lighting fixture outside to make it safe to move about the yard?
   Comments _____ Y ☐   N ☐
8. Is there any place around the house that is not fully secure? Are there any bushes up close to the house where someone could hide?
   Comments _____ Y ☐   N ☐
   _____Owner   _____Surveyor

Figure 12-2 Home Accessibility Survey Form (*Continued*)

This checklist highlights various measures you can take to make residential kitchens more usable for the disabled person.

1. Appliance considerations
   ___a. Provide platforms for front-opening appliances to allow reach into the appliance by the wheelchair user.
      (1) Clothes dryer
      (2) Compact upright freezer
      (3) Dishwasher

   ___ b. Refrigerator and freezer doors are equipped with magnetic gaskets to create a firm seal, maintain even temperatures, and conserve energy. The strong suction may make opening these doors very difficult for people with reduced strength in their arms and hands.
      (1) Specify a vacuum break that can be placed along the gasket to reduce the suction.
      (2) If vacuum break is unavailable, apply electrical tape across the lower door gasket in one or two places.

   ___ c. Cooktops, built-in ovens, and microwave ovens should be installed at a height most convenient for the individual using the space. These appliances should be usable from a seated or standing position. Microwaves may be built-in or placed on a movable table.

   ___ d. Counter and floor space surrounding appliances should provide adequate hand grip to support and balance a person on crutches or using a walker. This space should be provided in addition to the space needed to remove cooking pans and dishes.

   ___ e. Provide visual control of cooking pots by installing an adjustable mirror over the range or cooktop that permits the cook to see into the pots on the back burners. The mirror may be tilted by use of a chain and hook.

   ___ f. Exhaust hood controls must be installed at counter level for use by those in wheelchairs.

2. a. Counters and base cabinets
   ___ (1) Depth not to exceed 24 in. (60.96 cm).
   ___ (2) Height ranging from 2 ft 4 in. to 3 ft 6 in. (71.12 to 106.68 cm).

   b. Wall-hung cabinets
   ___ (1) Height above counter top 1 in. to 4 in. (2.54 to 10.16 cm).
   ___ (2) Maximum storage height not to exceed 48 in. (121.92 cm) above the floor.

Figure 12-3 Checklist for Barrier-Free Kitchen Design

3. Organizers
a. Specify and design organizers that allow items to be stored near the front or back of cabinets.
    ___ (1) Pull-out baskets or shelves (minimum 40 cu ft (1.13 cu m))
    ___ (2) Plate racks
    ___ (3) Suction-held turntables
    ___ (4) Hanging baskets
    ___ (5) Dispensers for cans and bottles

4. Operating information
    ___a. Provide appliance operational information in braille on the front of the appliance at the control center.

    ___b. Provide ridges or other tactile cues for those with loss of feeling in fingertips.

    ___c. Care and use of appliances may also be tape recorded.

5. Reaching aids
    People who have limitations in reaching, bending, or stooping may need a reaching tool to operate high controls, turn faucets, or remove items from shelves.
    ___ a. Knob turners: may be 12 in. to 18 in. (30.48 to 45.72 cm) long with an attachment that fits over the knob on one end.

    ___b. "Push-pullers" allow users to push oven racks in and pull racks out when laden with hot pots and pans.

    ___c. Tongs allow reaching into refrigerators and to high shelves.

Figure 12-3 Checklist for Barrier-Free Kitchen Design (*Continued*)

Parking

1. Is there off-street parking for the handicapped?
   Comments _____ Y ☐   N ☐
2. Is there parking for the handicapped close to the facility?
   Comments _____ Y ☐   N ☐
3. Is the designated parking space large enough to meet the requirements of a recommended parking space for the handicapped?
   Comments _____ Y ☐   N ☐
4. Is there an approved sign that designates this space as reserved for the handicapped?
   Comments _____ Y ☐   N ☐
5. Are there curb cuts in the travel path? Are they of the approved design?
   Comments _____ Y ☐   N ☐
6. Does the area that is designated as a reserved space have a firm surface? If not, what is the surface material?
   Comments _____ Y ☐   N ☐
7. Is the path of travel from the parking area steep? Does it have any steps or obstacles?
   Comments _____ Y ☐   N ☐
8. Is the walk at least 48-in. wide?
   Comments _____ Y ☐   N ☐
9. Does the walkway slope no more than 1 in 20?
   Comments _____ Y ☐   N ☐
10. Is the walkway free of cracks or broken pieces?
    Comments _____ Y ☐   N ☐
11. Is the walkway illuminated along the route of travel to the front entrance?
    Comments _____ Y ☐   N ☐
12. Are the curb-cut areas well-lit for safety?
    Comments _____ Y ☐   N ☐
13. Are there any steps between the walkway and the front entrance?
    Comments _____ Y ☐   N ☐
14. Is there a ramp that allows the front entrance to be used by the wheelchair-bound person?
    Comments _____ Y ☐   N ☐
15. Does the ramp have a maximum slope of 1 in 12?
    Comments _____ Y ☐   N ☐
16. Are there handrails on both sides? On one side? How high is the ramp from the ground?
    Comments _____ Y ☐   N ☐
17. Are the handrails at least 1-1/2-in. in diameter?
    Comments _____ Y ☐   N ☐
18. Does the surface of the ramp have a nonslip surface?
    Comments _____ Y ☐   N ☐
19. Is there a level area of 60 in. × 60 in. at the head of the ramp? Is it just before the entrance door?
    Comments _____ Y ☐   N ☐

Figure 12-4 Accessibility Survey Form for Commercial Applications

Entrance

1. Is the entrance door at least 32-in. clear from frame to frame?
   Comments _____ Y ☐ N ☐
2. Is there an automatic door opener?
   Comments _____ Y ☐ N ☐
3. Are there any interior steps to climb at the front entrance?
   Comments _____ Y ☐ N ☐
4. What type of surface material is on the entrance floor?
   Carpet?   Tile?   Ceramic Tile?
   Comments _____
5. Is there any type of floor grate or drain that could cause a person on crutches or using a walker to trip?
   Comments _____ Y ☐ N ☐
6. Is the entrance to the facility well-defined by some exterior signage?
   Comments _____ Y ☐ N ☐
7. Is the door easy to pull open? Can it be opened with less than a 5-(½)-lb-pull?
   Comments _____ Y ☐ N ☐
8. Are there benches on either side of the front entrance? Is there any seating in the foyer area? Other kinds of rest areas?
   Comments _____ Y ☐ N ☐
9. Is the entire facility on one floor? Is there any change of level in the facility's interior facility?
   Comments _____ Y ☐ N ☐
10. Are all interior halls at least 36-in. wide? Are some halls wider?
    Comments _____ Y ☐ N ☐
11. Is there an elevator?
    Comments _____ Y ☐ N ☐
12. What are the dimensions of the elevator? How many elevators are there in the facility?
    Comments _____ Y ☐ N ☐
13. Where is the elevator located? Is it for public use? Is it a freight elevator?
    Comments _____ Y ☐ N ☐
14. Does the elevator have an audible signal? Does it signal the floor number? How does it signal?
    Comments _____ Y ☐ N ☐
15. Is there a visual signal? Does it signal what floor you are on?
    Comments _____ Y ☐ N ☐
16. At what height is the exterior call-button? Are the call-buttons illuminated?
    Comments _____ Y ☐ N ☐
17. Is there braille writing on the door frame of each level?
    Comments _____ Y ☐ N ☐
18. Is the interior control board set 54-in. high?
    Comments _____ Y ☐ N ☐
19. Is there a telephone in the elevator cab for use in emergencies?
    Comments _____ Y ☐ N ☐

Figure 12-4 Accessibility Survey Form for Commercial Applications (*Continued*)

20. Is there a special vehicle to assist those who are disabled?
Comments _____ Y ☐ N ☐
21. Is there staff available to help the disabled?
Comments _____ Y ☐ N ☐

Public Telephones
Is there a telephone for public use? What is the height to the coin insert?
Comments _____ Y ☐ N ☐

Public Restrooms
How many public restrooms are on each floor? Is there one for each sex?
                                           Male ☐   Female ☐
Comments _____ Y ☐ N ☐
2. Is there an unobstructed direct route to the restrooms?
Comments _____ Y ☐ N ☐
3. Is there a door-assist opening device on the restroom door?
Comments _____ Y ☐ N ☐
4. Does the door operate with less than 5-1/2-lb of pull?
Comments _____ Y ☐ N ☐
5. Does the door opening have 32-in. of clear space from frame to frame?
Comments _____ Y ☐ N ☐
6. Is there a clear space of at least 32 in. × 48 in. in front of the lavatory?
Comments _____ Y ☐ N ☐
7. Can the faucets be reached from a wheelchair?
Comments _____ Y ☐ N ☐
8. Does the water faucet shut itself off automatically?
Comments _____ Y ☐ N ☐
9. Is there a tilting mirror? A standard mirror? At what height is the bottom edge?
Comments _____ Y ☐ N ☐

Other Considerations for Making the Facility Accessible
1. Are the water fountains accessible to the handicapped? Is it set no higher than 36 in. from the floor?
Comments _____ Y ☐ N ☐
2. Are the signs inside the building easy to read and do they have good contrast?
Comments _____ Y ☐ N ☐
3. Are interpreters available and/or are they provided for special performances? For lectures and seminars?
Comments _____ Y ☐ N ☐
4. Are hearing aids provided for the hearing impaired?
Comments _____ Y ☐ N ☐
5. Are audio cassettes or written material provided for special performances?
Comments _____ Y ☐ N ☐

Figure 12-4 Accessibility Survey Form for Commercial Applications (*Continued*)

6. Can a person rent a wheelchair?
   Comments _____ Y ☐   N ☐
7. Are the emergency alarm systems equipped to provide both audible and visual signals? A fire alarm? Are all exit signs illuminated? Are there directional signs showing emergency exits?
   Comments _____ Y ☐   N ☐
8. In places of assembly, are at least 1 percent of the seats adaptable to accommodate wheelchairs?
   Comments _____ Y ☐   N ☐
9. Are gift shops, dining rooms, and other places to eat, such as cafeterias, accessible to wheelchairs? Are there provisions to allow people in wheelchairs to use a food line?
   Comments _____ Y ☐   N ☐

Other comments on this facility:

_____

_____

_____

_____

_____

_____

_____Owner   _____Surveyor

Figure 12-4 Accessibility Survey Form for Commercial Applications (*Continued*)

ILLUSTRATIONS

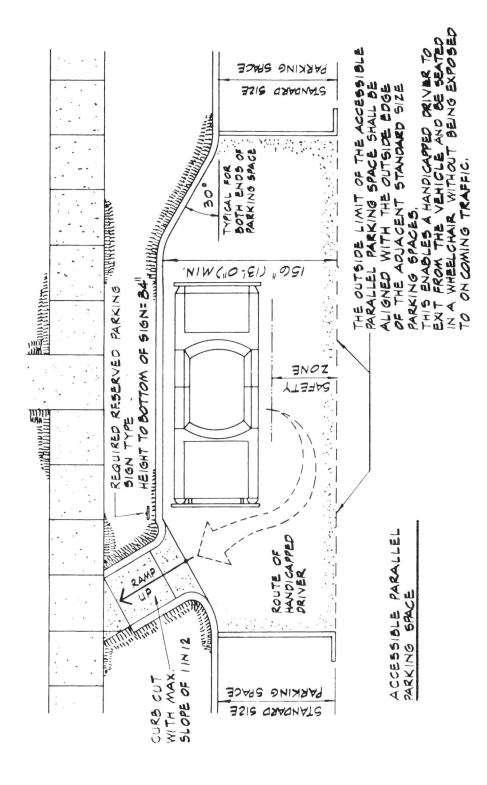

The outside limit of the accessible parallel parking space shall be aligned with the outside edge of the adjacent standard size parking spaces. This enables a handicapped driver to exit from the vehicle and be seated in a wheelchair without being exposed to oncoming traffic.

30°

TYPICAL FOR BOTH ENDS OF PARKING SPACE

STANDARD SIZE PARKING SPACE

156" (13'-0") MIN.

REQUIRED RESERVED PARKING SIGN TYPE HEIGHT TO BOTTOM OF SIGN= 84"

SAFETY ZONE

RAMP UP

CURB CUT WITH MAX. SLOPE OF 1 IN 12

ROUTE OF HANDICAPPED DRIVER

STANDARD SIZE PARKING SPACE

ACCESSIBLE PARALLEL PARKING SPACE

Figure 1-1 Parking Space requirements.

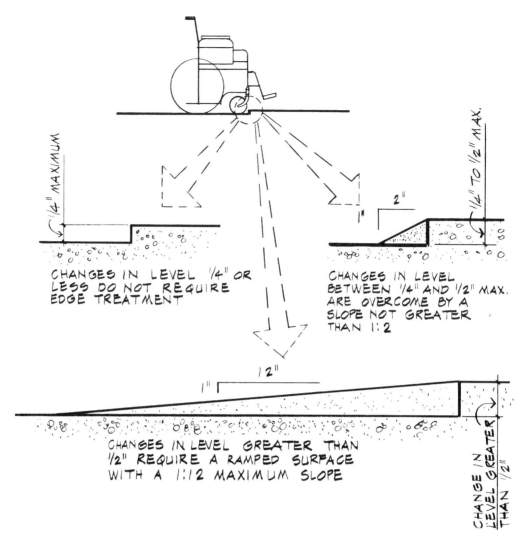

Figure 1-2 Changes in level.

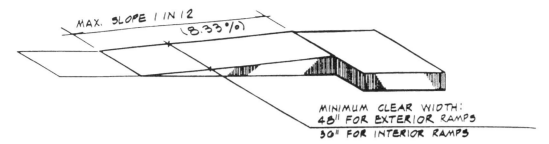

MAX. SLOPE 1 IN 12
(8.33%)

MINIMUM CLEAR WIDTH:
48" FOR EXTERIOR RAMPS
36" FOR INTERIOR RAMPS

——— MAXIMUM SLOPE OF A RAMP SHALL NOT EXCEED 1" VERTICAL RISE FOR EACH 12" HORIZONTAL RUN.

——— EXTERIOR RAMPS SHALL HAVE A MINIMUM CLEAR WIDTH OF 48 INCHES; INTERIOR RAMPS, AND RAMPS IN RENOVATIONS WHERE SPACE IS NOT AVAILABLE, SHALL HAVE A MINIMUM CLEAR WIDTH OF 36 INCHES.

RAMPS MAY HAVE A MAXIMUM CROSS SLOPE OF 1/4" PER FOOT.
RAMPS, REGARDLESS OF SLOPE, SHALL HAVE A MINIMUM LIVE LOAD OF 100 P.S.F.

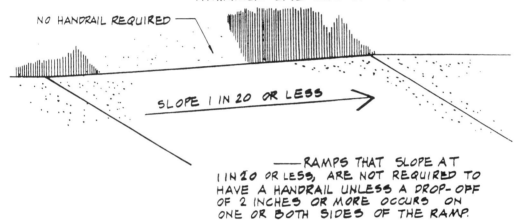

NO HANDRAIL REQUIRED

SLOPE 1 IN 20 OR LESS

——— RAMPS THAT SLOPE AT 1 IN 20 OR LESS, ARE NOT REQUIRED TO HAVE A HANDRAIL UNLESS A DROP-OFF OF 2 INCHES OR MORE OCCURS ON ONE OR BOTH SIDES OF THE RAMP.

Figure 1-3 Ramp designs.

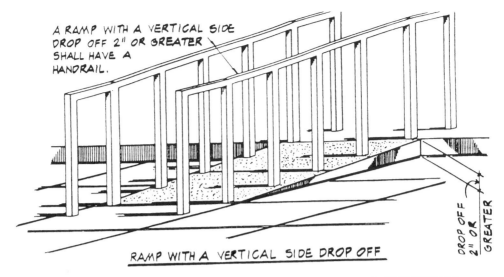

A RAMP WITH A VERTICAL SIDE DROP OFF 2" OR GREATER SHALL HAVE A HANDRAIL.

DROP OFF 2" OR GREATER

RAMP WITH A VERTICAL SIDE DROP OFF

A DROP OFF THAT HAS A VERTICAL CHANGE IN ELEVATION 2" OR GREATER, OR A SLOPE GREATER THAN 2 IN 12, SHALL REQUIRE A HANDRAIL.
THIS DOES NOT APPLY TO CURB RAMPS OR CURB CUTS LEADING TO ACCESSIBLE WALKS   OR ACCESSIBLE PARKING SPACES

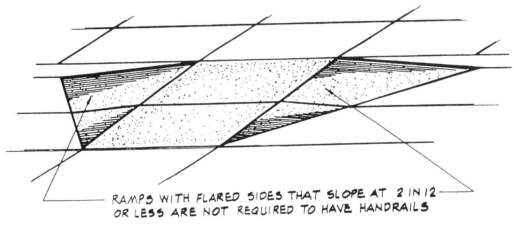

RAMPS WITH FLARED SIDES THAT SLOPE AT 2 IN 12 OR LESS ARE NOT REQUIRED TO HAVE HANDRAILS

Figure 1-4 Ramp designs.

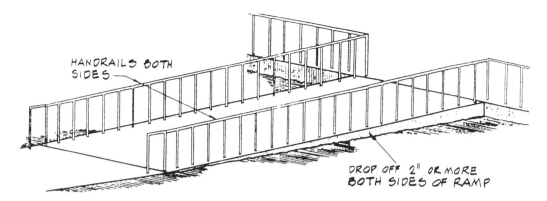

HANDRAILS BOTH SIDES

DROP OFF 2" OR MORE BOTH SIDES OF RAMP

———— WHEN A DROP-OFF OF 2" OR GREATER OCCURS ON BOTH SIDES OF A RAMP THAT SLOPES AT I IN 20 OR MORE, HANDRAILS ARE REQUIRED ON BOTH SIDES OF THE RAMP.

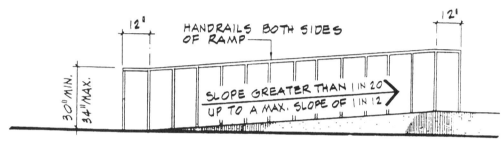

12"   HANDRAILS BOTH SIDES OF RAMP   12'

30" MIN. 34" MAX.

SLOPE GREATER THAN I IN 20 UP TO A MAX. SLOPE OF I IN 12

———— HANDRAILS ARE REQUIRED ON BOTH SIDES OF A RAMP WHEN THE SLOPE IS STEEPER THAN I IN 20.

———— RAMP HANDRAILS SHALL BE BETWEEN 30" TO 34" IN HEIGHT WITH 12" HORIZONTAL EXTENSIONS AT THE TOP AND BOTTOM LANDINGS.

Figure 1-5 Handrails and curb details.

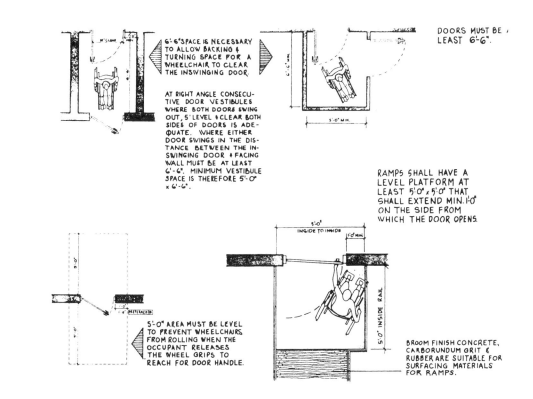

DOORS MUST BE AT LEAST 6'-6".

6'-6" SPACE IS NECESSARY TO ALLOW BACKING & TURNING SPACE FOR A WHEELCHAIR TO CLEAR THE INSWINGING DOOR.

AT RIGHT ANGLE CONSECUTIVE DOOR VESTIBULES WHERE BOTH DOORS SWING OUT, 5' LEVEL & CLEAR BOTH SIDES OF DOORS IS ADEQUATE. WHERE EITHER DOOR SWINGS IN THE DISTANCE BETWEEN THE INSWINGING DOOR & FACING WALL MUST BE AT LEAST 6'-6". MINIMUM VESTIBULE SPACE IS THEREFORE 5'-0" x 6'-6".

RAMPS SHALL HAVE A LEVEL PLATFORM AT LEAST 5'-0" x 5'-0" THAT SHALL EXTEND MIN. 1'-0" ON THE SIDE FROM WHICH THE DOOR OPENS.

5'-0" AREA MUST BE LEVEL TO PREVENT WHEELCHAIRS FROM ROLLING WHEN THE OCCUPANT RELEASES THE WHEEL GRIPS TO REACH FOR DOOR HANDLE.

BROOM FINISH CONCRETE, CARBORUNDUM GRIT & RUBBER ARE SUITABLE FOR SURFACING MATERIALS FOR RAMPS.

AN ENTRANCE TO BE USABLE BY THE PHYSICALLY HANDICAPPED MUST BE APPROACHED BY A CONTINUOUS COMMON SURFACE

[*PREFERRED] DOOR MATS & GRATES SHOULD NOT BE BARRIERS

THICK BRISTLY DOOR MATS OF HEMP OR PLASTIC BUNCH UP UNDER SMALL WHEELS OF CHAIRS PRESENTING A FORMIDABLE BARRIER. OFTEN MATS ARE THICKER THAN THE ½" MAXIMUM ALLOWABLE VERTICAL LEVEL CHANGE.

THICK DOOR MATS (GREATER THAN ½") SHOULD BE RECESSED INTO THE SURFACE AT LEAST ½ THEIR THICKNESS OR THIN MATS OF WOVEN RUBBER SHOULD BE USED.

GRATES AT DOORS FOR SNOW AND SAND TRAPS SHOULD BE AVOIDED UNLESS THE MAXIMUM GRID OPENING IS NO MORE THAN 3/8" x 3/8". LARGER OPENINGS ARE HAZARDOUS TO THOSE WITH CRUTCHES AND CANES AND MAKE WHEELCHAIR TRAVEL EXTREMELY DIFFICULT.

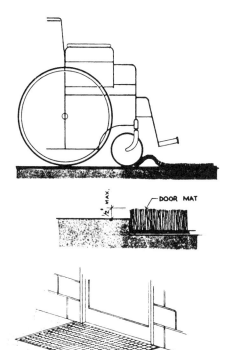

DOOR MAT

32" CLEAR

AN ADULT WHEELCHAIR AVERAGES 27" WIDE REQUIRED 32" CLEAR DOOR WIDTH ALLOWS CLEARANCE ON EACH SIDE FOR HANDS.

Figure 1-6 Road-to-sidewalk helpers.

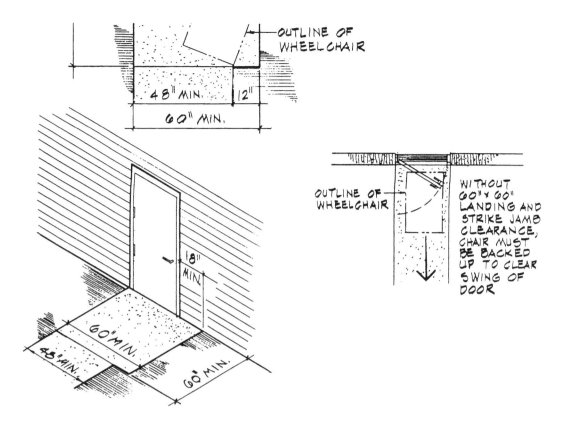

- WALKS TERMINATING AT DOORS SHALL HAVE A 60"x 60" LEVEL PLATFORM THAT EXTENDS A MINIMUM OF 18" BEYOND THE STRIKE JAMB ON THE PULL SIDE OF THE DOOR.

Figure 2-1 Site development walks and landings.

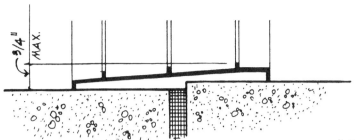

— MAXIMUM EXTERIOR THRESHOLD HEIGHT FOR SLIDING GLASS DOORS IS 3/4 INCH.

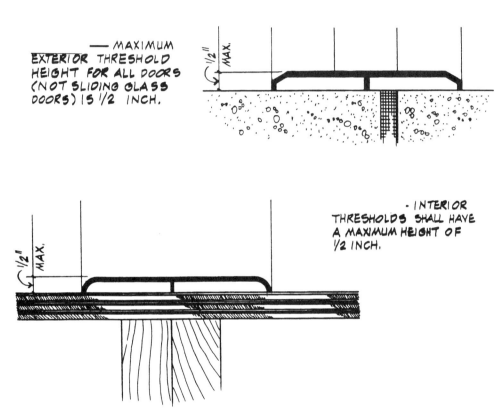

— MAXIMUM EXTERIOR THRESHOLD HEIGHT FOR ALL DOORS (NOT SLIDING GLASS DOORS) IS 1/2 INCH.

- INTERIOR THRESHOLDS SHALL HAVE A MAXIMUM HEIGHT OF 1/2 INCH.

Figure 2-2 Thresholds.

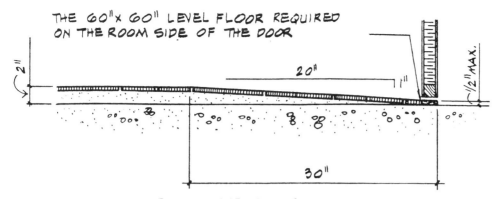

THE 60" x 60" LEVEL FLOOR REQUIRED
ON THE ROOM SIDE OF THE DOOR

20"

30"

2"

1"

1/2" MAX.

─── INTERIOR THRESHOLDS

CERAMIC TILE FLOORS IN SETTING BEDS MAY USE
A WARPED FLOOR IN PLACE OF A THRESHOLD.
THE MAXIMUM SLOPE OF THESE WARPED FLOORS
SHALL BE 5%.

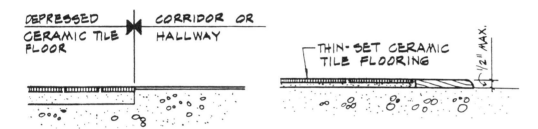

DEPRESSED
CERAMIC TILE
FLOOR

CORRIDOR OR
HALLWAY

THIN-SET CERAMIC
TILE FLOORING

1/2" MAX.

Figure 2-3 Interior thresholds.

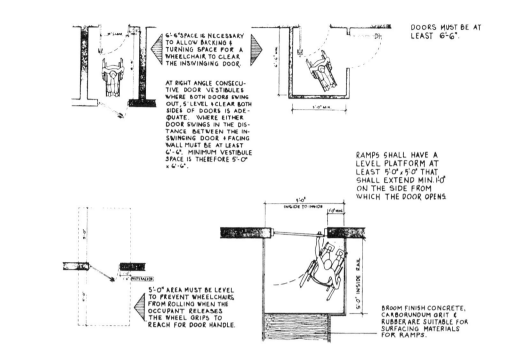

6'-6" SPACE IS NECESSARY TO ALLOW BACKING & TURNING SPACE FOR A WHEELCHAIR TO CLEAR THE INSWINGING DOOR.

AT RIGHT ANGLE CONSECUTIVE DOOR VESTIBULES WHERE BOTH DOORS SWING OUT, 5' LEVEL & CLEAR BOTH SIDES OF DOORS IS ADEQUATE. WHERE EITHER DOOR SWINGS IN THE DISTANCE BETWEEN THE INSWINGING DOOR & FACING WALL MUST BE AT LEAST 6'-6". MINIMUM VESTIBULE SPACE IS THEREFORE 5'-0" x 6'-6".

DOORS MUST BE AT LEAST 6'-6".

RAMPS SHALL HAVE A LEVEL PLATFORM AT LEAST 5'-0" x 5'-0" THAT SHALL EXTEND MIN. 1'-0" ON THE SIDE FROM WHICH THE DOOR OPENS.

5'-0" AREA MUST BE LEVEL TO PREVENT WHEELCHAIRS FROM ROLLING WHEN THE OCCUPANT RELEASES THE WHEEL GRIPS TO REACH FOR DOOR HANDLE.

BROOM FINISH CONCRETE, CARBORUNDUM GRIT & RUBBER ARE SUITABLE FOR SURFACING MATERIALS FOR RAMPS.

AN ENTRANCE TO BE USABLE BY THE PHYSICALLY HANDICAPPED MUST BE APPROACHED BY A CONTINUOUS COMMON SURFACE

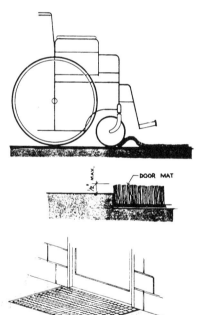

[*PREFERRED] DOOR MATS & GRATES SHOULD NOT BE BARRIERS

THICK BRISTLY DOOR MATS OF HEMP OR PLASTIC BUNCH UP UNDER SMALL WHEELS OF CHAIRS PRESENTING A FORMIDABLE BARRIER. OFTEN MATS ARE THICKER THAN THE 1/2" MAXIMUM ALLOWABLE VERTICAL LEVEL CHANGE.

THICK DOOR MATS (GREATER THAN 1/2") SHOULD BE RECESSED INTO THE SURFACE AT LEAST 1/2 THEIR THICKNESS OR THIN MATS OF WOVEN RUBBER SHOULD BE USED.

GRATES AT DOORS FOR SNOW AND SAND TRAPS SHOULD BE AVOIDED UNLESS THE MAXIMUM GRID OPENING IS NO MORE THAN 3/8" x 3/8". LARGER OPENINGS ARE HAZARDOUS TO THOSE WITH CRUTCHES AND CANES AND MAKE WHEELCHAIR TRAVEL EXTREMELY DIFFICULT.

AN ADULT WHEELCHAIR AVERAGES 27" WIDE. THE REQUIRED 32" CLEAR DOOR WIDTH ALLOWS 2 1/2" CLEARANCE ON EACH SIDE FOR HANDS.

Figure 2-4 Doors and doorways.

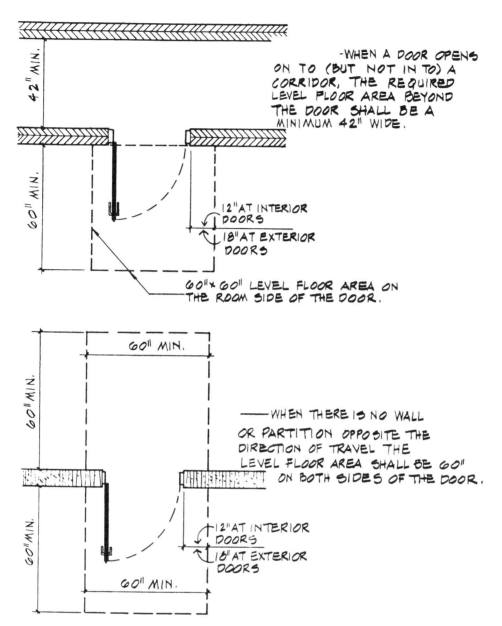

-WHEN A DOOR OPENS ON TO (BUT NOT IN TO) A CORRIDOR, THE REQUIRED LEVEL FLOOR AREA BEYOND THE DOOR SHALL BE A MINIMUM 42" WIDE.

42" MIN.

60" MIN.

12" AT INTERIOR DOORS

18" AT EXTERIOR DOORS

60" x 60" LEVEL FLOOR AREA ON THE ROOM SIDE OF THE DOOR.

60" MIN.

60" MIN.

60" MIN.

—WHEN THERE IS NO WALL OR PARTITION OPPOSITE THE DIRECTION OF TRAVEL THE LEVEL FLOOR AREA SHALL BE 60" ON BOTH SIDES OF THE DOOR.

12" AT INTERIOR DOORS

18" AT EXTERIOR DOORS

60" MIN.

Figure 2-5 Door and doorway design.

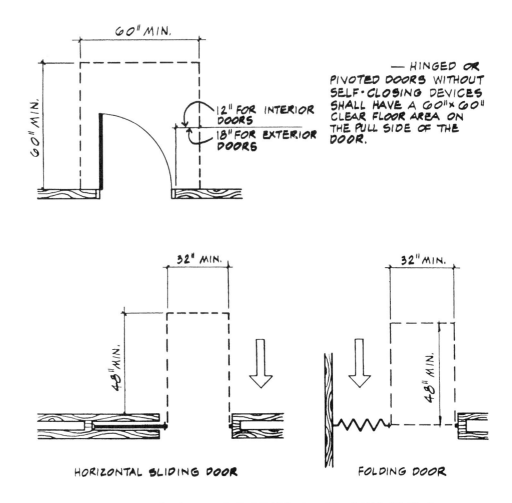

— HINGED OR PIVOTED DOORS WITHOUT SELF-CLOSING DEVICES SHALL HAVE A 60" x 60" CLEAR FLOOR AREA ON THE PULL SIDE OF THE DOOR.

60" MIN.

60" MIN.

12" FOR INTERIOR DOORS

18" FOR EXTERIOR DOORS

32" MIN.

48" MIN.

HORIZONTAL SLIDING DOOR

32" MIN.

48" MIN.

FOLDING DOOR

— SLIDING OR FOLDING DOORS SHALL HAVE A MINIMUM 32"W x 48"L CLEAR FLOOR AREA ON THE APPROACH SIDE OF THE DOOR. (THAT IS, BOTH SIDES OF THE DOOR, IF APPLICABLE)

Figure 2-6 Door and entrance design.

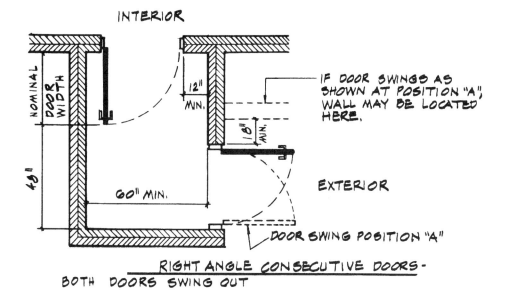

INTERIOR

NOMINAL DOOR WIDTH

48"

60" MIN.

12" MIN.

18" MIN.

IF DOOR SWINGS AS SHOWN AT POSITION "A", WALL MAY BE LOCATED HERE.

EXTERIOR

DOOR SWING POSITION "A"

RIGHT ANGLE CONSECUTIVE DOORS-
BOTH DOORS SWING OUT

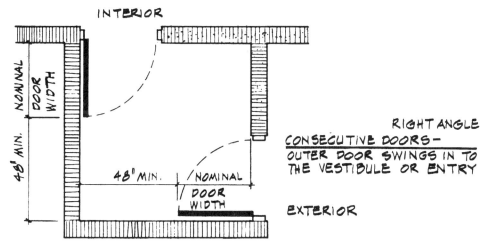

INTERIOR

NOMINAL DOOR WIDTH

48' MIN.

48" MIN.

NOMINAL DOOR WIDTH

RIGHT ANGLE CONSECUTIVE DOORS—
OUTER DOOR SWINGS IN TO THE VESTIBULE OR ENTRY

EXTERIOR

Figure 2-7 Consecutive doorways: outer door swings *in* to the vestibule or entry; right angle consecutive door swings *out*.

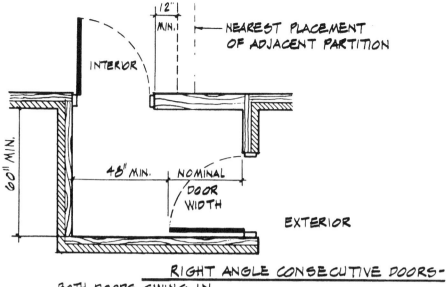

NEAREST PLACEMENT
OF ADJACENT PARTITION

INTERIOR

12" MIN.

60" MIN.

48" MIN.

NOMINAL DOOR WIDTH

EXTERIOR

RIGHT ANGLE CONSECUTIVE DOORS-
BOTH DOORS SWING IN

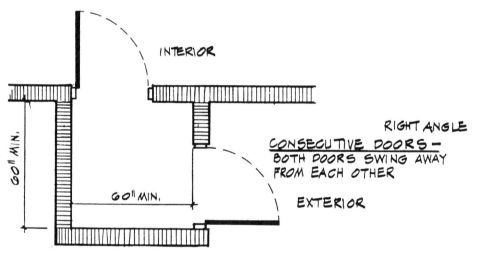

INTERIOR

60" MIN.

60" MIN.

RIGHT ANGLE
CONSECUTIVE DOORS -
BOTH DOORS SWING AWAY
FROM EACH OTHER

EXTERIOR

Figure 2-8 Consecutive doorways: both consecutive doors swing *away* from each other; right angle consecutive doors swing *in*.

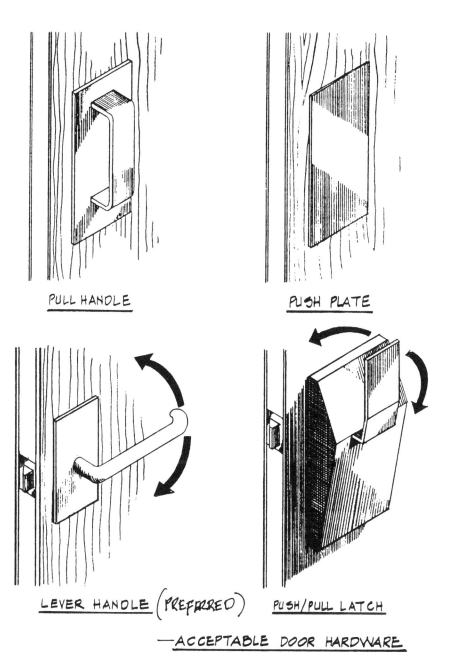

PULL HANDLE

PUSH PLATE

LEVER HANDLE (PREFERRED)

PUSH/PULL LATCH

—ACCEPTABLE DOOR HARDWARE

Figure 2-9 Acceptable door hardware.

—ACCEPTABLE DOOR HARDWARE

TOGGLE

KNURLED OR ROUGHENED
(EITHER PARTIALLY OR
TOTALLY COVERED)

CARBORUNDUM-EPOXY
COATING
(EITHER PARTIALLY OR
TOTALLY COATED)

—DOORS TO HAZARDOUS AREAS

Figure 2-10 Door hardware for hazardous areas.

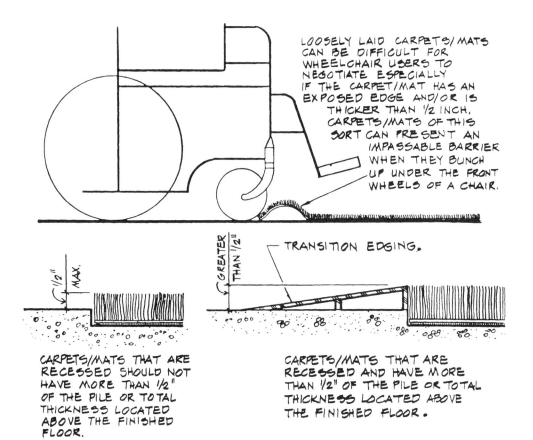

LOOSELY LAID CARPETS/MATS
CAN BE DIFFICULT FOR
WHEELCHAIR USERS TO
NEGOTIATE ESPECIALLY
IF THE CARPET/MAT HAS AN
EXPOSED EDGE AND/OR IS
THICKER THAN 1/2 INCH.
CARPETS/MATS OF THIS
SORT CAN PRESENT AN
IMPASSABLE BARRIER
WHEN THEY BUNCH
UP UNDER THE FRONT
WHEELS OF A CHAIR.

1/2" MAX.

GREATER THAN 1/2"

TRANSITION EDGING.

CARPETS/MATS THAT ARE
RECESSED SHOULD NOT
HAVE MORE THAN 1/2"
OF THE PILE OR TOTAL
THICKNESS LOCATED
ABOVE THE FINISHED
FLOOR.

CARPETS/MATS THAT ARE
RECESSED AND HAVE MORE
THAN 1/2" OF THE PILE OR TOTAL
THICKNESS LOCATED ABOVE
THE FINISHED FLOOR.

Figure 3-1 Carpet problems.

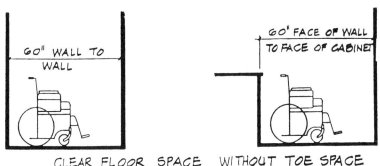

CLEAR FLOOR SPACE WITHOUT TOE SPACE

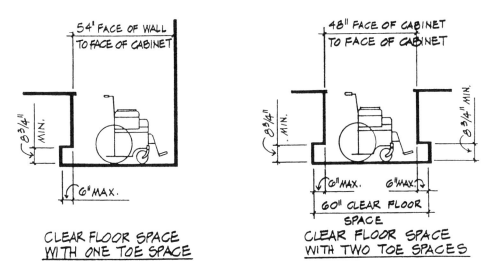

CLEAR FLOOR SPACE
WITH ONE TOE SPACE

CLEAR FLOOR SPACE
WITH TWO TOE SPACES

——THE MINIMUM 60" x 60" CLEAR FLOOR SPACE
MAY BE PARTIALLY REPLACED BY A 6" DEEP (MAX.) BY 8¾" HIGH (MIN.)
TOE SPACE ON ONE OR BOTH SIDES OF THE CLEAR FLOOR AREA.

Figure 4-1 Floor space in the kitchen.

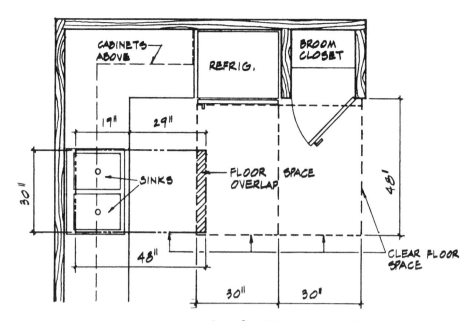

———A 30" × 48" CLEAR FLOOR SPACE
SHALL BE PROVIDED AT ALL APPLIANCES, FIXTURES
AND STORAGE SHELVES. FLOOR AREAS FOR ADJACENT
ELEMENTS MAY OVERLAP.

NOTE: THE 60" × 60" CLEAR FLOOR AREA AND THE
30" × 48" CLEAR FLOOR SPACE ARE NOT SEPARATE
AREAS WITHIN THE KITCHEN.
THE 30" × 48" PARKING SPACE IS CONTAINED
WITHIN THE 60" × 60" MANEUVERING AREA.

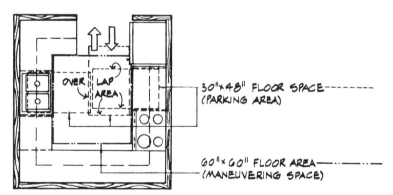

Figure 4-2 Arrangement of clear spaces.

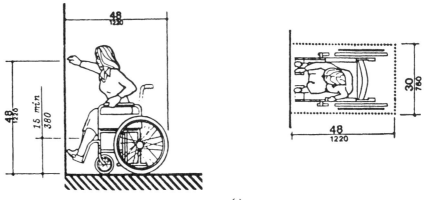

(a)
High Forward Reach Limit

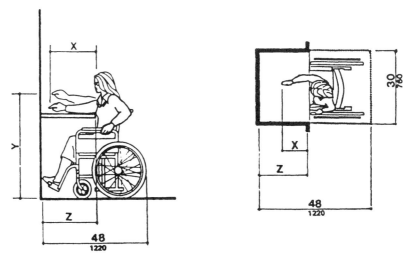

NOTE: x shall be <25 in (635 mm); z shall be >x. When x < 20 in (510 mm), then y shall be 48 in (1220 mm) maximum. When x is 20 to 25 in (510 to 635 mm), then y shall be 44 in (1120 mm) maximum.

(b)
Maximum Forward Reach over an Obstruction

Figure 4-3 Reach criteria, federal standards.

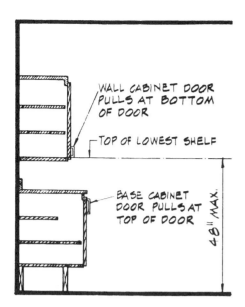

WALL CABINET DOOR PULLS AT BOTTOM OF DOOR

TOP OF LOWEST SHELF

BASE CABINET DOOR PULLS AT TOP OF DOOR

48" MAX.

—— THE BOTTOM SHELF OF ALL WALL CABINETS SHALL BE AT 48" MAX. ABOVE THE FINISHED FLOOR. (SEE ILLUSTRATION BELOW FOR ALLOWABLE EXCEPTION.)

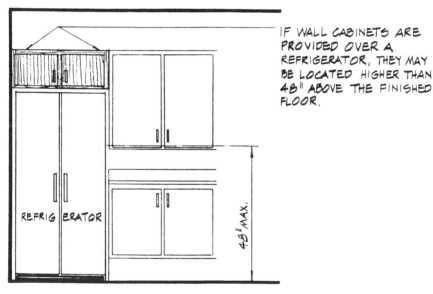

REFRIGERATOR

48" MAX.

IF WALL CABINETS ARE PROVIDED OVER A REFRIGERATOR, THEY MAY BE LOCATED HIGHER THAN 48" ABOVE THE FINISHED FLOOR.

Figure 4-4 Cabinet design for accessible shelving.

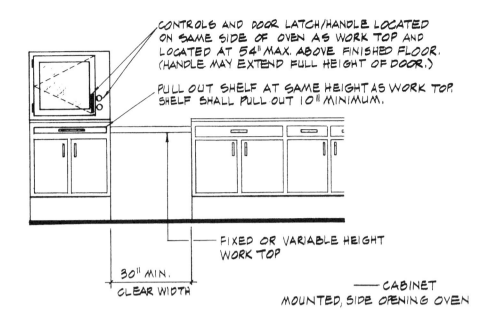

CONTROLS AND DOOR LATCH/HANDLE LOCATED ON SAME SIDE OF OVEN AS WORK TOP AND LOCATED AT 54" MAX. ABOVE FINISHED FLOOR. (HANDLE MAY EXTEND FULL HEIGHT OF DOOR.)

PULL OUT SHELF AT SAME HEIGHT AS WORK TOP. SHELF SHALL PULL OUT 10" MINIMUM.

FIXED OR VARIABLE HEIGHT WORK TOP

30" MIN. CLEAR WIDTH

CABINET MOUNTED, SIDE OPENING OVEN

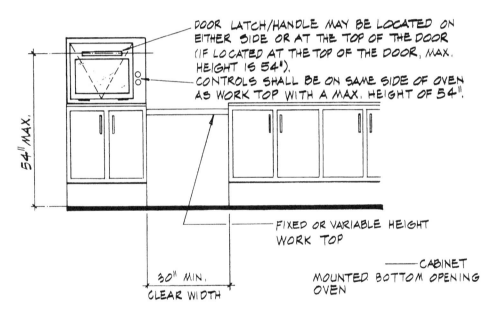

DOOR LATCH/HANDLE MAY BE LOCATED ON EITHER SIDE OR AT THE TOP OF THE DOOR (IF LOCATED AT THE TOP OF THE DOOR, MAX. HEIGHT IS 54").

CONTROLS SHALL BE ON SAME SIDE OF OVEN AS WORK TOP WITH A MAX. HEIGHT OF 54".

54" MAX.

FIXED OR VARIABLE HEIGHT WORK TOP

30" MIN. CLEAR WIDTH

CABINET MOUNTED, BOTTOM OPENING OVEN

Figure 4-5 Cabinet design: improved accessibility to controls and in work area.

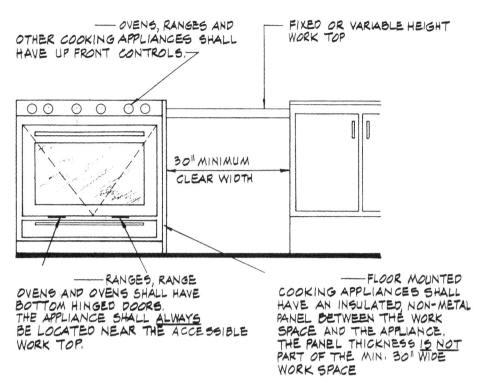

OVENS, RANGES AND OTHER COOKING APPLIANCES SHALL HAVE UP FRONT CONTROLS.

FIXED OR VARIABLE HEIGHT WORK TOP

30" MINIMUM CLEAR WIDTH

RANGES, RANGE OVENS AND OVENS SHALL HAVE BOTTOM HINGED DOORS. THE APPLIANCE SHALL ALWAYS BE LOCATED NEAR THE ACCESSIBLE WORK TOP.

FLOOR MOUNTED COOKING APPLIANCES SHALL HAVE AN INSULATED, NON-METAL PANEL BETWEEN THE WORK SPACE AND THE APPLIANCE. THE PANEL THICKNESS IS NOT PART OF THE MIN. 30" WIDE WORK SPACE

Figure 4-6 Ranges and space requirements.

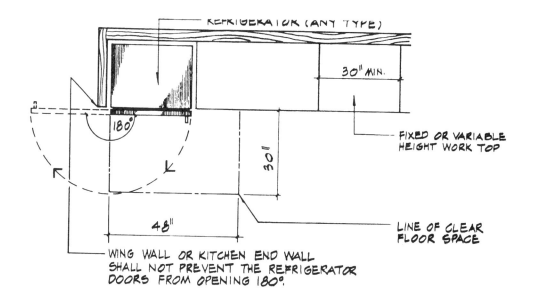

REFRIGERATOR (ANY TYPE)

180°

30" MIN.

30"

48"

FIXED OR VARIABLE HEIGHT WORK TOP

LINE OF CLEAR FLOOR SPACE

WING WALL OR KITCHEN END WALL SHALL NOT PREVENT THE REFRIGERATOR DOORS FROM OPENING 180°.

-REFRIGERATORS SHALL BE LOCATED WITHIN THE KITCHEN SO THAT THE DOOR (OR DOORS) CAN OPEN 180° WITHOUT OBSTRUCTION.

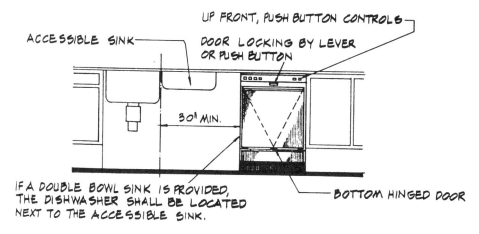

ACCESSIBLE SINK

UP FRONT, PUSH BUTTON CONTROLS

DOOR LOCKING BY LEVER OR PUSH BUTTON

30" MIN.

IF A DOUBLE BOWL SINK IS PROVIDED, THE DISHWASHER SHALL BE LOCATED NEXT TO THE ACCESSIBLE SINK.

BOTTOM HINGED DOOR

AUTOMATIC DISHWASHERS TRASH COMPACTORS

Figure 4-7 Appliance space requirements.

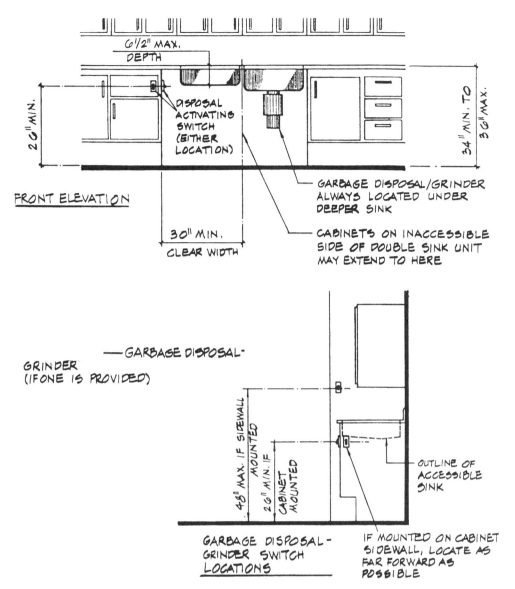

Figure 4-8 Sinks and garbage disposal installations.

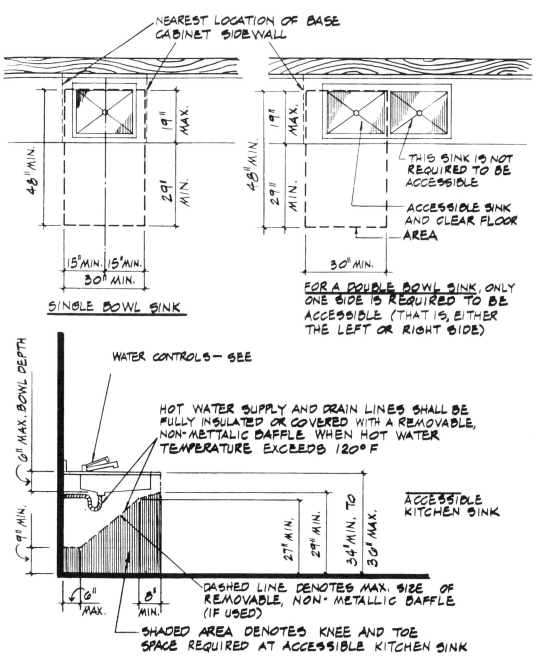

NEAREST LOCATION OF BASE CABINET SIDEWALL

19" MAX.

48" MIN.

29" MIN.

15" MIN. | 15" MIN.

30" MIN.

SINGLE BOWL SINK

48" MIN.

19" MAX.

29" MIN.

THIS SINK IS NOT REQUIRED TO BE ACCESSIBLE

ACCESSIBLE SINK AND CLEAR FLOOR AREA

30" MIN.

FOR A DOUBLE BOWL SINK, ONLY ONE SIDE IS REQUIRED TO BE ACCESSIBLE (THAT IS, EITHER THE LEFT OR RIGHT SIDE)

6" MAX. BOWL DEPTH

WATER CONTROLS – SEE

HOT WATER SUPPLY AND DRAIN LINES SHALL BE FULLY INSULATED OR COVERED WITH A REMOVABLE, NON-METTALIC BAFFLE WHEN HOT WATER TEMPERATURE EXCEEDS 120° F

9" MIN.

27" MIN.

29" MIN.

34" MIN. TO 36" MAX.

ACCESSIBLE KITCHEN SINK

6" MAX.

8" MIN.

DASHED LINE DENOTES MAX. SIZE OF REMOVABLE, NON-METALLIC BAFFLE (IF USED)

SHADED AREA DENOTES KNEE AND TOE SPACE REQUIRED AT ACCESSIBLE KITCHEN SINK

Figure 4-9 Sink installations.

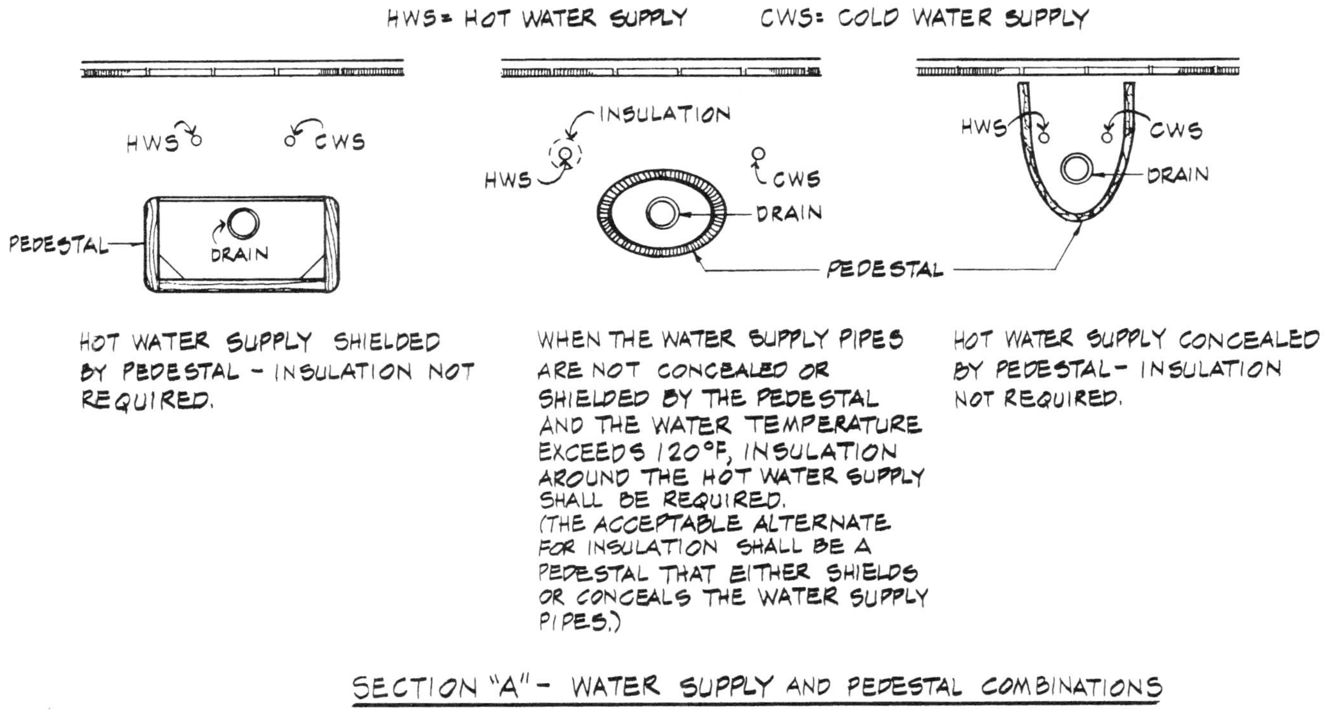
HWS= HOT WATER SUPPLY
CWS: COLD WATER SUPPLY
HWS
CWS
PEDESTAL
DRAIN
HOT WATER SUPPLY SHIELDED BY PEDESTAL - INSULATION NOT REQUIRED.
INSULATION
HWS
CWS
DRAIN
PEDESTAL
WHEN THE WATER SUPPLY PIPES ARE NOT CONCEALED OR SHIELDED BY THE PEDESTAL AND THE WATER TEMPERATURE EXCEEDS 120°F, INSULATION AROUND THE HOT WATER SUPPLY SHALL BE REQUIRED.
(THE ACCEPTABLE ALTERNATE FOR INSULATION SHALL BE A PEDESTAL THAT EITHER SHIELDS OR CONCEALS THE WATER SUPPLY PIPES.)
HWS
CWS
DRAIN
HOT WATER SUPPLY CONCEALED BY PEDESTAL - INSULATION NOT REQUIRED.
SECTION "A" - WATER SUPPLY AND PEDESTAL COMBINATIONS

Figure 4-10 Sink installations.

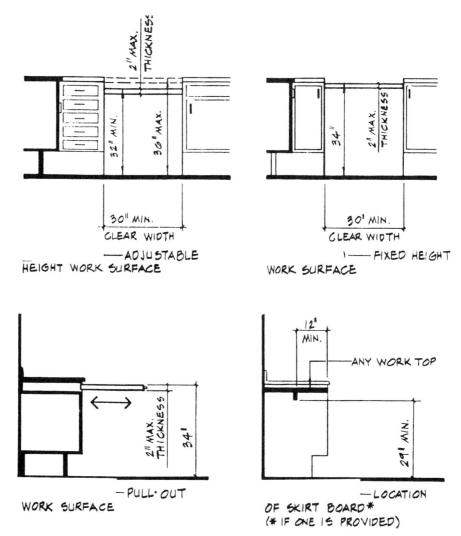

Figure 4-11 Work-space requirements in the kitchen.

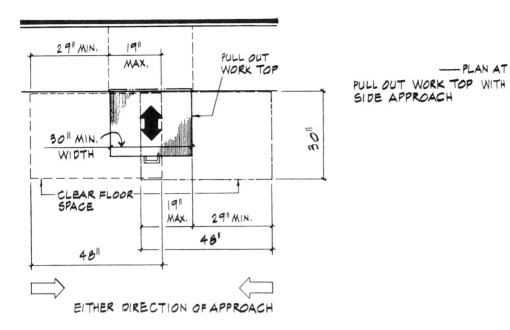

29" MIN. | 19" MAX.

PULL OUT WORK TOP

——PLAN AT
PULL OUT WORK TOP WITH
SIDE APPROACH

30" MIN. WIDTH

30"

CLEAR FLOOR SPACE

19" MAX. | 29" MIN.

48'

48"

EITHER DIRECTION OF APPROACH

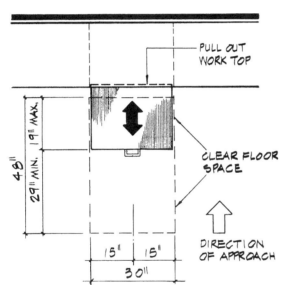

PULL OUT WORK TOP

——PLAN AT
PULL OUT WORK TOP WITH
FRONT APPROACH

48" | 19" MAX. | 29" MIN.

CLEAR FLOOR SPACE

DIRECTION OF APPROACH

15" | 15"

30"

Figure 4-12 Kitchen workspaces.

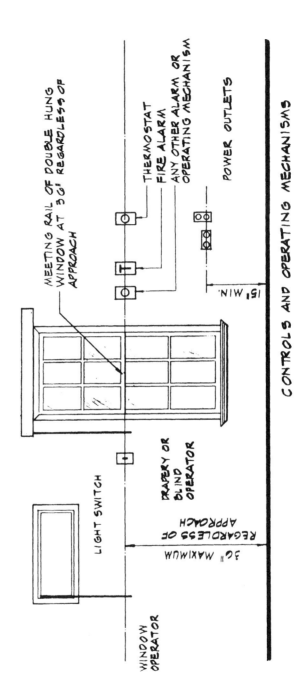

Figure 4-13 Height requirements for controls and operating mechanisms.

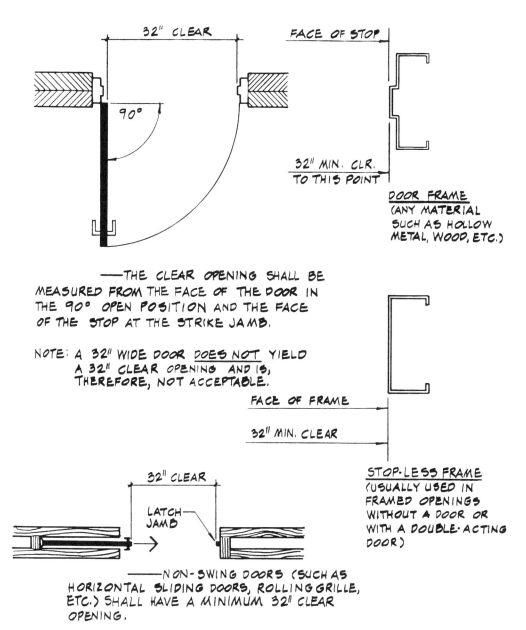

32" CLEAR

FACE OF STOP

90°

32" MIN. CLR.
TO THIS POINT

DOOR FRAME
(ANY MATERIAL
SUCH AS HOLLOW
METAL, WOOD, ETC.)

———THE CLEAR OPENING SHALL BE
MEASURED FROM THE FACE OF THE DOOR IN
THE 90° OPEN POSITION AND THE FACE
OF THE STOP AT THE STRIKE JAMB.

NOTE: A 32" WIDE DOOR DOES NOT YIELD
A 32" CLEAR OPENING AND IS,
THEREFORE, NOT ACCEPTABLE.

FACE OF FRAME

32" MIN. CLEAR

STOP-LESS FRAME
(USUALLY USED IN
FRAMED OPENINGS
WITHOUT A DOOR OR
WITH A DOUBLE-ACTING
DOOR)

32" CLEAR

LATCH
JAMB

———NON-SWING DOORS (SUCH AS
HORIZONTAL SLIDING DOORS, ROLLING GRILLE,
ETC.) SHALL HAVE A MINIMUM 32" CLEAR
OPENING.

Figure 6-1 Bathroom doors.

Technical Provisions

4.2: SPACE ALLOWANCE AND REACH RANGES

4.2.1* WHEELCHAIR PASSAGE WIDTH. The minimum clear width for single wheelchair passage shall be 32 in (815 mm) at a point and 36 in (915 mm) continuously (see Fig. 1 and 24(e).

4.2.2 WIDTH FOR WHEELCHAIR PASSING. The minimum width for two wheelchairs to pass is 60 in (1525 mm) (see Fig. 2).

4.2.3* WHEELCHAIR TURNING SPACE. The space required for a wheelchair to make a 180 degree turn is a clear space of 60 in (1525 mm) diameter (see Fig. 3(a)) or a T-shaped space (see Fig. 3(b)).

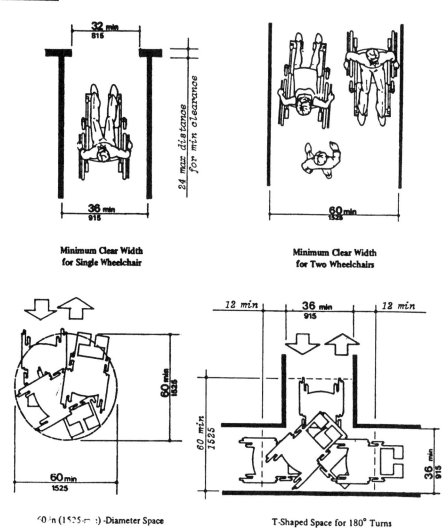

Minimum Clear Width
for Single Wheelchair

Minimum Clear Width
for Two Wheelchairs

60 in (1525 mm) -Diameter Space

T-Shaped Space for 180° Turns

Figure 6-2 Space allowances and reach ranges.

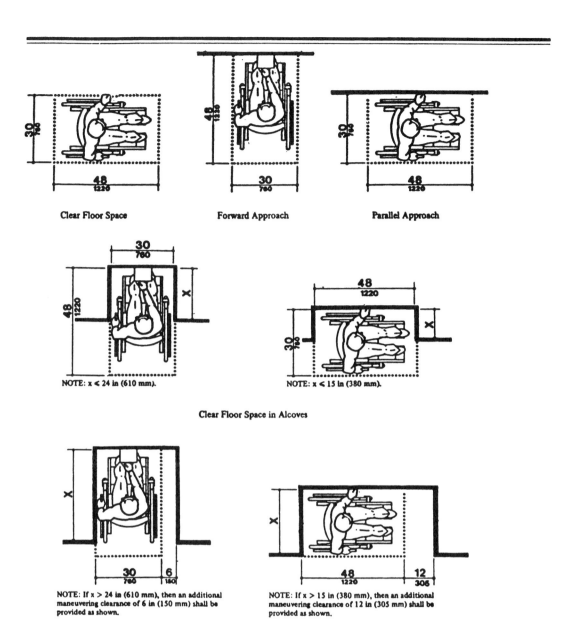

Clear Floor Space   Forward Approach   Parallel Approach

NOTE: x ≤ 24 in (610 mm).

NOTE: x ≤ 15 in (380 mm).

Clear Floor Space in Alcoves

NOTE: If x > 24 in (610 mm), then an additional maneuvering clearance of 6 in (150 mm) shall be provided as shown.

NOTE: If x > 15 in (380 mm), then an additional maneuvering clearance of 12 in (305 mm) shall be provided as shown.

Additional Maneuvering Clearances for Alcoves

Figure 6-3 Space allowances.

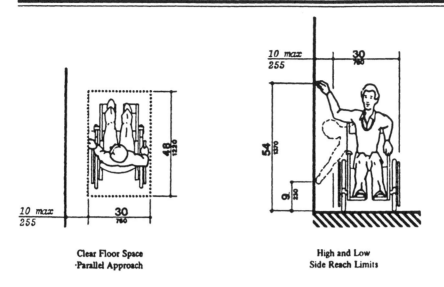

Clear Floor Space
·Parallel Approach

High and Low
Side Reach Limits

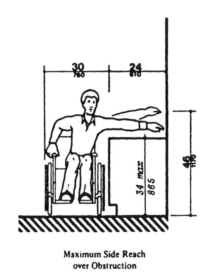

Maximum Side Reach
over Obstruction

Figure 6-4 Reach ranges.

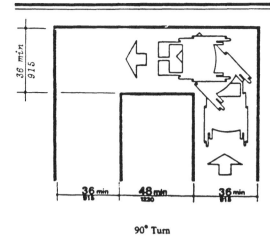

90° Turn

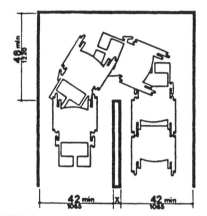

NOTE: Dimensions shown apply when x < 48 in (1220 mm).

Turns around an Obstruction

Figure 6-5 Accessible routes.

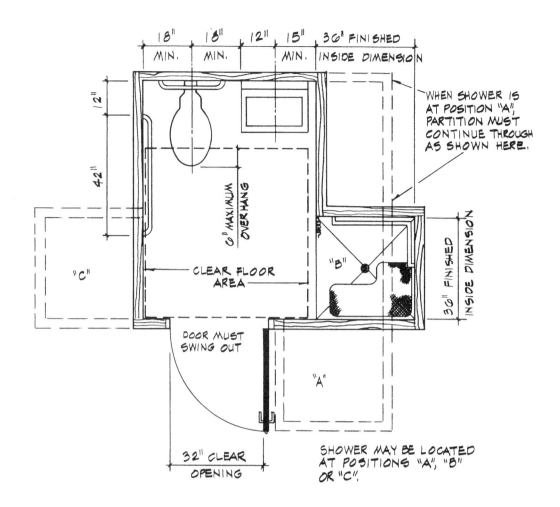

SMALL TOILET ROOM AND SHOWER
WITH 60" x 60" CLEAR FLOOR AREA

Figure 6-6 Plan for small bathroom and shower.

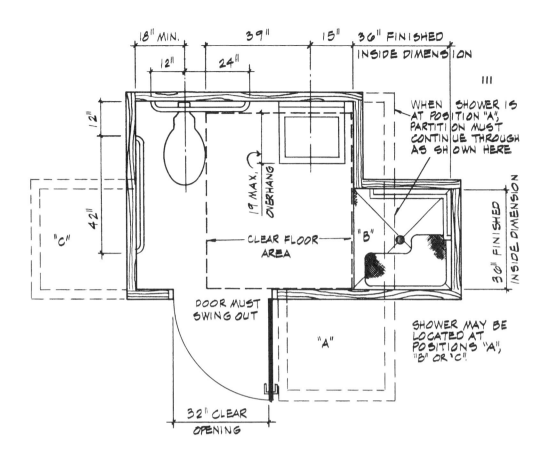

18" MIN.

39"

15"

36" FINISHED
INSIDE DIMENSION

12"

24"

III

12"

WHEN SHOWER IS
AT POSITION "A",
PARTITION MUST
CONTINUE THROUGH
AS SHOWN HERE

42"

19 MAX. OVERHANG

30" FINISHED INSIDE DIMENSION

"C"

CLEAR FLOOR
AREA

"B"

DOOR MUST
SWING OUT

"A"

SHOWER MAY BE
LOCATED AT
POSITIONS "A",
"B" OR "C".

32" CLEAR
OPENING

SMALL TOILET ROOM AND SHOWER
WITH A 54" WIDE × 63" LONG CLEAR FLOOR AREA

Figure 6-7 Plan for small bathroom and shower.

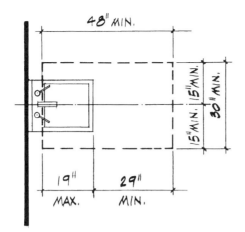

ACCESSIBLE LAVATORIES SHALL HAVE A MINIMUM CLEAR FLOOR SPACE OF 30"x 48". THE CLEAR FLOOR SPACE SHALL EXTEND A MAXIMUM 19" UNDER THE LAVATORY.

CLEAR FLOOR SPACE

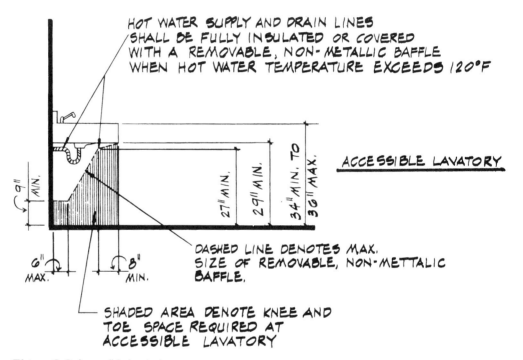

HOT WATER SUPPLY AND DRAIN LINES SHALL BE FULLY INSULATED OR COVERED WITH A REMOVABLE, NON-METALLIC BAFFLE WHEN HOT WATER TEMPERATURE EXCEEDS 120°F

ACCESSIBLE LAVATORY

DASHED LINE DENOTES MAX. SIZE OF REMOVABLE, NON-METTALIC BAFFLE.

SHADED AREA DENOTE KNEE AND TOE SPACE REQUIRED AT ACCESSIBLE LAVATORY

Figure 6-8 Accessible lavatories.

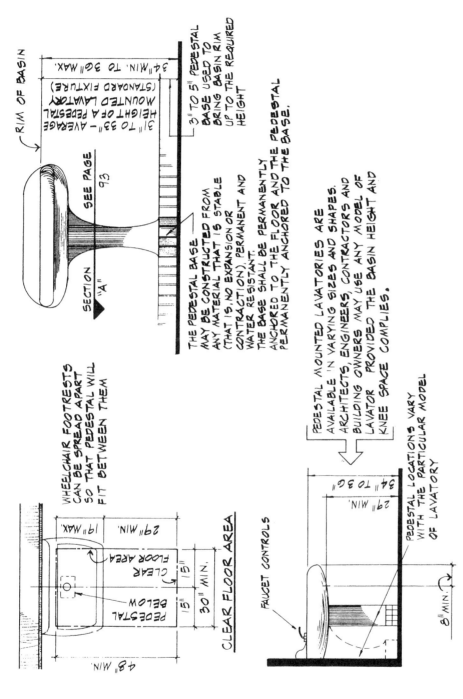

Figure 6-9 Pedestal lavatories.

RIM OF BASIN

34" MIN. TO 36" MAX.

HEIGHT OF A PEDESTAL MOUNTED LAVATORY (STANDARD FIXTURE)

31" TO 33"—AVERAGE

SECTION "A"

SEE PAGE 93

3" TO 5" PEDESTAL BASE USED TO BRING BASIN RIM UP TO THE REQUIRED HEIGHT

THE PEDESTAL BASE MAY BE CONSTRUCTED FROM ANY MATERIAL THAT IS STABLE (THAT IS, NO EXPANSION OR CONTRACTION), PERMANENT AND WATER RESISTANT. THE BASE SHALL BE PERMANENTLY ANCHORED TO THE FLOOR AND THE PEDESTAL PERMANENTLY ANCHORED TO THE BASE.

WHEELCHAIR FOOTRESTS CAN BE SPREAD APART SO THAT PEDESTAL WILL FIT BETWEEN THEM

19" MAX.

29" MIN.

CLEAR FLOOR AREA

15" MIN.

15"

30" MIN.

PEDESTAL BELOW

48" MIN.

CLEAR FLOOR AREA

PEDESTAL MOUNTED LAVATORIES ARE AVAILABLE IN VARYING SIZES AND SHAPES. ARCHITECTS, ENGINEERS, CONTRACTORS AND BUILDING OWNERS MAY USE ANY MODEL OF LAVATOR PROVIDED THE BASIN HEIGHT AND KNEE SPACE COMPLIES.

FAUCET CONTROLS

34" TO 36"

29" MIN.

PEDESTAL LOCATIONS VARY WITH THE PARTICULAR MODEL OF LAVATORY

8" MIN.

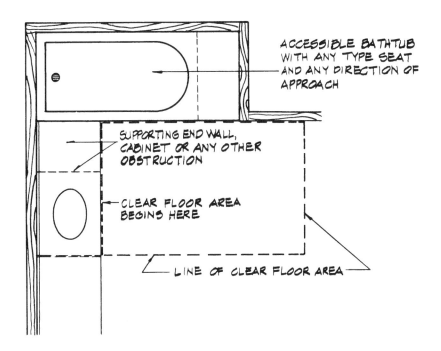

ACCESSIBLE BATHTUB
WITH ANY TYPE SEAT
AND ANY DIRECTION OF
APPROACH

SUPPORTING END WALL,
CABINET OR ANY OTHER
OBSTRUCTION

CLEAR FLOOR AREA
BEGINS HERE

LINE OF CLEAR FLOOR AREA

—IF THE SUPPORTING END WALL OF A
VANITY IS NOT LOCATED DIRECTLY AGAINST THE OUTSIDE
FACE OF THE BATHTUB, THEN THE CLEAR FLOOR AREA
SHALL BEGIN AT THE FORWARD EDGE OF THE VANITY
PROJECTED VERTICALLY TO THE FLOOR.

Figure 6-10 Accessible bathtub.

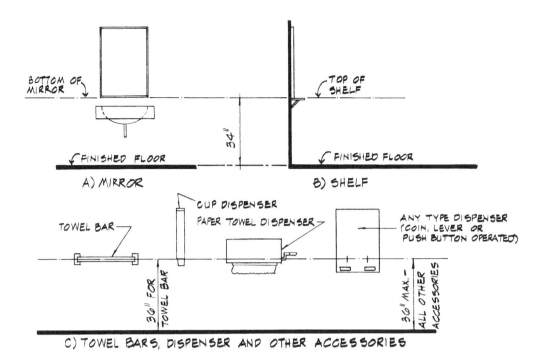

A) MIRROR

B) SHELF

C) TOWEL BARS, DISPENSER AND OTHER ACCESSORIES

TOILET ACCESSORIES

Figure 6-11 Accessible toilet accessories.

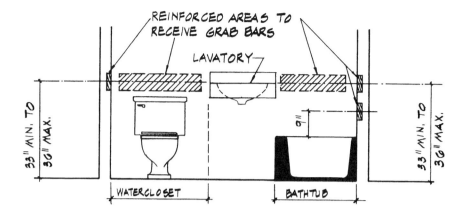

REINFORCED AREAS TO
RECEIVE GRAB BARS

LAVATORY

WATERCLOSET

BATHTUB

33" MIN. TO
36" MAX.

9"

33" MIN. TO
36" MAX.

———WALLS OR PARTITIONS ADJACENT TO
AND BEHIND WATERCLOSETS AND SURROUNDING
BATHTUBS SHALL BE SUITABLY REINFORCED
TO SUPPORT BOTH THE GRAB BAR ITSELF
AND A 250 POUND LOAD.

Figure 6-12 Blocking for grab bars.

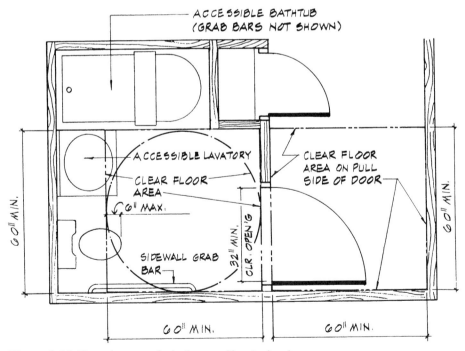

ACCESSIBLE BATHTUB
(GRAB BARS NOT SHOWN)

ACCESSIBLE LAVATORY

CLEAR FLOOR
AREA ON PULL
SIDE OF DOOR

CLEAR FLOOR
AREA

60" MAX.

SIDEWALL GRAB
BAR

60" MIN.

32" MIN. CLR. OPEN'G

60" MIN.

60" MIN.

60" MIN.

Figure 6-13 Floor clearances for bathroom with outswing door.

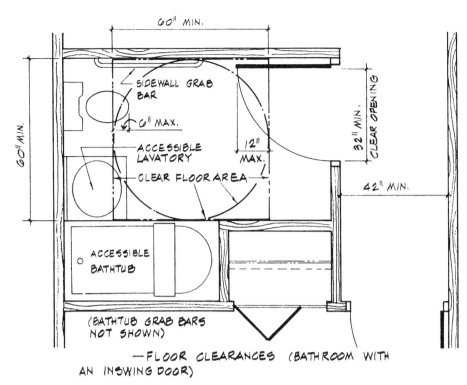

Figure 6-14 Floor clearances for bathroom with inswing door.

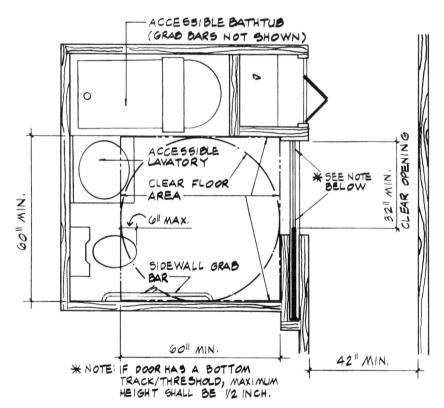

Figure 6-15 Floor clearances for bathroom with sliding door.

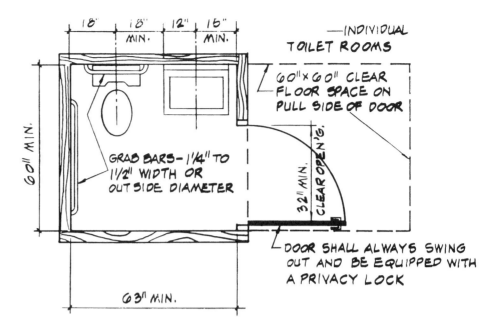

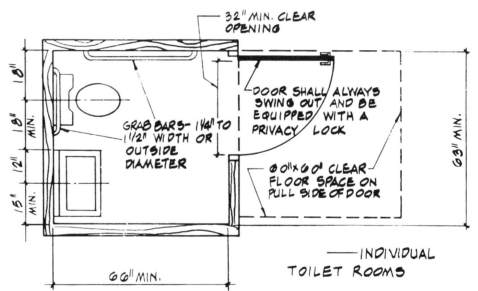

Figure 6-16 Individual toilet rooms.

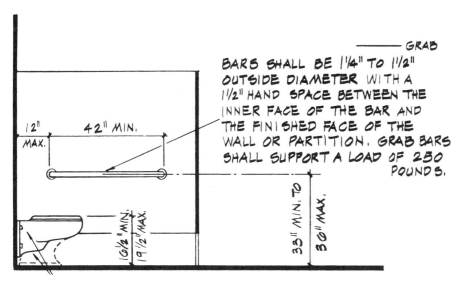

———— GRAB BARS SHALL BE 1¼" TO 1½" OUTSIDE DIAMETER WITH A 1½" HAND SPACE BETWEEN THE INNER FACE OF THE BAR AND THE FINISHED FACE OF THE WALL OR PARTITION. GRAB BARS SHALL SUPPORT A LOAD OF 250 POUNDS.

—ACCESSIBLE WATERCLOSETS, WHETHER FLOOR MOUNTED OR WALL MOUNTED, SHALL HAVE THE SEAT (NOT THE RIM) AT 16½" MINIMUM TO 19½ INCHES MAXIMUM ABOVE THE FINISHED FLOOR.

-GRAB BARS IN STANDARD SIZE TOILET STALLS SHALL HAVE ONE GRAB BAR LOCATED ON EACH SIDEWALL.

Figure 6-17 Toilet stall grab bars.

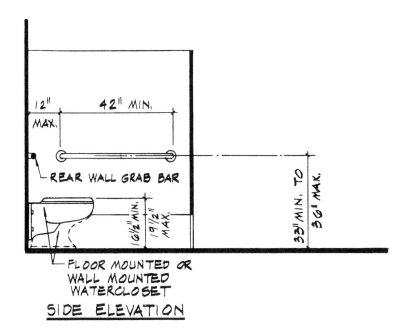

12" MAX. 42" MIN.

REAR WALL GRAB BAR

16½" MIN. 19½" MAX.

33" MIN. TO 36" MAX.

FLOOR MOUNTED OR
WALL MOUNTED
WATERCLOSET

SIDE ELEVATION

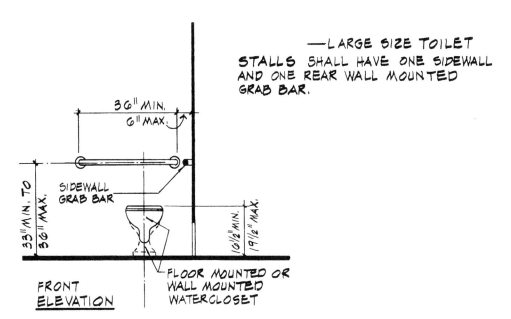

—LARGE SIZE TOILET
STALLS SHALL HAVE ONE SIDEWALL
AND ONE REAR WALL MOUNTED
GRAB BAR.

36" MIN.
6" MAX.

SIDEWALL
GRAB BAR

33" MIN. TO 36" MAX.

16½" MIN. 19½" MAX.

FRONT
ELEVATION

FLOOR MOUNTED OR
WALL MOUNTED
WATERCLOSET

Figure 6-18 Toilet stall grab bars.

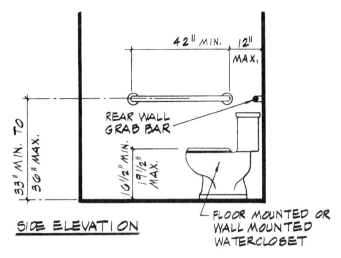

SIDE ELEVATION

—INDIVIDUAL **TOILET ROOMS** SHALL HAVE A 24" LONG REAR WALL GRAB BAR AND A 42" LONG SIDEWALL GRAB BAR.

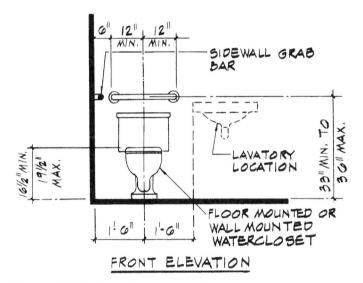

FRONT ELEVATION

Figure 6-19 Individual toilet room grab bars.

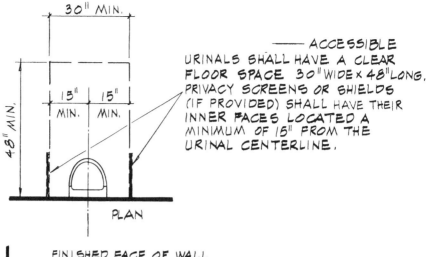

——— ACCESSIBLE
URINALS SHALL HAVE A CLEAR
FLOOR SPACE 30" WIDE × 48" LONG.
PRIVACY SCREENS OR SHIELDS
(IF PROVIDED) SHALL HAVE THEIR
INNER FACES LOCATED A
MINIMUM OF 15" FROM THE
URINAL CENTERLINE.

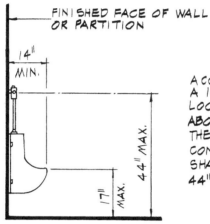

ACCESSIBLE URINALS SHALL HAVE
A 14" MINIMUM ELONGATED BOWL
LOCATED A MAXIMUM OF 17"
ABOVE THE FINISHED FLOOR.
THE CENTERLINE OF THE FLUSH
CONTROL OPERATING MECHANISM
SHALL NOT BE HIGHER THAN
44" ABOVE THE FINISHED FLOOR.

Figure 6-20 Accessible urinals.

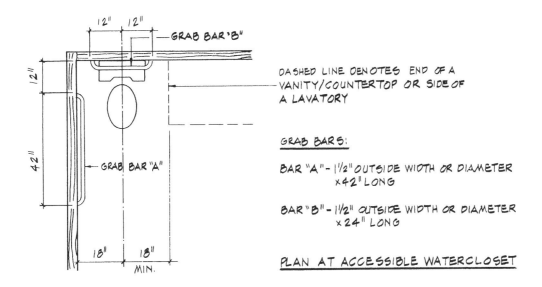

DASHED LINE DENOTES END OF A
VANITY/COUNTERTOP OR SIDE OF
A LAVATORY

GRAB BARS:

BAR "A" - 1½" OUTSIDE WIDTH OR DIAMETER
×42" LONG

BAR "B" - 1½" OUTSIDE WIDTH OR DIAMETER
×24" LONG

PLAN AT ACCESSIBLE WATERCLOSET

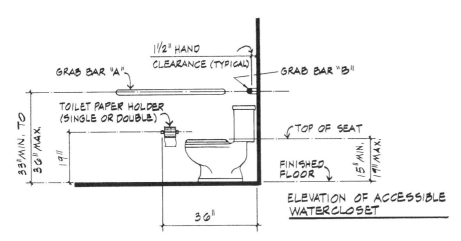

ELEVATION OF ACCESSIBLE
WATERCLOSET

Figure 6- 21 Accessible water closet, showing requirements of the ANSI code.

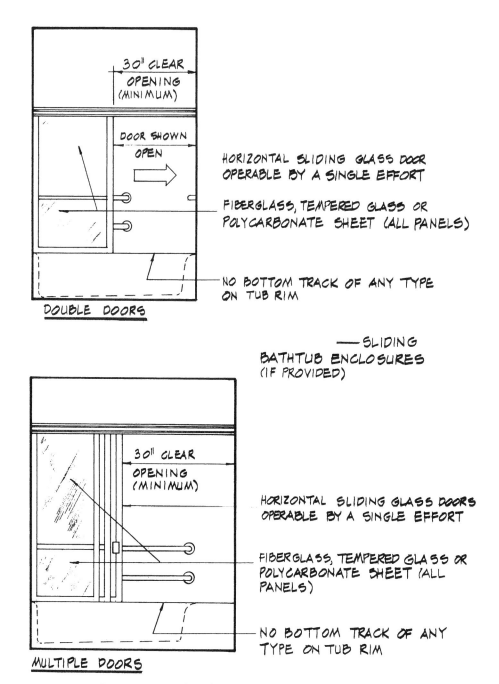

30" CLEAR
OPENING
(MINIMUM)

DOOR SHOWN
OPEN

HORIZONTAL SLIDING GLASS DOOR
OPERABLE BY A SINGLE EFFORT

FIBERGLASS, TEMPERED GLASS OR
POLYCARBONATE SHEET (ALL PANELS)

NO BOTTOM TRACK OF ANY TYPE
ON TUB RIM

DOUBLE DOORS

SLIDING
BATHTUB ENCLOSURES
(IF PROVIDED)

30" CLEAR
OPENING
(MINIMUM)

HORIZONTAL SLIDING GLASS DOORS
OPERABLE BY A SINGLE EFFORT

FIBERGLASS, TEMPERED GLASS OR
POLYCARBONATE SHEET (ALL
PANELS)

NO BOTTOM TRACK OF ANY
TYPE ON TUB RIM

MULTIPLE DOORS

Figure 6-22 Sliding door bathtub enclosures.

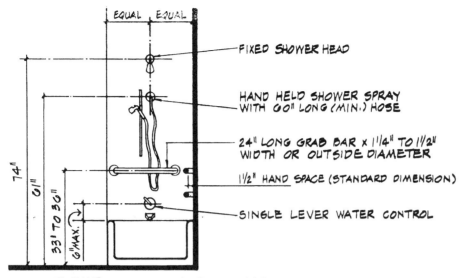

EQUAL EQUAL

FIXED SHOWER HEAD

HAND HELD SHOWER SPRAY
WITH 60" LONG (MIN.) HOSE

24" LONG GRAB BAR x 1¼" TO 1½"
WIDTH OR OUTSIDE DIAMETER

1½" HAND SPACE (STANDARD DIMENSION)

SINGLE LEVER WATER CONTROL

74"

61"

33" TO 36"

6" MAX.

ELEVATION OF CONTROL WALL

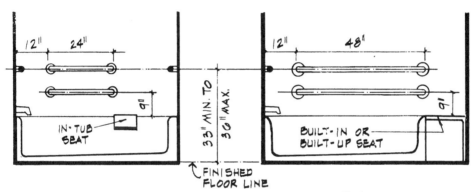

12" 24"

9"

33" MIN. TO 36" MAX.

12" 48"

9"

IN-TUB SEAT

BUILT-IN OR
BUILT-UP SEAT

FINISHED
FLOOR LINE

ELEVATION - BACK WALL OF BATHTUB

———— TWO GRAB BARS SHALL BE INSTALLED,
PARALLEL TO THE FINISHED FLOOR, ON THE WALL PARALLEL TO THE
LENGTH OF THE BATHTUB. FOR AN IN-TUB SEAT, THE BARS SHALL
BE 24" LONG; FOR A BUILT-IN OR BUILT-UP SEAT, THE BARS
SHALL BE 48" LONG.
ALL GRAB BARS SHALL BE 1¼" TO 1½" WIDTH OR OUTSIDE
DIAMETER.

Figure 6-23 Bathtub grab bar locations.

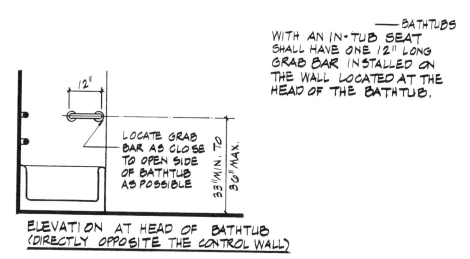

BATHTUBS WITH AN IN-TUB SEAT SHALL HAVE ONE 12" LONG GRAB BAR INSTALLED ON THE WALL LOCATED AT THE HEAD OF THE BATHTUB.

12"

LOCATE GRAB BAR AS CLOSE TO OPEN SIDE OF BATHTUB AS POSSIBLE

33" MIN. TO 36" MAX.

ELEVATION AT HEAD OF BATHTUB
(DIRECTLY OPPOSITE THE CONTROL WALL)

Figure 6-24 Grab bar location for bathtub with built-in seat.

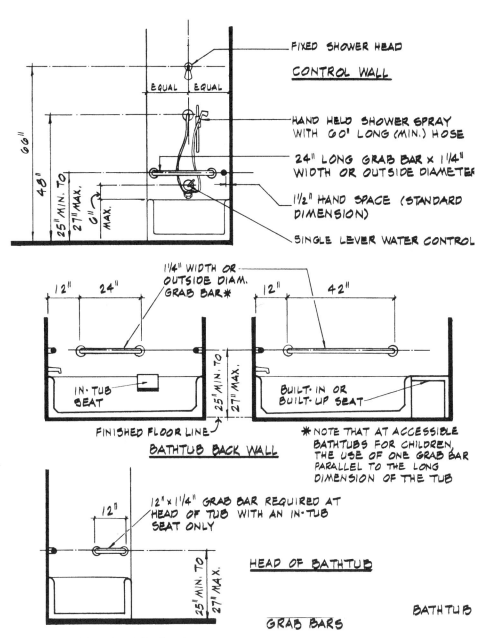

FIXED SHOWER HEAD

CONTROL WALL

HAND HELD SHOWER SPRAY WITH 60" LONG (MIN.) HOSE

24" LONG GRAB BAR x 1 1/4" WIDTH OR OUTSIDE DIAMETER

1 1/2" HAND SPACE (STANDARD DIMENSION)

SINGLE LEVER WATER CONTROL

1 1/4" WIDTH OR OUTSIDE DIAM. GRAB BAR *

IN·TUB SEAT

FINISHED FLOOR LINE

BATHTUB BACK WALL

BUILT·IN OR BUILT·UP SEAT

* NOTE THAT AT ACCESSIBLE BATHTUBS FOR CHILDREN, THE USE OF ONE GRAB BAR PARALLEL TO THE LONG DIMENSION OF THE TUB

12" x 1 1/4" GRAB BAR REQUIRED AT HEAD OF TUB WITH AN IN·TUB SEAT ONLY

HEAD OF BATHTUB

GRAB BARS   BATHTUB

Figure 6-25 Bathtub grab bar locations.

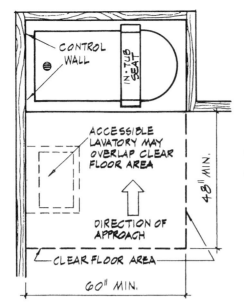

FRONT APPROACH TO
ACCESSIBLE BATHTUB
WITH AN IN-TUB SEAT

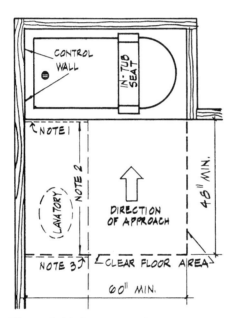

ACCESSIBLE BATHTUB WITH
VANITY OR COUNTERTOP
ADJACENT MAY HAVE THE CLEAR
FLOOR AREA EXTEND UNDER THE
COUNTER PROVIDED:
NOTE 1: THE SUPPORTING END WALL
IS DIRECTLY AGAINST THE
BATHTUB
NOTE 2: THERE ARE NO UNDER
COUNTER OBSTRUCTIONS

NOTE 3: SUPPORT WALL SHALL NOT
BE LOCATED WITHIN THE
CLEAR FLOOR AREA

FRONT APPROACH TO
ACCESSIBLE BATHTUB
WITH AN IN-TUB SEAT

Figure 6-26 Front approach to bathtub.

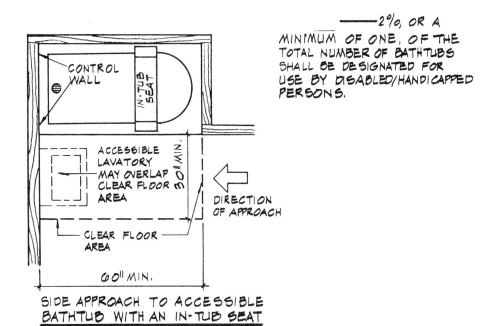

—2%, OR A MINIMUM OF ONE, OF THE TOTAL NUMBER OF BATHTUBS SHALL BE DESIGNATED FOR USE BY DISABLED/HANDICAPPED PERSONS.

CONTROL WALL

IN-TUB SEAT

ACCESSIBLE LAVATORY MAY OVERLAP CLEAR FLOOR AREA

30" MIN.

DIRECTION OF APPROACH

CLEAR FLOOR AREA

60" MIN.

SIDE APPROACH TO ACCESSIBLE BATHTUB WITH AN IN-TUB SEAT

CONTROL WALL

IN-TUB SEAT

NOTE 1

(LAVATORY)

NOTE 2

30" MIN.

DIRECTION OF APPROACH

NOTE 3

VANITY OR COUNTERTOP

CLEAR FLOOR AREA

60" MIN.

SIDE APPROACH TO ACCESSIBLE BATHTUB WITH AN IN-TUB SEAT

ACCESSIBLE BATHTUB WITH VANITY OR COUNTERTOP ADJACENT MAY HAVE THE CLEAR FLOOR AREA EXTEND UNDER THE COUNTER PROVIDED:

NOTE 1: THE SUPPORTING END WALL IS DIRECTLY AGAINST THE BATHTUB

NOTE 2: THERE ARE NO UNDER COUNTER OBSTRUCTIONS

NOTE 3: SUPPORT WALL SHALL NOT BE LOCATED WITHIN THE CLEAR FLOOR AREA

Figure 6-27 Side approach to bathtub.

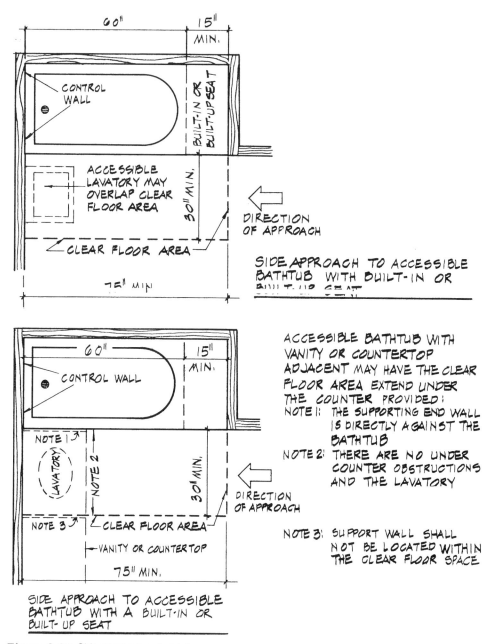

Figure 6-28 Side approach to bathtub.

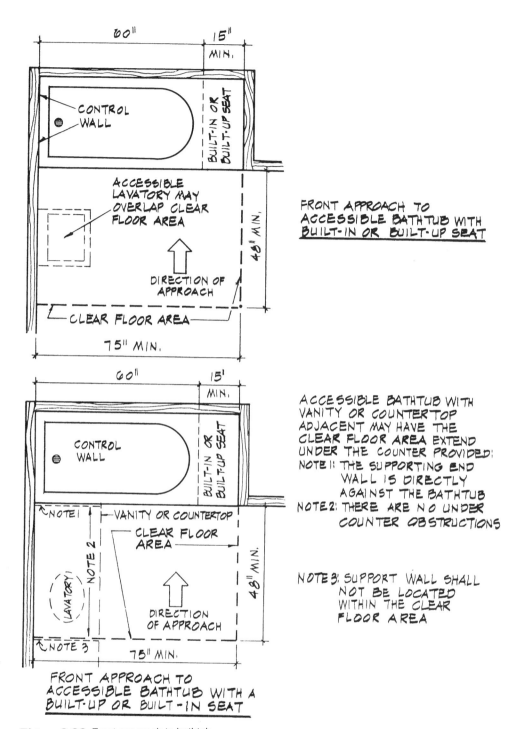

Figure 6-29 Front approach to bathtub.

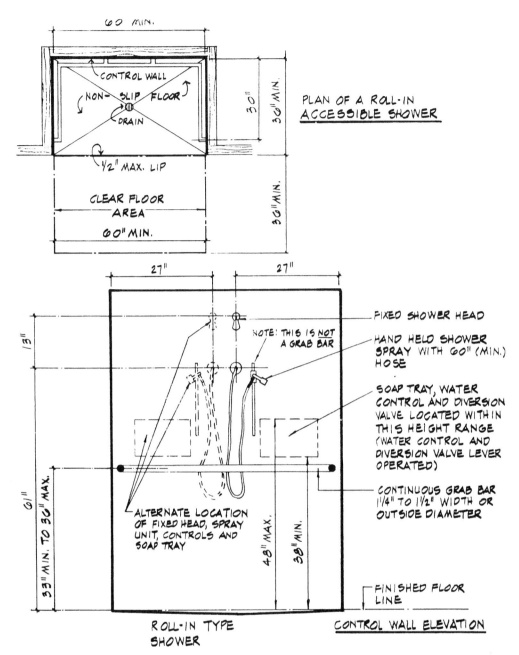

PLAN OF A ROLL-IN
ACCESSIBLE SHOWER

60 MIN.

CONTROL WALL

NON-SLIP FLOOR

DRAIN

30"

36" MIN.

½" MAX. LIP

CLEAR FLOOR AREA
60" MIN.

36" MIN.

27"   27"

13"

FIXED SHOWER HEAD

NOTE: THIS IS NOT A GRAB BAR

HAND HELD SHOWER SPRAY WITH 60" (MIN.) HOSE

SOAP TRAY, WATER CONTROL AND DIVERSION VALVE LOCATED WITHIN THIS HEIGHT RANGE (WATER CONTROL AND DIVERSION VALVE LEVER OPERATED)

CONTINUOUS GRAB BAR 1¼" TO 1½" WIDTH OR OUTSIDE DIAMETER

60"

33" MIN. TO 36" MAX.

ALTERNATE LOCATION OF FIXED HEAD, SPRAY UNIT, CONTROLS AND SOAP TRAY

48" MAX.

38" MIN.

FINISHED FLOOR LINE

ROLL-IN TYPE SHOWER

CONTROL WALL ELEVATION

Figure 6-30 Roll-in showers.

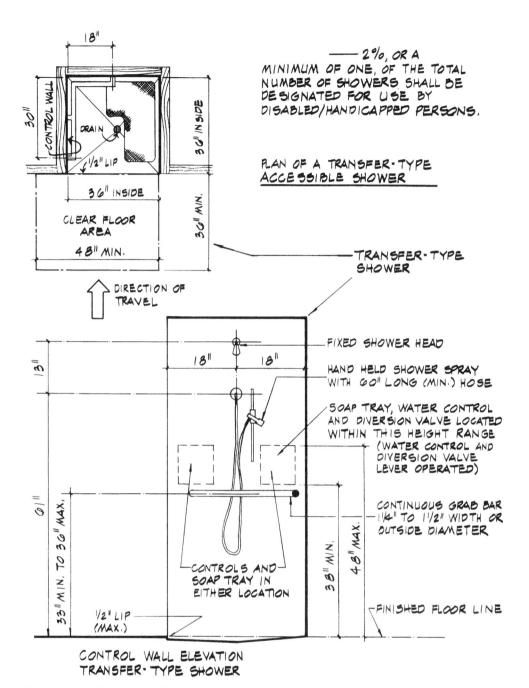

18"

30"
CONTROL WALL

DRAIN

1/2" LIP

36" INSIDE

36" INSIDE

CLEAR FLOOR
AREA

48" MIN.

36" MIN.

2%, OR A
MINIMUM OF ONE, OF THE TOTAL
NUMBER OF SHOWERS, SHALL BE
DESIGNATED FOR USE BY
DISABLED/HANDICAPPED PERSONS.

PLAN OF A TRANSFER-TYPE
ACCESSIBLE SHOWER

TRANSFER-TYPE
SHOWER

DIRECTION OF
TRAVEL

13"

60"

33" MIN. TO 36" MAX.

1/2" LIP
(MAX.)

18"   18"

CONTROLS AND
SOAP TRAY IN
EITHER LOCATION

38" MIN.

48" MAX.

FIXED SHOWER HEAD

HAND HELD SHOWER SPRAY
WITH 60" LONG (MIN.) HOSE

SOAP TRAY, WATER CONTROL
AND DIVERSION VALVE LOCATED
WITHIN THIS HEIGHT RANGE
(WATER CONTROL AND
DIVERSION VALVE
LEVER OPERATED)

CONTINUOUS GRAB BAR
1 1/4" TO 1 1/2" WIDTH OR
OUTSIDE DIAMETER

FINISHED FLOOR LINE

CONTROL WALL ELEVATION
TRANSFER-TYPE SHOWER

Figure 6-31 Transfer-type showers.

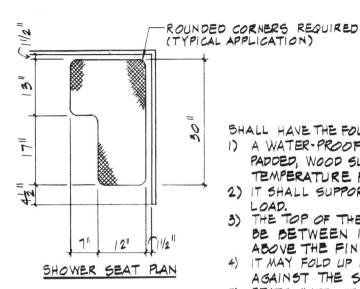

ROUNDED CORNERS REQUIRED
(TYPICAL APPLICATION)

SHOWER SEAT PLAN

— SHOWER SEATS

SHALL HAVE THE FOLLOWING FEATURES:
1) A WATER-PROOF SEAT (EITHER PADDED, WOOD SLATS OR HIGH-TEMPERATURE PLASTIC).
2) IT SHALL SUPPORT A 250 POUND LOAD.
3) THE TOP OF THE SEAT SHALL BE BETWEEN 17" AND 19" ABOVE THE FINISHED FLOOR.
4) IT MAY FOLD UP OR DOWN AGAINST THE SUPPORTING WALL.
5) SEATS MADE OF WOOD OR HIGH TEMPERATURE PLASTIC SHALL HAVE ALL CORNERS ROUNDED AND NO SHARP EDGES.

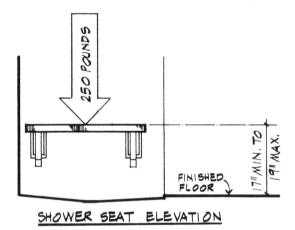

SHOWER SEAT ELEVATION

Figure 6-32 Shower seats.

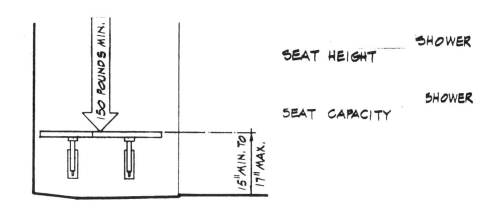

SEAT HEIGHT ————— SHOWER

SEAT CAPACITY ————— SHOWER

150 POUNDS MIN.

15" MIN. TO 17" MAX.

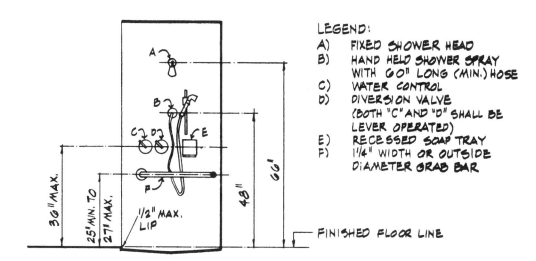

LEGEND:
A) FIXED SHOWER HEAD
B) HAND HELD SHOWER SPRAY
   WITH 60" LONG (MIN.) HOSE
C) WATER CONTROL
D) DIVERSION VALVE
   (BOTH "C" AND "D" SHALL BE
   LEVER OPERATED)
E) RECESSED SOAP TRAY
F) 1¼" WIDTH OR OUTSIDE
   DIAMETER GRAB BAR

FINISHED FLOOR LINE

36" MAX.

25" MIN. TO 27" MAX.

½" MAX. LIP

48"

66"

(LOCATION OF ELEMENTS APPLIES TO ANY TYPE SHOWER.

Figure 6-33 Accessible showers.

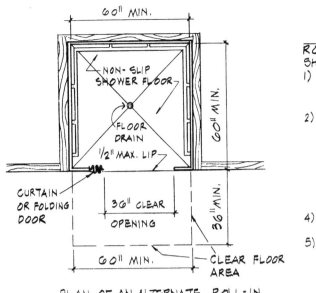

ALTERNATE
ROLL-IN TYPE SHOWER
SHALL HAVE:
1) A 60" x 60" OR 60" DIAM. CLEAR, INTERNAL FLOOR AREA
2) A CONTINUOUS THREE-WALL GRAB BAR OR THREE, 48" LONG GRAB BARS THAT ARE 1¼" TO 1½" IN WIDTH OR DIAMETER AT 33" TO 36" ABOVE THE SHOWER FLOOR
4) A 36" CLEAR OPENING FOR ENTRY AND EXIT
5) A FIXED SHOWER HEAD, HAND HELD, SHOWER SPRAY WITH 60" MIN. HOSE, LEVER OPERATED CONTROLS AND A RECESSED SOAP TRAY

PLAN OF AN ALTERNATE ROLL-IN SHOWER WITH CURTAIN OR FOLDING DOOR

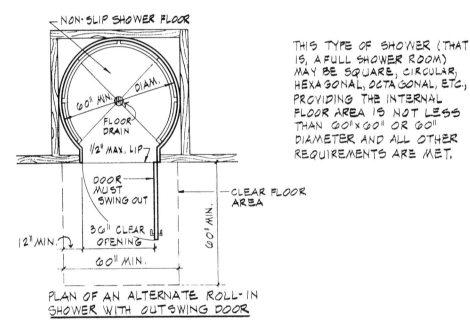

THIS TYPE OF SHOWER (THAT IS, A FULL SHOWER ROOM) MAY BE SQUARE, CIRCULAR, HEXAGONAL, OCTAGONAL, ETC., PROVIDING THE INTERNAL FLOOR AREA IS NOT LESS THAN 60" x 60" OR 60" DIAMETER AND ALL OTHER REQUIREMENTS ARE MET.

PLAN OF AN ALTERNATE ROLL-IN SHOWER WITH OUTSWING DOOR

Figure 6-34 Roll-in showers.

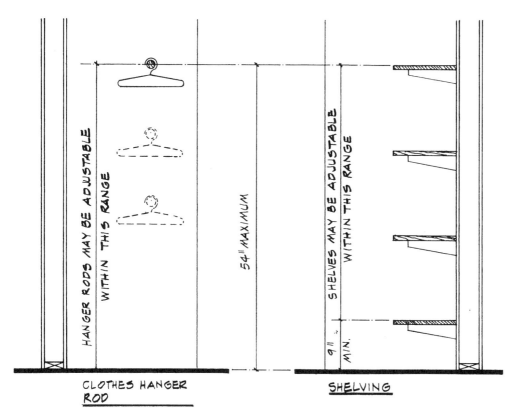

HANGER RODS MAY BE ADJUSTABLE WITHIN THIS RANGE

54" MAXIMUM

SHELVES MAY BE ADJUSTABLE WITHIN THIS RANGE

9" MIN.

CLOTHES HANGER ROD

SHELVING

Figure 7-1 Accessible closets.

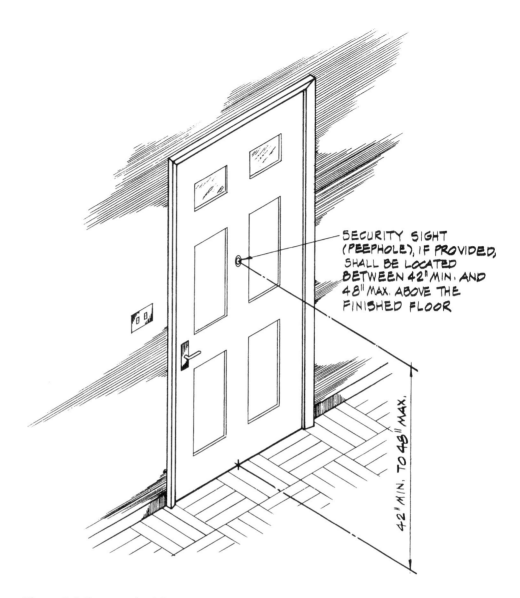

SECURITY SIGHT (PEEPHOLE), IF PROVIDED, SHALL BE LOCATED BETWEEN 42" MIN. AND 48" MAX. ABOVE THE FINISHED FLOOR

42" MIN. TO 48" MAX.

Figure 8-1 Door security sight.

INDEX

ABOUT THE AUTHOR

Albert A. Peloquin is a registered architect in Wisconsin and North Carolina with extensive experience in building design and facilities management. Most recently the Division Architect for Parks and Recreation for the State of North Carolina, where he was responsible for administering barrier-free design standards, Mr. Peloquin served for many years as a consulting architect for the University of North Carolina. He holds a degree in urban planning from the University of Wisconsin.